Parents and the
Dynamics of Child Rearing

Developmental Psychology Series

Series Editor, Wendell E. Jeffrey, UCLA

Parents and the Dynamics of Child Rearing

George W. Holden

UNIVERSITY OF TEXAS AT AUSTIN

WestviewPress

A Division of HarperCollins*Publishers*

Developmental Psychology Series

Copyright © 1997 by Westview Press, A Division of HarperCollins Publishers, Inc.

Published in 1997 in the United States of America by Westview Press, 5500 Central Avenue, Boulder, Colorado 80301-2877, and in the United Kingdom by Westview Press, 12 Hid's Copse Road, Cumnor Hill, Oxford OX2 9JJ

This book was typeset by Letra Libre, 1705 14th Street, Suite 391, Boulder, Colorado 80302.

Library of Congress Cataloging-in-Publication Data
Holden, George W.
  Parents and the dynamics of child rearing / George W. Holden.
    p. cm. — (Developmental psychology series)
  Includes bibliographical references and index.
  ISBN 0-8133-3030-0 (hardcover). — ISBN 0-8133-3031-9
  (pbk.)
  1. Parent and child. 2. Parenting. I. Title. II. Series.
BF723.P25H65 1997
155.6'46—dc20   96-43122
                                                                                      CIP

The paper used in this publication meets the requirements of the American National Standard for Permanence of Paper for Printed Library Materials Z39.48-1984.

10   9   8   7   6   5   4   3   2   1

To my mother, Elizabeth W. Holden,
and the memory of my father, Reuben A. Holden IV

Contents

Tables and Figures

Preface

This book concerns one of the oldest questions of intellectual inquiry. It is a question of universal interest, paramount importance, and widespread speculation. At the same time, it is an extremely difficult and complex one to answer. That question is: How do parents affect the development of their children? This book examines the scientific evidence concerning this question and related issues.

Human history encompasses a long tradition of thought regarding parents and their impact on children. The classical Greek philosophers pondered parental impact on children, as have numerous other philosophers, physicians, educators, and laypersons. In fact, it is difficult to imagine individuals who have not spent at least some time wondering how their own upbringing influenced their development. And what parent has not worried about the effects of some child-rearing practice on his or her child?

Despite the broad-based and sustained interest in the effects of parental behavior, constructing a science about parent-child relationships has been difficult and slow. Therefore, the primary goal of this book is to provide a cogent summary and synthesis of the current status of the scientific knowledge that has accumulated on the topic of parents and child rearing.

The research literature is voluminous, spanning more than half a century and from a number of disciplines (e.g., psychology, sociology, anthropology, education, psychiatry, and pediatrics). Within psychology alone, developmentalists do not lay the sole claim to an interest in parent-child relationships. Rather, psychologists from diverse orientations and training; including human behavioral genetics and social, educational, community, personality, and clinical psychology; have investigated the topic. Consequently, by necessity this book can introduce and describe the topics and issues only with a relatively broad brush stroke.

Besides addressing the fundamental question of how parents affect their children, this book examines four other basic and related questions. These are as follows: (1) Why do parents act the way they do? (2) What are the attributes of effective parents? (3) Why do some parents maltreat their children? (4) How have societal changes affected families?

The study of parents and child rearing represents a surprisingly formidable task. Until recently, one key reason for slow progress made in the field was the failure to recognize the complexities and difficulties inherent in the study of child rearing and its effects. It must be remembered that the study of child rearing is not comparable to charting the reaction of an amoeba to light or observing the electrical change in neurons with a magnetic resonance imaging machine. The complexity comes from a variety of sources, the foremost being a focus on two changing organisms: the parent and the child.

In fact, the perspective adopted in this book is on variability and change in the parent-child system. This orientation reflects a dynamic view, one that focuses on sources of variation as well as processes inherent in the parent-child relationship. As will become evident, a dynamic viewpoint is considerably more complex than a static or deterministic perspective. However, it is also a more accurate approach for capturing and understanding parent-child relationships.

Besides focusing on change, variability, and processes, this book takes a largely parent-centered perspective to parent-child relationships. In contrast to a child-centered perspective, which might address how children perceive their parents or how other nonparental environmental variables affect the developing child, this book's primary focus is on the parent. Consequently, the types of research reviewed and questions addressed will center primarily on parents' issues and their child-rearing behavior.

Scholars of parent-child relationships may recognize the similarity between the title of this book and the titles of two earlier books. The first book, by Percival Symonds (1949), was entitled *The Dynamics of Parent-Child Relationships*. However, the similarity ends there: Symonds's approach was a neo-Freudian one organized around the proposition that "parent-child relationships are determined primarily by the attitudes of parents and that these attitudes spring from the dynamic forces within the parents' personalities" (Symonds, 1949, p. v). As will be shown, such a view represents only a small part of what determines parental behavior.

This book shares more with the second book that has a similar title, *The Dynamics of Behavioral Development*, by the American-educated Chinese developmental psychologist Zing-Yang Kuo (1968). Kuo developed a dynamic epigenetic theoretical orientation to ontogeny, viewing an individual's development as a continual transformation of the organism across time. Throughout its life, the organism experiences a constant interplay between its genetic material and the environment such that either component cannot be readily separated out. Consequently, Kuo advocated a focus on the dynamic interaction of developmental processes.

I have adopted a similar dynamic approach in this book, and I hope the volume will serve as an introduction to the current research in parent-child relationships. The first three chapters provide introductory and background material necessary for consideration of the central questions addressed in the book. Chapter 1 focuses on how the basis of our understanding of child rearing has changed from unsubstantiated beliefs to

scientific investigation. Chapter 2 describes the different theories for assessing parent-child relationships, each with its own focus, strengths, and
limitations. Chapter 3 describes six basic approaches to the study of parents. These competing conceptualizations yield different types of information about parents and children.

Chapter 4 addresses the question of influences on parental behavior. It
organizes the multiple determinants in a theoretical model that serves to
identify different but nested levels of influence on child rearing. The multiplicity of influences attests to the many potential sources of change—as
well as stability—of parental behavior. Chapter 5 addresses the central
question of the book: In what ways do parents affect their children? The
evidence to date is mostly correlational, so the chapter more accurately addresses the associations that have been found between parental characteristics and children's positive and negative outcomes. Many parent-child associations are moderated by characteristics of the parent and child.

Chapter 6 builds on the previous chapter by integrating what is known
about the attributes of effective parents. A model of effective parenting that
incorporates the change inherent in child rearing is presented. The topic of
Chapter 7 concerns maltreating parents; the chapter addresses some of the
reasons and ways their behavior has mutated from that of other parents.
Chapter 8 reviews recent changes in American families and examines how
social policy has responded—as well as needs to respond—to the contemporary needs of families. A final chapter summarizes the major points and
discusses the implications of a dynamic perspective of parents.

Throughout the book, most of the demographic data concerns the
United States. There are two reasons for this focus. First, it is anticipated
that the primary consumers of the book will reside in the United States.
Second, the United States maintains the most current and readily available
statistical data about issues related to parents. Instructors who use the
book in other countries might want to search for comparable data from
their own countries.

This book is primarily intended to provided an advanced introduction to
the study of parent-child relationships for upper-level undergraduate students or perhaps first-year graduate students in psychology, human development, or education programs. However, it also should be of interest to
researchers who want an introduction to the empirical work concerning
parent-child relationships; clinicians, practitioners, and others who work
with parents; and even parents who have some background in psychology.
For all these potential readers, the chapters are intended to provide an
overview of research and a coherent portrait of our current understanding
of parents and their role in children's development.

It is not possible to do justice to the complex literature in a relatively
short book. Specifically, little space is devoted to such topics as adults' fer-

tility decisions, the transition to parenthood, role theory, alternative family structures (e.g., stepfamilies, gay parents), or feminist perspectives. Similarly, owing to space limitations, many important contributors to the research literature could not be included or are only briefly mentioned. However, whenever possible, attempts are made to credit many of the originators, innovators, and leaders in the field of parenting research. Readers seeking a more detailed, in-depth understanding will need to consult the references listed, such as the four-volume *Handbook of Parenting* (Bornstein, 1995).

Instructors who use the book in their classes may want to supplement each chapter with readings from cited or related empirical or review articles. Similarly, instructors may want to provide supplemental readings to fill in some of the inevitable gaps concerning topics barely mentioned. Alternatively, this book can be used in conjunction with other books, such as other volumes in this series, that go into more detail about particular issues associated with parent-child relationships.

George W. Holden

Acknowledgments

A number of individuals were instrumental in the completion of this book. Foremost, I am indebted to my wife, Anne Cameron. Anne's assistance was multifold, including tutoring me in clinical child psychology, editing chapters, and bringing to life many of the ideas discussed here, with the assistance of our children, Margaret, John, and Paul. Conversations with various colleagues at the University of Texas have enriched my understanding of social development; in particular, Judith Langlois and Ted Dix have been significant influences. One concrete example is the material in Chapter 3, which represents the outcome of a series of discussions with Ted Dix. A number of graduate students have worked with me on empirical investigations and have commented on drafts of chapters. They are Susan Coleman, Pam O'Dell, Kathy Ritchie, Jai Shim, Josh Stein, and Bob Zambarano. In addition, research assistants Julie Schmidt and Susanna Hall helped out with library research. Finally, Joan Grusec at the University of Toronto, Leon Kuczynski at the University of Guelph, and Dave MacPhee at Colorado State University each provided excellent comments on a draft of the manuscript. They each pointed out all too many blind spots and made astute suggestions as to how the manuscript could be improved; what limitations remain are despite their efforts. To all those individuals, I am most grateful and appreciative.

Support for my own research and, hence, for preparation of this book has been provided by grants from the National Institutes of Child Health and Human Development, the H. F. Guggenheim Foundation, the Hogg Foundation, IBM, and the University of Texas Research Institute.

G. W. H.

1

The Development of Child-Rearing Research: From Mere Beliefs to a Dynamic Perspective

In 1962, a French historian named Philippe Ariès published a book titled *Centuries of Childhood*. In it, he proposed a revolutionary thesis: How we think about children and the special time of childhood is a relatively new cultural phenomenon afforded by a certain degree of affluence in our society. He argued that at least from the time of the Middle Ages and until the seventeenth century there was no concept of childhood. Once children were old enough to function independently (about age seven, he thought), they began to be treated like small adults. There was no special time for education or any special treatment owing to their youth; young children were expected to join in the work of adults. In short, there was little distinction based on the age of individuals and virtually no conception of the unique period of life that we call *childhood*.

Although Ariès's thesis has received criticism for its historical inaccuracies (deMause, 1974; Shahar, 1990), the basic premise is sound: The way we perceive children and think about child rearing is indeed a product of our times. As William Kessen (1979) and others have pointed out, beliefs about children and parent-child relationships represent *cultural inventions*. These inventions about the family and its members are shaped from a confluence of the beliefs of influential individuals as well as from the economics, demographics, politics, and ideology of a society (Mintz & Kellogg, 1988). Historically the individuals whose beliefs had the most powerful effects on conceptions of children and parenting were ministers, philosophers, and physicians.

Beliefs About Child Rearing in the Past

A dramatic demonstration of the influence of ministers' beliefs occurred in colonial America, where the Puritan ministers subscribed to the view that all children were tainted by original sin. This doctrine refers to the Biblical de-

1

piction of what happened in the Garden of Eden. Adam and Eve disobeyed God by engaging in an act of free will (eating the apple). Consequently their nature became corrupt. Because all infants are direct descendants of Adam and Eve, they were believed to inherit their sinful and guilty state.

The colonial ministers did not hesitate to preach about the link between child-rearing practices and religious ideology. John Robinson, a Puritan and spiritual leader of the early Plymouth colonists, adopted the view that if children were to grow up to have the Puritan moral virtues of respecting their parents and devotion to hard work, parents must break their children's sinful wills and mold them early in life. Robinson wrote the following in 1628: "And surely there is in all children, though not alike, a stubbornness, and stoutness of minds arising from natural pride, which must, in the first place, be broken and beaten down. . . . This fruit of natural corruption and root of actual rebellion both against God and man must be destroyed and no manner of way nourished" (Greven, 1973, p. 13).

During the next century, John Wesley (1703–1791), a founder of the Methodist Church, similarly saw disobedience as synonymous with moral disorder. He warned of the dangers of losing control of a child and recommended the frequent use of physical punishment:

> A wise parent, on the other hand, should begin to break their [child's] will the first moment it appears. In the whole of Christian education, there is nothing more important than this. The will of a parent is to a little child in the place of the will of God. Therefore, studiously teach them to submit to this while they are children, that they may be ready to submit to his will, when they are men (Greven, 1973, pp. 59–60).

Historians of the colonial period now believe that the severe, repressive, and authoritarian child-rearing practices advocated by Reverends Robinson, Wesley, and others were limited to a certain segment of the Puritan population and not representative of the modal child-rearing practices in colonial America (Greven, 1977); however, the colonial days provide a vivid illustration of the potential influence of religious beliefs on child rearing.

Similarly, the writings of philosophers have long been a primary source of beliefs about the nature of development and child rearing. It was Aristotle (384–322 B.C.) who advanced the idea that children were blank tablets, waiting to be written on by parents and life experience. Among his other writings about children's development, he argued that fathers, rather than mothers, play a special role in their sons' development (Borstelmann, 1983; French, 1977).

More than any other philosopher before or after, the British physician and philosopher John Locke (1632–1704) had a revolutionary and enduring impact on child-rearing practices, owing to his then controversial beliefs. The son of Puritan parents, Locke wrote a book, *Some Thoughts Concerning Education* (1693/1978), that became the dominant child-rearing manual in Western Europe and America during the first half of the eighteenth century. The book contains advice given to a father about raising his son. Besides advocating a blank slate position and thereby rejecting the notion of children as innately sinful, Locke proposed a novel view of children and provided a wide range of child-rearing recommendations. He appreciated the influence of the environment on development, recognized the need for early stimulation for children's development, and advocated encouragement of mature behavior: "The sooner you treat him as a man, the sooner he will begin to be one" (p. 78). Locke is best remembered for his belief that children are rational beings and that parents therefore should use reasoning as the principal disciplinary technique rather than physical punishment or material rewards.

Although much of his advice sounds sensible and beneficial, Locke also proposed child-rearing practices that are now regarded as unorthodox or even bizarre. Many pages of his manual are devoted to the virtues of "hardening" infants by immersing them in cold baths, building endurance and toughness by dressing them in light clothing and thin shoes in cold weather, administering low levels of pain as a way of firming up their minds, and avoiding certain fruits (peaches, melons, grapes) because of their "unwholesome" juice.

Another philosopher with highly influential ideas about child rearing was the Swiss-born Jean-Jacques Rousseau (1712–1778), who took exception to a number of Locke's ideas. In his book *Emile*, Rousseau (1762/1956) described the rearing of a boy by a tutor as a way of conveying both his theoretical views about development and his prescriptions for appropriate child-rearing methods. He, like Locke, rejected the idea of original sin in children. Children are born innocent and amoral; it is society that corrupts them, he said. But in contrast to Locke, Rousseau believed that children are not rational, at least not until age twelve. As he pointedly wrote, "If children appreciated reason, they would not need to be educated. . . . Nature wants children to be children before they are men" (1956, Vol. 2, p. 38). Consequently, punishment for wrong behavior made little sense to him. "Before the age of reason we do good or ill without knowing it, and there is no morality in our actions" (p. 34).

Rousseau's view of child rearing can be captured by the metaphor of gardening: Let children develop freely and with little assistance so that the maturational process can unfold naturally and benevolently (Borstelmann, 1983). The parental role is not to discipline, educate, or train; rather it is to facilitate natural development.

Physicians represent a third group of individuals who have provided a strong dose of child-rearing beliefs to society since antiquity. These directives all too often were based on unsubstantiated ideas rather than medical knowledge. Beginning with Hippocrates (460–370 B.C.), much of their advice concerned infant feeding and nutrition and can be found in historical reviews (Ruhrah, 1925; Wickes, 1953). Many physicians have freely dispensed child-rearing recommendations along with medical advice.

During the twentieth century, the child-rearing advice of two American physicians has been particularly influential. Luther Emmett Holt first published *The Care and Feeding of Children* in 1894. It became the leading book on child care for almost 50 years. It does indeed provide some medical information, such as daily care of infants, milestones of child development, feeding recommendations, and how to deal with certain common ailments. Much of Holt's advice sounds reasonable by today's standards. For example, in the sixth edition of his book (Holt, 1914), he advocated breast-feeding with the rationale that there was "no perfect substitute" and providing the justification that has been subsequently confirmed that breast-feeding results in lower rates of infant mortality.

Holt also made a number of recommendations that are now known to be medically or developmentally unsound. Among these are the following: initiating bowel training when infants are two months old, keeping infants on a liquid diet for the first year, giving children no raw vegetables and no meat until they reach the age of twelve, and avoiding kissing infants because "tuberculosis, diphtheria, syphilis, and many other grave diseases may be communicated in this way" (p. 174).

The influence of physicians' beliefs was captured by the early twentieth-century postcard reproduced in Figure 1.1. In this whimsical card, a physician is scolding a father for trying to feed cow's milk to his child directly from the cow. Of course, drinking milk in this way is physically impossible, a fact that highlights the message that parents should not give their children cow's milk.

One child raised strictly according to Dr. Holt's precepts became an even more renowned physician. After several years working as a pediatrician, Dr. Benjamin Spock recognized the need for a new and radically different guide to child care (Bloom, 1972). Titled *The Common Sense Book of Baby and Child Care*, Spock's parenting manual provided basic pediatric information and served to correct some of Holt's peculiar child-rearing recommendations. Like Holt's book, Spock's book included sections on basic milestones of development, daily care of infants, feeding, and ailments. The most recent edition (Spock & Rothenberg, 1992), however, is a 700-page tome that includes a considerable amount of "psychology," including sections on feelings the parent may experience, why children of different ages act the way they do, and how to manage young children.

It is interesting to speculate about how the individuals who made pronouncements about child rearing developed their beliefs. One primary

FIGURE 1.1   Early Twentieth-Century Postcard Depicting a Physician Warning of the Perils of Cow's Milk.

source of ideas is personal experience with children; some of the advice givers were parents, although many were not. Aristotle had two children, but Locke had none. The Reverend John Wesley was a bachelor most of his life, although he was married briefly to a woman with four of her own children. Rousseau was himself a father five times over; however, because the children were born out of wedlock (to the same mother), he placed his newborns in an orphanage. Apparently, Rousseau based his beliefs on three kinds of "evidence": his work as a tutor, observations of French peasant children, and what he heard about children in primitive cultures (Thomas, 1992).

It is likely that many of these early child-rearing "experts" were lacking in experience with children and based their views on casual rather than systematic observations. Even if they did have children, that experience did not automatically give them expertise. Mere experience and casual observation are not enough: Only careful research can generate a sound understanding of children and parenting.

Of all the influential child-rearing "authorities" cited in the preceding discussion, the only one who gained a rich background of experience with parents and children before writing his book was Benjamin Spock. Spock wrote his book only after working for a decade as a pediatrician and fathering two children. Even so, he questioned the wisdom of his own advice and admitted that "when a young man writes a book about how to raise children, in a sense it's his reflection on the way his mother raised him" (Spock & Morgan, 1989, p. 136).

To his credit, Spock began to investigate the validity of his advice. In 1958 he started an exploratory child-rearing study with twenty-one families (Bloom, 1972). Although it was not the first empirical study of child rearing and was not adequate to evaluate the effects of different parenting practices, it represented a developmental milestone among those "experts" dispensing child-rearing advice. That effort marked the recognition of the necessity to base child-rearing advice on scientific evidence.

The Advent of Child-Rearing Research

Only relatively recently has systematic research into child rearing begun to inform our views about children and parents. Beliefs about children and parents, once the province of ministers, philosophers, and physicians, now are based on research findings. It is difficult to pinpoint the exact date of the genesis of child-rearing studies, in part because of the multiple roots of and influences on the field of developmental psychology as a scientific discipline (Cairns, 1983; Kessen, 1979). If one defines *study* as careful observation, then diaries from the nineteenth century might qualify, such as Charles Darwin's essay about his son, published in 1877 (Kessen, 1965). However, if one defines *study* as systematic investigation involving more than one subject, the first such effort was under the direction of a pioneer of American psychology and one of the founders of developmental psychology, G. Stanley Hall. Charles H. Sears (1899) in collaboration with Hall at Clark University in Worcester, Massachusetts, developed a questionnaire to study parents' views about child punishment.

Another early parenting study was reported in a doctoral dissertation published in 1927 by Gertrude Laws. Her study focused explicitly on parents and their attitudes about their children's social adjustment. Shortly thereafter, a number of investigators began to publish studies about parenting. *Child Development,* the leading journal in the field of developmental psychology, was first published in 1930. By the end of the 1930s, investigations into the effects of different child-rearing practices on children began to appear, in part spurred by the developmental theories of Sigmund Freud and John Watson. Since that time, the amount of research on parenting has exploded.

The product of the research has been the construction of a psychology of parents and child rearing. This work has not been carried out by psychologists alone. Rather, biologists, physicians, educators, anthropologists, sociologists, and social workers have all contributed to the creation of a science of child psychology and child rearing (Cairns, 1983; Sears, 1975). Out of this heterogeneous research activity have come scientific "facts" about parents and children, representing what has been called another type of cultural invention (Scarr, 1985). As will be shown, however, this knowledge is not simply invented but reflects empirically derived findings. Some findings are discarded as a consequence of subsequent research, whereas others are refined, modified, or built on. In that way, our child-rearing knowledge has evolved rapidly with regard to theories, methods, and findings.

Four Trends of Change in Child-Rearing Research

As will become apparent in the subsequent chapters in this book, there have been a voluminous number of investigations into what has traditionally been called "socialization" but is more accurately labeled "child rearing." When taking a broad view of this area of study, four basic trends can be identified. Each of these trends reflects a different face of the same issue: an increasing appreciation for the variation that is inherent in the study of parents and child rearing.

Foremost, views of children and the parent-child relationship have changed. For instance, children are no longer considered innately sinful or corrupt as they were 350 years ago. More important, the very nature of the parent-child relationship is now regarded differently than it was just thirty years ago. Children are no longer considered passive receptacles awaiting parental influence. Researchers now recognize the active nature of children and the many ways in which children influence parents (Bell & Chapman, 1986; Russell & Russell, 1992; Scarr & McCartney, 1983). Consequently, the bidirectional and interdependent nature of the relationship is increasingly being recognized.

A second change-related trend contrasts with the earlier research focusing on static qualities of parenting. Today, researchers are giving much more attention to the marked change and variability that occurs in parental behavior. Rather than viewing parents as stable or even immutable, current investigations are documenting the ways in which parents modify their behavior. As will be discussed in a subsequent chapter, there is now strong evidence that parents change their behavior in response to a variety of factors in themselves, their children, and the context.

Over the past fifteen years or so, research findings have supported a third trend: Parents and their child-rearing behaviors are sensitive to changes or perturbations in their environment. The family is not protected from problems in the world around it. Similarly, a parent-child relationship may not be buffered from or immune to problems in the environment, such as a conflictual marital relationship. Rather, evidence is accumulating that the parent-child relationship is inextricably embedded in and affected by layers of larger social and societal contexts.

A fourth trend concerns recognition of the increasing number of behavioral features inherent in effective parenting. Early research tended to focus on single characteristics such as acceptance or overprotection. Subsequently, interest has focused on qualities of warmth, sensitivity, and control, to name a few of the popular constructs. However, as investigations have accumulated, it is increasingly clear that effective child rearing involves many attributes and different behaviors. New dimensions of parenting are periodically "discovered" such as power sharing (Kochanska, 1992), monitoring (Crouter, MacDermid, McHale, & Perry-Jenkins, 1990), or balancing parental needs with child needs (Dix, 1992; Maccoby, 1992). These newly discovered attributes of parents necessitate a change in our understanding about the nature of child rearing.

Each of these trends, which will be examined further in subsequent chapters, has contributed to the conclusion that parent-child relationships represent a complex phenomenon capable of modifications or even transformations. To understand child rearing, therefore, it is necessary to acknowledge and account for change in parenting. Only a dynamic perspective can do this.

A Dynamic Perspective on Child Rearing

Historically, the predominant view of parents has considered them to be largely inert entities that embody one or perhaps two static characteristics. A parent might be sensitive or strict or perhaps warm and firm. The possibility that a parent might show behavioral variability was not considered. Parents were also viewed as unchanging across time. Once a parent was assessed or classified, it was assumed that the parent had always been and would continue to be that same way. Similarly, until recently, parents were assumed to behave the same way toward their different children.

Such a static view is limited for a variety of reasons. Foremost, it ignores an essential characteristic of parenting, that of making behavioral adjustments during ongoing interactions. Static views fail to recognize that parents are thinking beings who modify their child-rearing behavior based on a variety of considerations, from transient emotions to long-term goals.

A dynamic perspective is oriented toward two features of a phenomenon: the capacity for change and the processes involved. A focus on change does not mean that stable qualities are ignored. Rather, stability is recognized as part of a system that at the moment is in equilibrium. Dynamic perspectives focus on the capacity for change and the types of adjustments made, with the expectation that such information can reveal much about the nature of the individual and the parent-child relationship.

There are many ways in which parents adjust their child-rearing behavior. A father may appear attentive and indulgent at one moment, but after a child's transgression, he may suddenly become angry and strict. A mother may be restrictive about her adolescents' peer relationships but permissive regarding chores and household rules. A parent might be lenient with one temperamentally difficult child as a strategy to avoid conflict but controlling with a compliant child. Change in parenting also occurs across larger time frames. The birth of another child, changing work demands, and revised beliefs about child rearing are just three examples of sources of modified parenting behavior over time.

Until relatively recently, the variability in child rearing was essentially ignored and not considered to be of scientific value. I argue, however, that change in parental behavior contains much important information about parents, the nature of child rearing, and even how parents affect their offspring. Change is intrinsic to parenting; to neglect it is to disregard one of the most prominent features of parenting.

Besides attending to change, a dynamic perspective focuses on the ongoing interactional processes. As this book will make clear, there are many different types of processes involved in parent-child relationships. For example, there are processes associated with multiple potential influences on caregiving behavior, processes concerning how parents think about their children, and processes concerning how parent and contextual variables combine to influence a child's development. By examining the process, one can begin to understand the interrelations among multiple variables.

One way to appreciate the nature of the ongoing processes in child rearing is to recognize the inherent tension caused by competing concerns, goals, or needs. For example, a mother who has taken her preschooler shopping in the supermarket is likely to be simultaneously concerned with maintaining her child's good behavior, planning menus, and selecting the groceries she needs. The quality of her child rearing is likely to be a reflection of how she deals with those competing demands. Similarly, parents often hold conflicting child-rearing goals. One of the most common sources of friction is in the competition between short- and long-term goals. Often the particular goal orientation of the parent results in different behaviors: For example, a short-term goal of placating a child may mean giving in to the child's inappropriate demands. A longer-term orientation dictates that the parent stand firm.

Dealing with the competing needs of a child or of different individuals is another fundamental dynamic of parenting. At all times a parent has the needs of two individuals at hand: the child and the parent. Parents who maximize their child's needs at the expense of their own needs would be labeled *child-centered,* in contrast to the opposite pattern of a *parent-centered* adult (Dix, 1992; Pulkkinen, 1982). In reality, rather than parents being one type or the other, there is a constant tension between the two orientations. Eleanor Maccoby (1992) recognized this dynamic when she argued that parenting involves the process of inducing the child "into a system of reciprocity ... [whereby the parent] assumes a deep and lasting obligation to behave so as to promote the best interests of the child, even when this means setting aside certain self-interests" (p. 1012). This process grows even more complex when other family members and their needs are added to the interaction.

Perhaps the most conspicuous indication of the tension inherent in parenting can be found in the qualities that have been identified as attributes of effective parents. As will be discussed in more detail in a subsequent chapter, there is research evidence that effective parents often must balance between two competing thoughts or behaviors. Studies have found that effective child-rearers must be warm but also firm, involved but not too intrusive, and consistent but also flexible in their disciplining (Grusec & Goodnow, 1994; Maccoby & Martin, 1983). Effective parents also promote the development of conscience in their children by inducing some, but not too much, affective discomfort (guilt or anxiety) following a child's misbehavior (Kochanska, 1993). How do effective parents accomplish these common balancing acts? A model depicting this process will be presented in Chapter 6.

A dynamic perspective provides a better account of the phenomenon of parenting and many of the research findings than a static model can. Such a view results in different implications as well. Instead of cataloging particular characteristics of parents, such as child-rearing attitudes and skills, what becomes important is how those predispositions and skills are used in ongoing situations. How does the parent appraise the child and situation? In what ways is child rearing affected by changes in the context? How do parental characteristics interact with qualities of the child? These questions are at the heart of a dynamic view of child rearing, which this book makes clear is the only approach to parents and child rearing that can adequately account for the complexity and changes inherent in the process.

2

Theories of
Parent-Child Relationships

Theoretical approaches to parent-child relationships differ widely on a variety of fundamental dimensions. They contrast in their scope, such as whether parent-child relationships are viewed from a phylogenetic (development of the species over time) or an ontogenetic (development of individuals over their life span) perspective. The approaches also differ markedly in the importance they attach to parents as environmental influences on their children's development. Many, but not all, of the theories propose a specific mechanism by which parents influence their offspring. The theories also differ dramatically concerning whether they lead to testable propositions and allow the generation of new hypotheses. These dimensions should be kept in mind as theories of parent-child relationships are described.

It is difficult to formulate categories of theories, given the multidimensional nature of the differences. However, there are five principal theoretical approaches in the area of parent-child relationships. The major contemporary theories are ethology, attachment, social learning, ecological systems, and behavioral genetics. Sometimes in concert with the preceding, but more often independent of them, are a number of narrower theoretical approaches to parent-child relationships. Three examples will be described: Lev Vygotsky's theory of zones of proximal development, Richard Bell's control system theory, and attribution theory.

The contributions of an outdated but influential theoretical orientation merit mentioning also. What is considered the first "modern" theory about parent-child relationships was developed by Sigmund Freud and subsequently refined by his followers (e.g., Karen Horney, Ernst Jones, & Margaret Ribble). Although Freud is famous for his rich theory of the conscious and unconscious mind, his developmental theory is less well known and more limited. At the centerpiece of his theory about how children develop are the five *psychosexual stages*. He hypothesized that children's development progressed in a fixed and orderly sequence through discrete stages. These stages are the oral (roughly, from birth to one year of age), anal (one to three years), phallic (three to six years), latency (six to twelve years), and

11

genital (beginning at about age twelve) stages. Each stage represented the locus of an individual's sexual energy.

Although maturation drove development, Freud also believed that parents played an important role in this developmental sequence. Parents must successfully guide their children through each stage in order for the children to proceed to the next one. If the parents did not negotiate a stage appropriately but instead frustrated their children, the children could become stuck, or "fixed," in that particular stage. An orally fixated person, for example, might exhibit such symptoms as excessive talking, gum chewing, or smoking.

Freud believed that both the mother and father were uniquely important for a child's development. He theorized that the mother-infant relationship was the prototypic one and that all subsequent relationships were based on that one. Fathers' importance came later; they played a prominent role in the moral development of their sons, according to his theory of *identification*. During the phallic stage, children identify with their same-sex parent. Freud developed a series of assumptions about boys' feelings of attraction to their mother, followed by anger at and fear of the father, commonly known as the *Oedipal complex*. These feelings are resolved by the boy's identifying with the father, a process that promotes superego, or conscience, development (Emde, 1992). Ironically, even though both mothers and fathers were given a prominent role in Freud's (1936) developmental theory, he wrote little about them.

Freud's legacy is mixed. Although his theoretical ideas stimulated research and theory development in a variety of domains, his developmental theory has not been supported by empirical research. The clearest example comes from the attempts to test the tenets of Freud's psychosexual theory. For example, studies have found no long-term ramifications of differences in feeding practices (e.g., breast- versus bottle-feeding, demand versus scheduled feeding, abrupt versus gradual weaning) in direct conflict with predictions based on Freudian theory (Sewell & Mussen, 1952). Despite that critical failing and other shortcomings of the theory, this first developmental theory helped to open the scientific door to the study of parental influences on children's behavior and the development of other theories.

Major Theories About Parent-Child Relationships

Currently, the five theoretical orientations mentioned previously guide much of the research in parent-child relationships. Although other theories have been used to explicate parent-child behavior, the five described here represent the most prominent theoretical orientations currently in use.

Ethology

From a chronological perspective, *ethological theory* is the most inclusive theoretical approach to parents, because it attempts to understand how parental behavior has evolved over tens of thousands of years. Developed from animal behavior research with a Darwinian root, it was initially extended into human behavior by Konrad Lorenz and Niko Tinbergen. It (and its offshoot, sociobiology) is intended to explain how forces of natural selection have modified behavior to enhance survival rates and reproductive fitness during the struggle for survival of the human species, *Homo sapiens.*

The ethological approach attempts to understand such questions as how the patterns of parenting that developed over the past 35,000 years represent successful adaptations to the environment. In particular, given that 99 percent of human generations lived in hunter-gatherer societies, the aim of the ethological approach is to explicate how contemporary parental behavior reflects and is affected by that evolutionary heritage (Fishbein, 1976).

Ethology's major tenets are that contemporary behavior reflects the adaptation of the organism to specific environments and that behavior should be observed in its naturally occurring setting. Therefore, ethologists analyze the mutual influences between organism and environment (Hinde, 1989). Through the mechanism of natural selection, individuals have evolved to be sensitive or particularly attuned to certain environmental events or stimuli. Consequently, both parents and their offspring should have characteristics and exhibit behaviors that are designed to promote the survival of the young.

Ethologists have studied the adaptive value of various attributes and qualities of parent-child behavior. It is easy to recognize that the cry of an infant is a powerful and aversive stimulus designed to elicit rapid caregiver attention. However, more subtle stimuli have also been linked to caregiving behavior. Some ethologists have argued that the unique facial characteristics of human infants and other young animals that we perceive as "cute" (e.g., large forehead, round cheeks, small nose and chin) represent a special class of stimuli that serve to turn on an "innate releasing mechanism" in adults and therefore result in caregiving (Eibl-Eibesfeldt, 1970). In a similar vein, Kevin MacDonald (1992) has proposed that the feeling of positive affect (i.e., love) is a characteristic that was selected over time to ensure cohesive family relationships and paternal investment in children.

Other ethologically oriented scientists have argued that evolutionary influences can result in different patterns of parenting behavior. According to some biologists, parents may invest more or less care in their offspring depending on assessments of the likelihood of the offspring's survival and ability to reproduce (e.g., Trivers, 1974). According to this view, it was adaptive for our ancestors with scarce resources not to provide many resources for premature or handicapped infants who were unlikely to survive.

A recent ethological view of child rearing builds on the idea that access to resources is associated with differential parenting practices. The provocative hypothesis links parental behavior, reproductive strategies, and children's physical and emotional development (Belsky, Steinberg, & Draper, 1991). It is proposed that there are two distinct and divergent evolutionary pathways designed to promote reproductive success. In contexts with relatively few resources (e.g., low-income families) and thus more stress, child rearing tends to be characterized by harshness, rejection, and insensitive and inconsistent parenting. In short, Belsky and his colleagues argue that parenting in stressful environments reflects a more limited investment strategy and a poorer quality of child care. This results in problematic parent-child relationships and, subsequently, earlier puberty, earlier sexual activity, and more offspring. Alternatively, in contexts of low stress (or more resources), parents are more sensitive and responsive to their children, which leads to fewer child behavior problems, later puberty, later sexual activity, and fewer progeny. Unlike some ethological theories, this hypothesis has several tenets that can be empirically tested; studies are under way to test the accuracy of these propositions.

Attachment Theory

Attachment theory has its roots in both neopsychoanalytic theory and ethology, but it is considerably more circumscribed. The theory was designed to address the establishment, maintenance, and consequences of the affectionate bonds between a parent and child. John Bowlby (1969), a British child psychiatrist, initially formulated the central ideas. As the theory evolved, it grew to reflect Bowlby's long-term collaboration with Mary Ainsworth, an American psychologist.

The core premise of the theory, as it stands today, is that attachment between a parent and infant reflects a behavioral system that has been adapted to promote survival and competent functioning of the offspring. One part of the system promotes the proximity between the infant and caregiver, serving the function of protecting and nurturing the infant. The system is also designed to facilitate the development of exploratory and independent behavior of an infant. This is achieved by caregivers providing a *secure base*. Such a base allows infants to feel comfortable exploring their environment because they know they can retreat to the safety of the caregiver if distressed or fearful. After regaining a sense of well-being, infants in the presence of the caregiver can then return to exploring the environment and developing competencies. Caregivers establish this feeling of a secure base over the first year of life by being sensitive to the cues emitted by infants, addressing the infants' needs, and providing emotional regulation. In turn, infants learn to trust that caregivers will take care of their needs. That trust develops into a secure attachment that promotes exploration of the environment, supports the development of social and cognitive competence, and establishes feelings of efficacy (Ainsworth & Bowlby, 1991).

The quality of this initial relationship translates into two fundamentally different types of attachment: securely attached and insecurely attached individuals. The theory holds that these attachment relationships have corresponding internal cognitive representations. As their social world expands, children bring with them this internal representation of the self and others, also called a *working model*. Because individuals base their interpersonal behavior on their working models (Bowlby, 1988), insecurely attached children behave differently from securely attached children when interacting with people other than their parents, such as peers or teachers.

The theory has been extended to capture how individuals' internal representation of self and others may influence their behavior in later childhood and adulthood (Ainsworth, 1989). In particular, investigations linking adults' working models with how they form romantic relationships and how they parent their own children have been increasing, as will be discussed in Chapter 5.

Attachment theory has recently been built on by Patrick Davies and Mark Cummings (1994) to include the effect of marital relationships on children's feelings of security. They propose that children's emotional security is based on their experiences with their parents' conflict. If parents are engaged in frequent acrimonious interactions, children will feel insecure and worry about the implications of the conflict. Alternatively, children who are exposed to no marital discord or to constructive conflict that gets resolved amicably are likely to develop feelings of emotional well-being and have improved capacities for emotional regulation.

Social Learning Theories

Social learning theories represent a group of theories that concern how behavior is modified through specific social experiences. Contemporary theories have evolved from a mixture of previous theories, including psychoanalysis, learning theories, and cognitive theories (Cairns, 1979; Grusec, 1992). One early influential approach reformulated some of Freud's ideas into testable hypotheses using Clark Hull's learning theory (Dollard, Doob, Miller, Mowrer, & Sears, 1939). Other early social learning theorists limited their attention to the principles of classical and operant conditioning.

The "father of behaviorism," John B. Watson (1880–1961), was also the father of the explicit link between social learning and child rearing. The learning mechanisms for his ideas came from the work of Ivan Pavlov and Edward Thorndike. Watson espoused an extreme environmental and mechanistic view of development. Humans were viewed as machines fueled by learning principles (Lomax, Kagan, & Rosenkrantz, 1978). His well-known boast about being able to determine the outcome of children appeared in 1926:

> Give me a dozen healthy infants, well-formed, and my own specified world to bring them up in and I'll guarantee to take any one at random and train him to become any type of specialist I might select—a doctor, lawyer, artist, merchant-chief and, yes, even into beggar-man and thief, regardless of his talents, penchants, tendencies, abilities, vocations and race of his ancestors (Watson, 1926, p. 10).

A few years later, Watson tempered his claim but not his view when he wrote that "it is what happens to individuals after birth that makes one a hewer of wood and a drawer of water, another a diplomat, a thief, a successful business man or a far-famed scientist" (1930, p. 270). His child-rearing manual, *Psychological Care of Infant and Child* (1928), was intended to guide parents in rearing psychologically healthy children and to sit on the shelf next to Dr. Holt's book.

Watson's social learning theory was primarily one of classical conditioning. He saw the learning principle as a method for controlling fears in children and curing such common problems as shyness. Parents also needed to be warned of the dangers of "coddling" or giving affection to infants, because he was convinced it resulted in learned "invalidism." Watson believed that the prudent use of classical conditioning represented a powerful environmental tool to allow parents to influence their children's development (Horowitz, 1992).

Watson's theory largely neglected operant conditioning as a learning principle; however, after the work of B. F. Skinner, no social learning theory could be complete without it. Skinner's functional analysis of behavior and the delineation of the three-term contingency relation (antecedent stimulus, behavior, consequent stimulus) are core components of social learning theories (Gewirtz & Pelaez-Nogueras, 1992). The identification of how positive and negative reinforcement as well as punishment influence the probability of a behavior recurring has frequently seen applications in parent-child relationships. As will be discussed in Chapter 3, operant conditioning theory has been used to account for such topics as how children acquire bad habits from their parents and how parents inadvertently reinforce behaviors they do not like, such as whining or noncompliance.

Among the different social learning theories, some have remained largely limited to the application of learning principles to interpersonal relationships (Bijou & Baer, 1961), and others have attempted to integrate stimulus-response learning theory with psychoanalytic theory (Sears, Rau, &

Alpert, 1965). Currently, the broadest social learning theory is the one articulated by Albert Bandura (1989; Bandura, Ross, & Ross, 1963). His pioneering learning studies of the impact of modeling greatly advanced the social learning perspective. In his famous "Bobo doll" studies, Bandura and his colleagues demonstrated that children only need to observe an act in order to acquire it. Subsequently, he showed that children are more likely to imitate models who are perceived as nurturant and powerful, attributes common to parents (Bandura, 1965).

Bandura recognized the fundamental role that direct learning and observational learning play in the establishment of new behavior. Observational learning is an efficient way of learning because it has few costs for the individual. What is observed may or may not be modeled, depending on a series of cognitive components (e.g., attention, memory, imagery, and motivation). Once a behavior is established, it can readily be maintained through reinforcement. As Bandura's theory has developed, it has grown progressively more cognitively oriented; he now calls it *social cognitive theory* (Bandura, 1989). His theory currently emphasizes the cognitive and information-processing capacities of an individual that mediate social behavior (e.g., attention, memory). In particular, Bandura proposes that individuals' feelings of self-efficacy, or beliefs about their ability to effect changes in the environment, constitute one of the key ingredients to understanding human behavior (Grusec, 1992). As will be seen, this cognitive attribute has been effectively applied to understanding parental behavior.

Ecological Systems Theory

One of the limitations of attachment and social learning theories is that they do not explicitly recognize the role of the context. Ecological systems theory, as developed by Urie Bronfenbrenner (1979, 1989), was designed to do just that. At its most fundamental level, the theory was intended to expand on Kurt Lewin's (1935) classical formula of behavior, $B = f(PE)$, meaning that behavior is a joint function of the person and the environment. Ecologists believe that one cannot and should not separate out the person from the environment; the two are integrally connected. This constant connection or interaction between the two results in *transactional* influence. In the case of parent-child relationships, this means that a child's behavior or characteristics can influence both the parent and the contexts in which the interactions occur. In turn, these experiences influence the child's subsequent behavior and characteristics. For example, an athletic child may persuade her parents to allow her to join a soccer team. That involvement, in turn, may result in new friendships and family trips to attend weekend games.

The formal ecological systems theory consists of a number of principles, propositions, and corollaries (Bronfenbrenner, 1979). The central contribution of the theory lies in explicating how a child's development occurs within a nested series of contextual levels. These levels of context that impinge on an individual are hierarchically organized. At the most proximal level is the *microsystem,* referring to behavior and interactions occurring in the immediate setting. A parent playing with his or her child represents an interaction at the microsystem level. The second level is the *mesosystem,* which refers to the processes or linkages taking place between two or more settings that contain the individual; it is the system of microsystems. An example of the links between two settings is the situation in which events taking place in the home (e.g., marital discord) affect a child's performance in school and vice versa (Bronfenbrenner, 1986). Another example is provided by the fact that children may behave quite differently in different contexts. Understanding the reasons underlying these cross-situational behavioral variations and similarities is at the heart of the mesosystem analysis.

The third level of context is the *exosystem,* which represents domains that impinge on or encompass the immediate context of interaction but do not ordinarily contain the child. As will be discussed in Chapter 4, a parent's job is one such external societal structure that can indirectly affect a child and the quality of parent-child interaction. The final level of Bronfenbrenner's theory is the *macrosystem.* This level concerns the most distal determinants and is used to refer to the major, overarching characteristics or structures of a culture or subculture. Cultural institutions, general cultural beliefs about children and parenting, and subcultural traditions involving child-rearing practices are captured at this level of analysis.

The ecological systems model has been particularly useful in two ways. First, it has helped to focus attention on the role that the context plays in the lives of children and their parents. Second, it has afforded a theoretical structure within which to integrate diverse research results, such as the influence of different types of external environments (e.g., work, social networks, and neighborhoods) on the adaptive or maladaptive functioning of families (Belsky, 1993).

Behavioral Genetics Theory

Behavioral genetics theory stands in stark contrast to the previous theories on several dimensions. Most important, the overarching goal of the theory is to understand the genetic influences on human behavior (Goldsmith, 1994; Plomin, 1990). Toward that end, the behavioral geneticists typically employ within-family research designs, such as comparing monozygotic and dizygotic twins, siblings, or adoptive children with their biological and adoptive parents. These comparisons allow assessments of the degree of similarity among the family members on such measures as intelligence, personality, and social behavior.

This orientation toward genetic determinants rather than environmental influences can be clearly traced back to one of the forefathers of the approach, Arnold Gesell (1880–1961). Gesell, trained as an educator, developmental psychologist, and physician, proposed a nativist theory of development. He believed that children's genetic constitution determined the natural unfolding of their inherited predispositions. Parents' central role was to support this unfolding by providing an environment appropriately matched to the child's state of maturational readiness (Thelen & Adolph, 1992).

Gesell's legacy can be readily seen in contemporary behavioral genetics; however, in contrast to Gesell, who was primarily interested in charting the normative course of development, behavioral geneticists have focused on individual differences within both normal and abnormal populations. Through statistical analyses comparing individuals' characteristics within families, behavioral geneticists have found that for a variety of cognitive and personality variables, the heritability between parent and child is in the range of 30 to 60 percent. Nongenetic factors, including the environment and error variance, must account for the rest of the statistical differences. Consequently, behavioral geneticists are beginning to turn their attention to understanding the influence of the environment, such as the impact of child rearing (Plomin, 1994).

Within any family, the environment is composed of *shared* (among family members) and *nonshared* environmental influences. Behavioral geneticists reason that if child rearing has strong effects, all the children within a family should be affected alike and develop similar characteristics. However, siblings are often found to be dramatically different from one another on a variety of indices (Dunn & Plomin, 1990). There appears, therefore, to be a strong influence of nonshared, idiosyncratic environmental factors on children's development. As will be discussed in Chapter 5, this lack of shared child-rearing influence has led some to argue that within the normal range, parenting behavior and parental characteristics have little impact on children's development (Rowe, 1994; Scarr, 1992).

Narrower Theoretical Approaches Addressing Child Rearing

In addition to the aforementioned major theories addressing parent-child relationships, there are many other, narrower theories about child rearing. These theories have a more limited focus on particular aspects of child rearing. Three prominent examples of such theories are discussed in the following sections: Vygotsky's concept of the zone of proximal development, Bell's theory of control systems, and attribution theory.

Vygotsky's Theory

Although the Russian psychologist Lev Vygotsky (1896–1934) did not live long enough to formulate a comprehensive theory of development, his conception of the role parents play in their children's development has been influential (Van der Veer & Valsiner, 1988; Wertsch, 1985). Vygotsky's work focused on understanding children's cognitive development, and he gave parents and other social agents a prominent role in that developmental process. He believed that social interactions provide the primary arena for development.

The central role that parents play in this developmental process is captured by the concept of the *zone of proximal development.* This concept refers to the more advanced behavior a child is capable of exhibiting while in the presence of and with the assistance of adults or more mature peers. According to Vygotsky, children's development is driven by their experiences in this zone (Wertsch, 1985). The idea of the zone can be readily appreciated when one compares the following two images: First, picture the havoc that would occur if a child were left alone in a toy store. Now consider what children's behavior is actually like in toy stores. Parents take children to such stores all the time; only rarely do children become unmanageable there. Vygotsky believed that the very act of taking children to places like toy stores or engaging them in more advanced tasks than they could perform on their own was one of the main "motors" of development.

The fundamental way parents are able to elicit more mature behavior is through the process of *scaffolding.* Parents erect a structure around a desired behavior to support children's more advanced behavior. As children grow more advanced in their linguistic, cognitive, or social interactional ability, parents can dismantle the scaffolding. Eventually, children are able to navigate through a toy store on their own, without parents closely monitoring their every action. Vygotsky believed that repeatedly exposing their children to the zone of proximal development was a key part of the role that parents play.

Bell's Control System Model

A second example of a narrow theory of parent-child relationships is one that was designed to explicate the nature of ongoing parent-child interactions. Rather than viewing parents as determining their children's behavior or children as determining their parents' behavior, Richard Bell developed the control system model to account for the ongoing reciprocal nature of interactions (Bell, 1971; Bell & Chapman, 1986). The model reflects the view that parents and children regulate each other's behavior. According to Bell, parents have an upper and lower limit of tolerance for the intensity, frequency, and situational appropriateness of their children's behavior. These limits are based on expectations and largely determined by previous interactions. Parents attempt to keep their children within the ideal boundary set by upper and lower limits.

Most often, children violate parents' upper limits. This might mean the child is too loud, too active, or engaged in an unacceptable behavior. The parent reacts by reducing or redirecting the child's excessive behavior so it falls back into the acceptable range. Bell argued that the model holds equally well from the child's perspective. If a parent gives a child inadequate attention, approaching the child's lower limit, the child may act in a way to prime or stimulate the parent to action.

This theory of mutual regulation has received support from observational studies of parents and children focusing on such child characteristics as activity level, independence, and responsiveness (Bell & Chapman, 1986). However, the model is best suited to account for parent-child relationships during times of disequilibrium (Maccoby & Martin, 1983). When the parent-child dyad is in a period of stability and the individuals are meeting each other's expectations, the model has little explanatory power.

Attribution Theory

A third example of a narrow theory addressing child rearing comes from the domain of parents' social cognition. To date, the most fruitful theoretical approach to understanding parental thinking and, in turn, child rearing has come from applications of social psychology's attribution theory. More accurately, several different attribution theorists (e.g., Fritz Heider, Bernard Weiner, Harold Kelley, Edward Jones) have provided the conceptual framework for examining the way that parents explain and evaluate their own and their children's behavior.

Attribution theory has guided studies addressing a variety of questions about the immediate and long-term determinants of parent and child behavior as well as the perceived causes of social and cognitive outcomes in children (see review by S. Miller, 1995). Parental attributions are important because the types of socialization practices adopted are presumably based on those perceptions. Consequently, the types of attributions parents make may eventually result in particular developmental outcomes for their children.

One of the strengths of attribution theory is that it yields clear and testable hypotheses. For example, an attributional analysis of children's misbehavior leads to the predictions that the seriousness of the misdeed should be based on parental assessments of the child's motivation, knowledge, and ability (Dix & Grusec, 1985). Furthermore, attribution theory leads to predictions about parental affect: The types of attributions parents make regarding child misdeeds should be related to parental emotional responses to that behavior, as will be indicated in Chapter 3.

Theories and Parent-Child Dynamics

How well do the theories account for the dynamics of parent-child relationships? Each of the three narrower theoretical approaches focuses on different aspects of ongoing parent-child interactions and therefore captures different qualities of the dynamic nature of parent-child interactions. Bell's model is clearly the most dynamic, because it focuses on adjustments made when the parent-child system is in disequilibrium. Similarly, Vygotsky's model of the zone of proximal development focuses on a dynamic process whereby parents draw the child into a more advanced level of functioning. Attribution theories also recognize the ongoing process whereby parents interpret and reassess their own and their children's behavior.

The ability of the five major theories to account for the interactional nature of parent-child relationships is more varied. Attachment and social learning theories recognize ongoing parent-child interactions as the central determinant of future behavior. In contrast, behavioral genetics until recently has not considered family interactions to be important. However, with the recognition of the role of nonshared environmental influences on development, the theoretical orientation is more open to recognizing the importance of interactions. The ethological theory intends to reveal how interactions are adaptive (or maladaptive) across time. Finally, ecological systems theory sees interaction as a core focus but examines how behavior is embedded and nested within larger contexts. The theory also appreciates that changes at higher contextual levels can result in modifications at the microsystem level.

To varying degrees, each of the theories recognizes that the dynamics of parent-child interactions is the core phenomenon of interest. That commonality raises the question of how the eight theories are interrelated. In some cases, the competing theoretical accounts complement each other, as in the case of ethology and attachment theories. More often the theories reside independently, without impinging on one another. The last way the theories can coexist is in conflict. Nowhere is the theoretical conflict in sharper contrast than in the perspectives taken by two of the theories on the classical problem of how to deal with a crying infant.

A strict social learning interpretation would warn parents that after infants' basic needs have been addressed, further attention serves only to reinforce the crying behavior and increase the likelihood that the infant will cry more in the future. The danger is that parents are "spoiling" the infant by teaching that a cry will be rewarded with parental attention. Consequently, the learning theory perspective would recommend that parents ignore a crying infant to extinguish the behavior (Gewirtz & Boyd, 1977).

Attachment theory dictates a very different response. Crying is a distress signal sent to a caregiver. It is important that caregivers respond quickly and appropriately so that infants will learn to trust caregivers and understand that their needs will be taken care of (Ainsworth & Bell, 1977). For a child to develop a healthy attachment and trust in the secure base, it is imperative for parents to respond to the crying.

Directions Toward Theoretical Integration

How might contrasts among the theories be resolved or the theories synthesized? A synthesis is a long way off, but one common piece of turf among many contemporary theories is the increasing appreciation that behavior and development need to be considered from the perspective that the organism is in constant transaction with the environment (Cairns, 1991). Interaction between parents and children does not occur in a vacuum; the fact that behavior is continually being influenced by the environment will likely get heightened theoretical recognition in the future.

A second direction for future theoretical growth is a recognition of the unique qualities of parent-child relationships. With the exception of attachment theory, theories of parent-child relationships do not adequately account for the unique history of prior interactions. Some efforts are under way to address this deficiency. *Social relationships theory* (Hinde, 1989) holds that the interactions that form interpersonal relationships represent the most important aspect of the environment. Interactions are embedded in long-term relationships; they are affected by both preceding interactions and expectations about future ones. Therefore, social interactions and the quality of the relationships must be the central topic of inquiry.

In each family, there is a series of relationships (mother-father, mother-child, father-child, sibling-sibling). Each relationship is composed of a set of interactions. Typically, most of the information about relationships and interactions goes ignored by researchers. Hinde (1976) argued that data about relationships can be collected on multiple dimensions, including the content (what the people do together), the diversity (the range of things done), the quality (the participants' responsiveness to each other), the relative frequency and patterning of interactions, the reciprocal or complementary nature (e.g., equality versus dominance), and the intimacy and commitment.

Another unique quality of parent-child relationships is that they occur within the context of the family. *Family systems theory,* a prominent theoretical approach in clinical psychology (Minuchin, 1985; Schultz, 1984), focuses on such relationships. Those who adhere to this approach hold that relationships among all members of the family must be recognized in order for the family structure and functioning to be understood. One cannot simply focus on one particular parent-child dyad within a family. Rather, all family members and their interrelationships must be examined for the behavioral dynamics operating within a family to be appreciated. For example, *coparenting* is a basic family systems concept. It refers to the extent that parents are mutually supportive and accommodate to the other parent's style. This aspect of family structure can be assessed only by observing all the members of the family interacting together (McHale, 1995). At some point in the future, it is likely that family systems theory and social relationships theory will fuse to help form an integrated theory of parent-child relationships.

Summary

Five principal theories addressing parent-child relationships were described: ethology, attachment, social learning, ecological systems, and behavioral genetics theories. Each encompasses a different theoretical scope, focus, and perspective on the parent-child relationship. With the exception of behavioral genetics, each theory recognizes the primary importance of parental behavior for children's development. However, views concerning what are the important characteristics of parental behavior and the processes through which children are affected differ dramatically across the theoretical horizons.

There are many other theories of parent-child relationships that focus on particular aspects of the interaction. Three narrower theories were presented: Vygotsky's theory of zones of proximal development, Bell's control systems model, and attribution theory. Each of these theories highlights the dynamic nature of child-rearing behavior but from the different viewpoints of promoting more advanced child behavior, regulating the other's behavior, and inferring causes of behavior, respectively.

Contemporary theories of child rearing are largely isolated from each other. Two directions that may provide an avenue for integration are focusing on the constant transactions with the environment and emphasizing the unique qualities of parent-child relationships. Until that integration is achieved, the particular theoretical perspective adopted will have direct implications for what is studied, how it is studied, and how phenomena are interpreted.

3

Different Approaches Used in Studying Parent-Child Relationships

Having discussed the theoretical perspectives on parent-child relationships, I turn now to the fruits of those orientations: how parents are conceptualized and studied by researchers. Given the heterogeneous roots of developmental research in general and parent-child research in particular (as indicated in Chapter 1), it is not surprising that there exist a number of competing conceptualizations about the nature of parents. Parents have been perceived and studied in remarkably disparate ways.

Six distinct approaches can readily be identified in the literature. As will be seen, these approaches adopt different assumptions and ask different questions about parents. These six approaches can be labeled the *trait, social learning, social address, momentary process, child effects,* and *parental beliefs* approaches. For each of these, the approach is defined, its origins are described, samples of representative work are reviewed, and its current status is discussed.

Six Prominent Approaches

The Trait Approach

This is the best-known approach used to study parents, although it sometimes appears with the label of parental *style, typology, syndrome,* or *pattern.* In this approach, parents are divided into different groups depending on the traits that characterize their child-rearing behavior. Although different parents may use the same child-rearing techniques (e.g., prohibitions, support), the way the technique is behaviorally expressed (e.g., warmly, harshly) helps to determine the parenting style. These traits can be thought of as providing differing contexts that moderate the effectiveness of particular child-rearing practices (Darling & Steinberg, 1993).

The trait approach can be traced back to the earliest of parenting studies. In the 1930s, a variety of parenting traits were identified, the most influential of which was *overprotection,* or excessive maternal care. The psychiatrist David Levy used the case study approach in an effort to link maternal overprotection with several different child behavior problems (e.g., tyrannical behavior, dependency; Levy, 1943). Levy's work set the stage for subsequent investigations of different parental traits and their relation to child behavior. In particular, the traits of parental acceptance (sometimes called warmth) and rejection were based on Levy's work and have continued to be popular trait constructs (Rohner, 1986; Symonds, 1938).

The first rigorous methodological effort to identify parental traits occurred in the 1940s and represented the first of three classical parenting studies. Using both interviews and observational ratings of parental behavior in the home, the Fels Research Institute in Ohio began a longitudinal study of influences on children's development. Three main dimensions of parental behavior were identified: democracy, indulgence, and acceptance. The most important of these was *democracy,* defined as having a high level of communication in the family, consulting the child on policy decisions, giving the child choices, and encouraging self-reliant behavior. Children in democratic families were found to be the most socially competent (Baldwin, 1948; Baldwin, Kalhorn, & Breese, 1945).

By the end of the 1950s, various other parenting traits had also been investigated (e.g., protectiveness, rejection, child-centeredness, affection). In an effort to organize these and other parenting traits, Earl Schaefer (1959) created a "circumplex" model, or circular order, to identify the different types of parenting traits. The advantage of this hypothetical model of traits is that it simultaneously depicts on a continuum the relations between what are commonly considered to be the two most important child-rearing dimensions: the degree of warmth and the degree of control. Most of the popular child-rearing traits can then be placed somewhere along the continuum of the two dimensions. The parent who was *high* on giving the child autonomy and warm toward the child would be classified as democratic, whereas a parent who was *low* on giving the child autonomy and exhibited less warmth toward the child would be labeled as authoritarian. Examples of where the major parenting traits would be placed on the circumplex model are presented in Figure 3.1.

The second classical study of parenting, conducted by Robert Sears, Eleanor Maccoby, and Harry Levin (1957), took a different approach to documenting parent effects in a sample of 379 mothers. They investigated three questions: (1) how mothers were rearing their children; (2) the effects of different forms of rearing (including feeding disturbances, toilet training problems, aggressive behavior, and conscience development); and (3) why mothers used one type of training rather than another. To answer those questions, the investigators relied solely on maternal interviews for information about the mothers' child-rearing practices (which were then reduced to child-rearing patterns and dimensions) and the children's behaviors. Their major finding concerning parenting traits, reported in the book *Patterns of Child Rearing,* was that maternal warmth had "pervasive" positive effects on the children, whereas coldness was associated with feeding and bed-wetting problems.

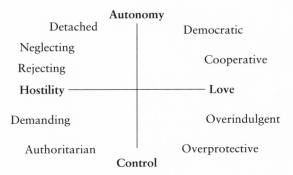

FIGURE 3.1 A Circumplex Model of Parenting Traits. (Adapted, with permission, from E. S. Schaefer, 1959, *Journal of Abnormal and Social Psychology*, 59, 226–235.)

The apex of the trait approach occurred with the publication of a monograph by Diana Baumrind (1971) reporting on the third classical parenting study. Based on an extensive, multimethod assessment of 133 parents of preschoolers in northern California, Baumrind developed a classification scheme primarily describing the amounts of control and warmth exhibited by parents. She identified three now well-known patterns of parenting. The three major classifications were authoritarian, authoritative, and permissive.

Authoritarian parents, representing about 20 percent of the sample, consisted of parents who insisted on obedience, used punishment, and typically exhibited little warmth toward their children. *Authoritative* parents, accounting for 19 percent of the sample, were warm but used firm control along with reasoning and encouraged their children's independence. Notice that both authoritarian and authoritative parents may have issued the very same prohibitions or commands to their children, but they differed dramatically in the style in which they administered them. *Permissive* parents, who made up 30 percent of the sample, were characterized as high on warmth but low on the control dimension. They rarely punished or restricted their children, and they did not require mature behavior; instead, permissive parents were warm and indulgent, letting their children make their own decisions. A fourth group, representing 8 percent of the sample, consisted of the *rejecting-neglecting* parents, who tended to reject their offspring and did not encourage independence. These four groups comprised three-quarters of the sample; the remaining parents could not be classified. Baumrind found that each of the three primary typologies was associated with different levels of child competence, as will be discussed in Chapter 5.

Maccoby and John Martin (1983) proposed that Baumrind's typology could be enhanced if parenting were thought of as varying systematically on two dimensions. One dimension was divided on the basis of the degree to which a parent made demands on or attempted to control the child. The other dimension concerned the extent to which a parent accepted the child and was responsive to the needs of that child. When these two dimensions are divided into high and low and then combined, the result is a fourfold scheme of parenting traits. Parents who are high on demanding and high on accepting are *authoritative.* Those who make high demands but are low on accepting are *authoritarian.* Parents who are low on demanding but high on acceptance are labeled *permissive* (or indulgent). Finally, those parents who are low on demanding and low on accepting are identified as *neglecting.*

Since the 1930s, well over thirty different parenting traits have been created by researchers in an effort to describe the nature of parents. The traits have ranged from accepting (Symonds, 1938) and child-centered (Pulkkinen, 1982) to aggressive (Sears et al., 1957) and punitive (McCord, 1988). The two trait approaches that have received the most attention are the one dealing with parental sensitivity and the one concerning parental warmth and control. *Sensitivity,* the appropriate and timely responsiveness of a parent, will be examined in Chapter 6.

Baumrind's well-known typology of parental traits not only has been used with parents of preschoolers but also has been applied to parents of adolescents (Fletcher, Darling, Dornbusch, & Steinberg, 1995; Hetherington & Clingempeel, 1992). As these studies that include parents of adolescents illustrate, the trait approach to parents continues to be a popular approach to assessing the nature of parents.

The Social Learning Approach

The *social learning* approach does not attempt to identify differences among parents but rather focuses on the learning principles that parents exhibit in their child-rearing behavior. Learning principles are embodied by parents in two ways. Foremost, parental influence occurs through dispensing of contingencies and through modeling. Second, parental behavior is determined through parents' own previous social learning experiences. Different proponents of this approach focus on different social learning principles, such as positive and negative reinforcement, punishment, or learning associations through classical conditioning. Although they espouse different learning mechanisms, researchers adopting this approach share the common belief that the essence of parenting can be captured by social learning constructs.

As discussed in Chapter 2, John B. Watson was the patriarch of this approach. Although his extremist views were not widely accepted (even by his wife), the learning approach to parents grew into a prominent perspective from the late 1950s through the 1970s. Early social learning theorists, including Robert Sears (1951; Sears et al., 1957) and John Whiting (Whiting & Child, 1953), applied learning principles to child rearing. In the 1960s and 1970s, the social learning theorists were influenced by B. F. Skinner and used learning principles to address a range of child-rearing problems. Researchers described how parents could reduce their infants' frequency of crying, eliminate "bratty" behavior, stop bed-wetting, and even get more sleep by using various learning principles, such as positive reinforcement, punishment, and discrimination learning (Pumroy & Pumroy, 1978). Before long, observational studies documented the naturally occurring incidence of reinforcement contingencies in the home and in the laboratory (Fagot, 1978; Lytton, 1979; Margolin & Patterson, 1975). For example, one socialization topic that has received considerable attention is the degree to which parents reinforce appropriate and punish inappropriate gender role behavior (Fagot, 1978; Langlois & Downs, 1980).

The social learning theory of Albert Bandura stimulated a variety of studies on the subject of imitation and uses of reward and punishment. Systematic experimental laboratory investigations of social learning processes became increasingly common in the 1960s and 1970s. Laboratory studies of modeling and analog experiments of punishment were also conducted, based on the learning approach (Parke, 1974). Childhood aggression and delinquency began to be interpreted as acquired behaviors learned from inappropriate interactions with parents (Eron, Huesmann, & Zelli, 1991).

The social learning approach toward parent-child relations continues to be actively pursued; the programmatic work by Gerald Patterson provides an excellent example. Since the 1970s, Patterson and his colleagues have investigated the origins of delinquent behavior in boys and how it is supported by subsequent parental behavior. His findings led to the development of a theory of "coercive cycles" in families, one that relies heavily on the principles of operant conditioning. Briefly, his coercion theory states that young boys often are trained to become uncontrollable by "inept" mothers (Patterson, 1980, 1982). Mothers who do not have adequate parenting skills resort to two types of behaviors that are ineffective for controlling their children. First, mothers "natter" (or fuss at) their sons either to do something (clean up their room) or not to do something (act aggressively). Their sons ignore the mothers' nattering, and often the mothers give up. If the mothers do not give up, they tend to escalate their efforts at control by raising their voices and then using physical punishment. However, the boys reciprocate by escalating their noxious behaviors. Both mother and child use force to try to get the other to back down. Generally, the sons outlast their mothers, who acquiesce.

According to the social learning interpretation, mothers are inadvertently reinforcing their sons' aversive behavior in these commonly occurring interactions. By terminating the nattering or their coercive efforts, the mothers are actually negatively reinforcing (removing a negative stimulus) their sons' behavior, which increases the likelihood that the behavior will be repeated in the future. Mothers of these aggressive boys have also been observed to positively reinforce noxious behavior by giving attention, laughing, or even verbally encouraging the misbehavior. In this manner, boys learn that coercive behavior is effective, and they use this acquired style of interaction when with peers and others.

The fault does not rest entirely on the shoulders of the mothers, however; they are "unacknowledged victims" (Patterson, 1980). These women are faced with the task of trying to deal with difficult children, whereas the fathers are largely passive or, as Patterson calls them, "resident guests." Putting blame aside, Patterson argues that the home represents a key early social learning influence that sets the stage for subsequent antisocial behavior in adolescence, as will be discussed in Chapter 5.

The Social Address Approach

The third prominent approach to parents can be labeled the *social address* approach, a term coined by Bronfenbrenner (1979). This approach typically involves comparing parents from different "addresses," whether they be different cultures, geographical locales, religious backgrounds, or socioeconomic status groups. The underlying assumption is that membership in a larger cultural group is the variable that not only determines how parents rear their children but also accounts for how parents affect their children's development. Variation within a cultural group is typically ignored. This approach is, in essence, a sociological approach to parents.

It was not sociologists who first used this approach, however, but cultural anthropologists. Cross-cultural studies of socialization began with Margaret Mead's (1928) study of people on the island of Samoa. She wanted to study the extent to which development was influenced by culture and had heard that, in contrast to American youth, adolescents there did not rebel. Mead's method was to interview carefully chosen informants as representatives of the culture. Although the data she collected, and particularly the accounts of sexual relations among the Samoan youth, have subsequently been criticized due to the apparent fabrications by the informants (Freeman, 1983), her study represented a watershed by laying the groundwork for other investigations exploring cultural differences in child-rearing practices and children's development. By the mid-1960s, a number of cross-cultural studies examining relations among cultures, child-rearing practices, and personality development had been published (Minturn & Lambert, 1964; Whiting, 1963).

Although cultural anthropologists were first on the scene, developmental psychologists soon began to conduct their own social address studies both across and within cultures. Geographic, economic, racial, and ethnic differences among parents in North America began to be studied. Studies investigated rural versus urban differences in parents (Stott, 1940) and social class differences in socialization practices such as feeding, toilet training, and disciplining (e.g., Davis & Havighurst, 1946).

Social address studies have also investigated racial and ethnic group differences in child-rearing practices. One early, classical study of both racial and socioeconomic differences in child rearing was conducted by Allison Davis and Robert Havighurst (1946). They used two- to three-hour interviews of 200 mothers to collect information about feeding, toilet training, and disciplinary practices in Caucasian and African-American middle- and working-class mothers. Comparing the social classes, they found that middle-class parents reportedly began training their children in self-responsibility, individual achievement, and cleanliness habits earlier than working-class parents. Within the two social classes, they found "striking similarities" as well as a few differences between the racial groups. Racial differences were found primarily in areas of feeding and cleanliness training. African-American parents were more relaxed about feeding and weaning their young children but stricter than Caucasian parents in toilet training.

Subsequent studies of racial differences have continued to catalog differences among African-American, Hispanic, and Caucasian parents. Evidence is accumulating, however, that as in the study of intelligence, there is considerable variation within cultural groups that typically is ignored in favor of studying the between-group variation (Ogbu, 1981). For example, researchers recently discovered wide variability in the disciplinary practices reported by a sample of low-income black mothers (Kelley, Power, & Wimbush, 1992). Maternal education, age, and religious beliefs as well as father absence were all found to be associated with particular disciplinary practices.

Contemporary examples of the social address approach can be found in cross-cultural efforts to identify different attitudes about child rearing. These studies are often based on relatively small and unrepresentative samples of parents from two countries. However, some recent cross-cultural studies differ from these traditional social address studies. Rather than simply contrasting two samples of parents, efforts are being made to identify the particular variables or processes that give rise to social address differences. For instance, a study by Amy Richman, Patrice Miller, and Robert LeVine (1992) was designed to assess the association between differing amounts of formal education and maternal sensitivity. Low-income Mexican mothers who had only two years of formal schooling were found to be less verbally responsive to their children than low-income mothers who had nine years of schooling (Richman et al., 1992). That study indicated that the experience of going to school provides both verbal skills and a model of adult-child conversation that women later use when they become mothers.

Many other contemporary social address studies have gone beyond the traditional approach of simply identifying group differences. Research is being designed to identify the processes that account for associations or even causal relations between culturally regulated child-rearing practices and developmental outcomes (Valsiner, 1989). One prominent example is in the area of academic achievement. Studies comparing families in Japan, China, and the United States are attempting to link parents' practices and expectations with their children's academic performance (Stevenson & Baker, 1987).

The Momentary Process Approach

A very different approach to the study of parents first appeared in the late 1960s. This approach focuses on the moment-to-moment sequences of interactions between parents and children. This work has sometimes been described more poetically as investigating the "dance" between a mother and her infant. The question of interest is, how is ongoing behavior regulated, modified, or influenced? To investigate this question, a "microanalytic" approach is taken to examine the specific sequences of interactional behavior.

Molecular variables, such as looking, smiling, turn taking, face-to-face play, or interactive matching, are often explored in *momentary process* studies of parent-infant relationships. These discrete behaviors serve to form the menu of the interaction. Sometimes, momentary process studies focus on abstract molar variables designed to capture enduring relationship characteristics that transcend any particular action sequence. *Synchrony* (actions of one person coordinated with and supportive of ongoing activity of the other), *reciprocity* (back and forth exchange of similar behaviors), and *complementarity* (back and forth exchange with individuals taking different roles) are three of the main molar variables used to describe the quality of dyadic relationships (Cairns, 1979; Kaye, 1982).

To document molecular or molar relationship variables, ongoing interactions are filmed or videotaped for precise coding. Each second (or tenth of a second) of behavior is coded to reveal the often subtle actions of interest. In one analysis of mother-infant interactions, the great majority of the behaviors of interest were fleeting: They lasted only from 0.3 to 1.0 second (Stern, 1977).

Early moment-to-moment investigations focused on how mothers modulate their infants' attention (Brazelton, Koslowski, & Main, 1974; Stern, 1971). Researchers studied such features as mothers' facial expressions, vocalizations, gazes, and head movements. The momentary process approach can be used to address questions concerning the origins, variability, and maintenance of social interactions. The tasks of engaging and modulating attention and the interactional qualities of reciprocity, complementarity, and synchrony have all been explored (e.g., Kaye & Fogel, 1980). With older children, the approach has also been put to service to examine how mothers can successfully time their bids for attention to gain compliance from their children (Schaffer & Crook, 1979). See Figure 3.2 for an example of the type of data collected from a microanalytic study of a twelve-week-old boy with his mother (Trevarthen, 1977). Vocalizations, smiles, and body movements from both infant and mother are analyzed at a rate of sixteen frames per second. The figure displays the conversation-like exchange between the two. Maternal sensitivity is illustrated by the mother's responses to her infant's vocalizations, her periods of quietness when the infant is vocalizing, and her own talking when the infant is quiet. Through exchanges like these, infants learn some of the basic components of social interaction, such as taking turns, imitation, and reciprocity. The microanalytic approach has exposed these and other short-lived actions that form the rudiments of social interactions.

The momentary process approach, although not used as frequently these days, continues to provide new information about parent-child relationships. It has been particularly helpful for examining the "microstructure" of the interactional consequences of maternal depression. Microanalytic studies have demonstrated that the behavioral repertoires (e.g., engagement, attention, quality of communication) of depressed caregivers can indeed be severely affected by affective disorders (Cohn & Tronick, 1983). Depressed mothers and their three-month-old infants have also been found to be more likely to match negative behavior states but less likely to match positive ones than nondepressed mothers and infants (Field, Healy, Goldstein, & Guthertz, 1990). In a study in which mothers were instructed to simulate depression, their toddlers were observed to become more negative and unfocused in their activities (Seiner & Gelfand, 1995). The implication from these microanalytic studies is that infants exposed to chronically depressed mothers will develop a depressed and problematic interactional style.

The Child Effects Approach
Anyone who has spent time with children knows that parents do not always control the interaction: Children often play a determining role in parental behavior. The *child effects* approach grew out of a reaction to the

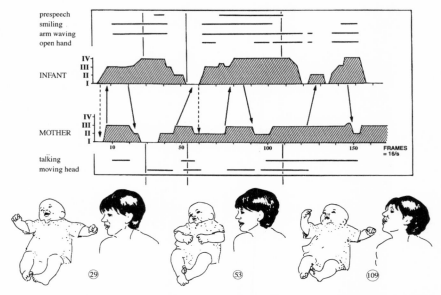

FIGURE 3.2   Microanalytic Study of Conversation-like Exchange Between an Infant and His Mother. (Reprinted, with permission, from C. Trevarthen, 1977, in H. R. Schaffer [Ed.], *Studies in Mother-Infant Interaction* [pp. 227–270], New York: Academic Press.)

unidirectional view of parental influence on child behavior. Such a one-sided conception dominated the parenting literature and is most obvious in the trait, learning, and social address approaches. As early as 1951, however, Robert Sears, in his American Psychological Association presidential address, prepared the ground for this approach when he advocated recognition of the dyadic nature of parent-child relations. Appreciation of this dyadic nature requires a bidirectional view of influence.

Despite the obvious truth of Sears's conceptualization, widespread adoption of a bidirectional view of influence has been slow. It was not until Richard Bell's (1968) landmark paper, "A Reinterpretation of the Direction of Effects in Studies of Socialization," that this approach became galvanized. In that paper and in subsequent papers and books, Bell and his colleagues (Bell, 1979; Bell & Chapman, 1986) as well as others (Rheingold, 1969) drew attention to the fact that many child characteristics can have a pivotal impact on parents and child-rearing behavior.

The first empirical demonstration of a "child effect" on parental behavior looked at the influence of both the age and the gender of children (Rothbart & Maccoby, 1966). Since that study, three categories of child characteristics have been investigated: general child characteristics, physical characteristics, and behavioral characteristics. The following list outlines the specific variables studied:

- General child characteristics
  - Age
  - Gender
  - Birth order
- Physical characteristics
  - Prematurity
  - Neonatal attributes
  - Physical attractiveness
- Behavioral characteristics
  - Activity level
  - Dependence
  - Responsiveness
  - Type of child misbehavior
  - Handicapping condition
  - Behavior problems

To date, the child behavioral variable that has received the most attention has been children's activity level. For example, studies have focused on boys with attention deficit hyperactivity disorder (ADHD) and their mothers, in an effort to understand the role parents play in their children's hyperactivity. In one "blind" study, hyperactive boys were assigned to receive either a medication or a placebo. The boys did indeed respond by behaving differently when medicated than when on a placebo pill (Barkley & Cunningham, 1979). In turn, mothers, who were unaware of the study condition their sons were in, acted differently depending on the condition. This experimental study provided clear evidence for the influence of child behavior on parent behavior.

The expression "driving one to drink" was investigated in another example of a child-effects study (Lang, Pelham, Johnston, & Gelernter, 1989). Two elementary school–aged boys were trained to act in one of two ways: normally or like children who suffered from ADHD and conduct disorder. Thirty-two adults were then randomly assigned to one condition for an eighteen-minute interaction with one of the boys. Following the interaction, the adults were given the opportunity to drink beer before they were to interact again with the same boy. When exposed to the deviant-acting child confederate, males drank significantly more beer than when interacting with the normal-acting child. This study provided experimental evidence of a child effect: Difficult children can motivate adults to drink alcohol.

In addition to eliciting reactions from their parents to their characteristics or behavior, children can have effects on their parents in two other, more subtle ways (Russell & Russell, 1992). First, through their personality and interests, children can contribute to the overall quality of the parent-child relationship. A parent may become a soccer coach in response to his daughter's interest in playing the sport. In turn, this new-found joint activity may enhance the quality of the parent-child relationship. An additional type of child effect lies in the characteristics of a particular child that can mediate parental behavior. Two children may perceive the same parental behavior differently and thus react differently to it. An aggressive child will likely perceive physical punishment differently than a withdrawn and shy child. To fully understand the role of the child in socialization, each type of child effect must be understood.

It should be remembered that the child effects approach was never intended to show that children determine parents' behavior. Rather, it was designed to provide an antidote to the contemporary research that focused exclusively on parent effects (Bell, 1979). Beyond that function, research into child effects has aided in the development of a theory of reciprocal socialization, sometimes called *transactional development* (Sameroff & Chandler, 1975). Figure 3.3 depicts the four major models of parent-child effects: parent effects, child effects, bidirectional effects, and transactional effects. Both parent- and child-effect models represent unidirectional concepts of influence. In contrast, bidirectional models acknowledge the constant mutual influence of one person on another. The control systems model by Bell (1971), described in Chapter 2, is an example of a bidirectional theory. Transactional models go a step further by suggesting that the ongoing mutual influences between individuals result in changes in each individual. In turn, the individual who has changed slightly modifies the other individual. The transactional model best represents the developmental concept of *epigenesis*—the continuous developmental process that results from the exchanges between the developing organism and its environment (Kuo, 1967).

Current work reported in the child-effects literature has been more inclusive by examining not just child effects but also parent effects and sometimes "relationship effects": the unique contribution attributed to the quality of the parent-child relationship (Bugental, Blue, & Lewis, 1990; Dix, Ruble, & Zambarano, 1989; Kenny, 1990). However, as Kenneth Dodge (1990) argued, it is both problematic and not constructive to attempt to specify the relative strength of one influence or another, much like choosing sides for the false dichotomy of nature versus nurture. A more useful orientation is to identify the mechanisms of influence associated with parent-child interactions and assess how they affect a child's development.

The Parental Beliefs Approach

The newest and most diverse approach to the study of parenting focuses on the cognitive activity of parents as a tool for understanding parental behav-

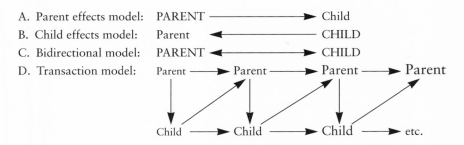

A. Parent effects model: PARENT ⟶ Child
B. Child effects model: Parent ⟵ CHILD
C. Bidirectional model: PARENT ⟷ CHILD
D. Transaction model: Parent ⟶ Parent ⟶ Parent ⟶ Parent
Child ⟶ Child ⟶ Child ⟶ etc.

FIGURE 3.3 Competing Models of Parent-Child Influence.

ior and, in turn, how children develop. Such studies represent a response to the criticism that researchers have ignored the fact that parents are indeed thinking participants in child rearing. As one researcher put it, "in our enthusiasm to give the infant proper recognition as a contributor to the interactive process, . . . it may have inadvertently been assumed that the cognitive capacities of the infant and parent could functionally be treated as similar" (Parke, 1978, p. 76).

The *parental beliefs* approach differs from traditional work on parental attitudes, because most of the attitude studies have been in service of the trait approach to parents (Holden, 1995). The parental beliefs approach emphasizes the cognitive mediation of behavior, or how immediate and ongoing thinking processes influence parent-child interactions. One of the pioneers of this approach was Lois Stolz (1967), whose interview study of mothers and fathers documented how child rearing was multiply influenced by parental values and beliefs, previous experience of parents, information sources (e.g., books), and other people.

Another pioneering approach was that taken by Elsie Broussard and Miriam Hartner (1971). They developed questionnaires to study maternal perceptions by examining the difference between mothers' views of their own babies and their views of average babies. These researchers found evidence that mothers' perceptions of their infants were predictive of the children's subsequent social and emotional development. Mothers who rated their own infants as average or below average were thought to place their infants at risk for later problems. Subsequent research identified various problems with this approach. Broussard and Hartner's conceptualization of perceptions could not account for mothers who accurately perceived their children as only average; the findings did not hold up in replication studies; and the instrument was found to have limited reliability and validity (Palisin, 1980). Nevertheless, the work generated much interest in the role of parents' perceptions.

A third pioneer was Walter Emmerich (1969), whose work presaged many of the subsequent areas of inquiry concerning parental beliefs. He was especially interested in understanding how parents' goals influenced parental roles. Toward that end, he developed an extensive question-naire assessing parents' child-rearing values and goals (e.g., obedience), beliefs about the efficacy of child-rearing methods, and perceptions of their ability to influence their child. Among his central findings was that parents subscribed to social learning theory: They believed, in principle, that changing the child-rearing environment can greatly modify the child's behavior.

The parental beliefs approach was not crystallized until the mid-1980s as manifested by the advent of several reviews and a book on the topic (Goodnow, 1984, 1988b; Sigel, 1985; Sigel, McGillicuddy-DeLisi, & Goodnow, 1992). Currently, the study of parental beliefs can be divided into five major domains: perceptions, attributions, beliefs, self-percep-tions, and problem solving. Listed in Table 3.1, these five areas are briefly described.

Parental behavior must be, to some extent, a function of how the parent is perceiving the child. To use an example from Chapter 1, if a colonial American parent perceived her child's personality to be sinful, she would behave differently from a parent influenced by Rousseau, who saw the child as fundamentally good but in need of guidance from the parent.

The most dramatic demonstrations of the impact of parental perceptions have been in the area of children's gender. The mere labeling of a newborn as a boy or a girl can elicit very different perceptions about the infant. In one of the first such studies, parents were asked to describe their newborns (Rubin, Provenzano, & Luria, 1974). Fathers in particular were more likely to adopt stereotypic views, describing their sons as big, strong, and hardy and their daughters as fine-featured, quiet, calm, and delicate.

Subsequent studies have improved on that original one by reporting on observations of how parental perceptions influence behavioral responses. In a design that has been used in numerous studies, an infant is recruited as a confederate. The child is dressed in gender-neutral clothes and labeled as either a boy or a girl. Children and adults are then observed interacting with the infant, and behavioral measures, such as talking, touching, and providing toys, are coded. A review of the literature (Stern & Karraker, 1989) concluded that gender labeling elicits sex-stereotyped responses but only on a minority of the variables measured. The adults' behavior was also influenced by other child characteristics (e.g., attractiveness), the child's actual behavior, and the extent that the adults' sex-role orientation was traditional.

Parental perceptions of other infant characteristics, such as prematurity and attractiveness, have also received some attention (Frodi, Lamb, Leav-

TABLE 3.1   Domains of Research into Parental Beliefs

Domains	Definition and Examples
Perceptions	The subjective and objective views parents have concerning their children (e.g., temperament, abilities)
Attributions	The casual interpretation a parent gives to a child's behavior, such as perception of intentionality. Examples include: • Role of intentionality in child misbehavior • Parenting versus child's disposition • Influences of achievement (e.g., talent, effort, or schooling)
Beliefs	The ideas, knowledge, or expectations a parent holds about children and child rearing, including: • Content—ideas about child development or parenting • Quality—structure, intensity, and accuracy of ideas • Sources—cultural, familial, or experiential origins of ideas • Effects—consequences of the ideas on children and parents
Self-perceptions	The parents' thoughts and feelings about parenting, including: • Stress—feelings of tension as they relate to parenting • Competence—confidence in one's skill as a parent • Satisfaction—the degree to which a parent finds parenting fulfilling
Problem solving, decisionmaking	The processes used in resolving child-rearing problems or making decisions (e.g., diagnosing problem, generating solutions, testing or revising solutions)

itt, & Donovan, 1978; Stern & Hildebrandt, 1984). The domain in which parental perceptions are most actively investigated is that of children's temperament. The most common method used to assess children's temperament is parent-report questionnaires. But how accurate are parents' perceptions of their infants? As Mary Rothbart and Hill Goldsmith (1985) pointed out, accurate reports are a function of several factors, including rater characteristics (e.g., knowledge of infant's behavior, memory), biases in the rater's perception (e.g., a very sociable mother may interpret a child's behavior differently than a chronically depressed mother), and the quality of the questionnaire. In all likelihood, parental reports consist of both objective and subjective components (Bates & Bayles, 1984). The challenge is to accurately differentiate between those two components of parental perception.

One specialized domain of parental perceptions concerns attributions, or assessments, of the determinants of children's immediate behavior. Attributions, as discussed in Chapter 2, reflect parents' theories about the causes of behavior and development. Parents frequently make attributions about their children's behavior. Crying in the middle of the night, urinating on the floor, drawing on a table, and slamming the door are common types of actions analyzed by parents for the intentionality and willfulness of the child.

A variety of different types of parent attributions have been investigated, including views about the relative roles of nature and nurture in development, the degree to which parents can influence their children, ingredients involved in successful school achievement, determinants of parents' own behavior, and most frequently, the causes of child misbehavior (Miller, 1995). Of these, the most important attributions concern parents' assessments of children's misbehavior.

These types of attributions have important implications for parents and children. The question most often addressed is whether parents interpret children's misbehavior as intentional or situationally induced. Theodore Dix and his colleagues (Dix, Ruble, Grusec, & Nixon, 1986) have demonstrated that parents' appraisals of children's misbehavior are dependent on the children's developmental level. As children get older, parents perceive misconduct as increasingly intentional and a reflection of the child's personality. In conjunction with those assessments, parents' affective reactions (i.e., how upset they are) become increasingly negative (Dix & Reinhold, 1991).

Although attribution research has clear implications for parental behavior and emotion, the preponderance of research into parental beliefs has focused on beliefs about children or child rearing. The term *beliefs* has been used synonymously with the terms *knowledge, ideas,* and *expectations.* The cataloging of beliefs held by parents has been the most active area of research within the parental beliefs approach. Beliefs about child development and parenting, like attributions, are likely to guide parental behavior. If parents believe that newborns cannot see until they are about six weeks old, a belief reported by some Kurdish women in Israel, their behavior toward newborns will likely be quite different from that of parents who hold different beliefs about newborns' capabilities (Frankel & Roer-Bornstein, 1982).

Investigations into parental beliefs can be categorized into four domains: the content, quality, sources, and effects of parental thoughts (Goodnow & Collins, 1990). The *content* of parental thoughts might include ideas about the nature of physical, motor, and cognitive development (Miller, 1988) or ideas about how parents influence their children's development (Russell & Russell, 1982). The *quality* of those beliefs includes their structure, intensity, and accuracy. The *sources* of the beliefs, such as culture, family, experience, or literature, represent a third focus of studies. Many cross-cultural studies have compared parents' attitudes and beliefs across ethnic groups and countries (e.g., Ninio, 1979). Such culturally derived beliefs have been labeled *parental ethnotheories* and represent powerful influences on behavior (Harkness & Super, 1995). The *effects* of those beliefs, the domain that has received the least amount of attention, concerns how parental beliefs translate into parental behavior and, in turn, influence children's development (Sigel, 1986). Children can be affected by their parents' beliefs in a variety of ways, from disciplinary responses to intergenerational transmission (Sigel et al., 1992).

Another area of parental beliefs consists of parents' self-perceptions, or thoughts about their own parenting. It is presumed that parents' perceptions about their own parenting can have a considerable impact on subsequent behavior. Consequently, investigators have measured such variables as parents' feelings of stress, efficacy, competence, and satisfaction in the parenting role (Bugental, Blue, & Cruzcosa, 1989; Johnston & Mash, 1989). These types of feelings are not just idle thoughts. Parents' self-judgments of their competence have been found to be related to their parenting abilities (Teti & Gelfand, 1991), depression and social supports (Cutrona & Troutman, 1986), and the number of problems parents perceive their children as having (Johnston & Mash, 1989).

The final domain of parental beliefs research examines the process of social cognition, or how parents solve problems or make child-rearing decisions. A common attribute of the parental experience is having to deal with minor child-rearing problems (e.g., how one responds to infant crying, child waking up in the night, child being aggressive). Similarly, beginning even before the child's birth, parents must make a variety of decisions about child rearing, such as whether to use anesthesia for the birth, circumcise their sons, breast- or bottle-feed. These and later decisions, such as child-care arrangements, the extent to which a home is childproofed, and exposure to potentially negative influences, are likely to have real consequences on their children's development.

To date, relatively few studies have explored parental problem solving or decisionmaking. One example was my investigation of how previous experience with infants influenced the ways in which adults solved a child-rearing problem (Holden, 1988). The problem was a common one for all parents of infants: diagnosing why a baby was crying. The study adopted an information-processing approach and was designed to reveal how differing levels of previous experience with infants affected the problem-solving process. Both parents and nonparents operated a computer simulation. The task was to acquire the fewest and most important information units (out of twenty-five units available) to determine which of nine competing causes of crying was the correct one (e.g., baby was hungry, tired, sick). The results indicated that mothers chose about eight pieces of information, on average, before correctly identifying the cause of the crying. Generally, fathers needed a little more information to solve the problem; as a group, they selected about ten information units. With regard to identifying the cause of the problem, both mothers and fathers usually picked the correct cause on their first attempt.

When nonparents were compared with parents, some interesting results emerged. Women who were not mothers but had baby-sitting experience performed similarly to the mothers. But the group of participants who stood out were the males who were not fathers. Although they selected about the same number of information units as the fathers, they made an average of two wrong guesses before choosing the right answer. This high rate of incorrect guesses revealed their limited problem-solving ability in this domain.

When the particular type of information selected was examined, another effect of experience was noted. Parents and experienced nonparents recognized early on that the information about the infant's age was important to learn; most selected it within their first five information choices. In comparison, the inexperienced nonparents tended to select it much later in their search or to ignore entirely that piece of information. This investigation illustrated that previous experience with infants does make individuals more efficient and accurate in solving a child-rearing task.

Currently, the parental beliefs approach is the approach most commonly taken in research concerning parents. Its popularity is largely due to the promise it holds for exposing the underlying basis of parental behavior and for revealing possible avenues for behavioral change. Research efforts are under way, focusing on a wide array of beliefs and attempting to understand how they impact parental behavior, parental emotions, and children's outcomes (Dix, 1991; Sigel et al., 1992).

Comparison and Evaluation of the Approaches

These approaches provide six distinctive perspectives for understanding the nature of parents and parent-child relationships. Some approaches are complementary and together provide a richer understanding of parents. Yet others, such as the trait and child effects approaches, are fundamentally incompatible. To compare the six approaches, I have evaluated them on the basis of answers to the following five key questions: (1) What is their primary question? (2) What assumptions are made about the determinants of parental behavior? (3) At what level of specificity do they analyze parental behavior? (4) What assumption is made about the direction of parent-child influence? and (5) What is the time frame for analysis of causal relations?

As can be seen in Table 3.2 each approach asks a different central question. The trait approach addresses the question of how individual differences in parenting affects children's development. In contrast, the momentary process approach focuses on how the parent and child modulate each

TABLE 3.2 Six Prominent Approaches to Child-Rearing Research Differentiated Across Five Key Dimensions

Approach	Primary Question	Level of Analysis or Aggregation of Parent	What Determines Parental Behavior	Direction of Influence	Time Frame for Analysis of Causal Relations
Trait	How do variations in parenting affect children's development?	Global, aggregated	Stable, core traits	Parent to child	Long term
Social learning	How do parents shape their children's behavior?	Some global and aggregated; others specific	Experiences with own parents and children	Predominantly parent to child	Immediate and short term
Social address	How and why do different groups of parents and children differ?	Global and aggregated	Beliefs and practices of the social group	Parent to child	Long term
Momentary process	How are parent-child interactions structured and regulated?	Specific and nonaggregated	Proximate events and experiences of children and parents	Bidirectional	Immediate
Child effects	In what ways do children modify their parents' behavior?	Specific and nonaggregated	Child's characteristics and behavior	Child to parent or bidirectional	Immediate and short term
Parental beliefs	How is parental thinking related to parent or child characteristics or behavior?	Specific and nonaggregated	Parents' beliefs and appraisals	Parent to child	Immediate

other's ongoing behavior. The child effects approach is designed to identify child characteristics that modify parental behavior. Similarly, each approach takes a different view of the etiology of parental behavior. The social learning approach assumes that parenting is determined by previous social experiences. In particular, the feedback parents receive from their own actions or experiences is said to determine what parents do. The social address approach, in contrast, takes the orientation that the beliefs or practices of the greater cultural group—whether they are due to ethnicity, nationality, or some other group membership—form a central basis of parenting. In contrast, the parental beliefs approach views parents' own thinking as the major determinant on behavior.

The approaches also differ on the level with which they examine parents. The momentary process approach consists of detailed analyses of a small segment of ongoing behavior. In contrast, the trait approach makes generalizations about typical patterns of child-rearing behavior. The parental beliefs and social learning approaches take the middle road, typically focusing on the adjustments or changes parents are capable of making. Assumptions about the direction of influence constitute a fourth issue that can be compared across the approaches. The trait, social learning, social address, and parental beliefs approaches assume that the parent has more influence on the child than the child on the parent. The two exceptions are the child effects approach, which (as its name reveals) adopts the opposite view, and the momentary process approach, which assumes a bidirectional nature of influence.

A fifth dimension on which the approaches can be compared is the time frame implicated for causal relations between parent and child. Some approaches (e.g., social address and trait) assume that parents affect their children only after years of interactions. In contrast, the momentary process approach focuses on the present and looks at effects over a time span of seconds or minutes.

Table 3.2 helps to reveal the relative strengths and weaknesses of the approaches. For instance, the trait approach has enjoyed the most popularity, in part because it addresses the most basic question: How do different parenting practices affect child outcomes? However, there are also a number of drawbacks that often go unacknowledged. One problem is that of exclusion: Trait schemes are unable to classify all parents. For example, in what some consider the best parent trait study conducted, Baumrind (1971) was able to classify only 76 percent of the parents into one of four basic patterns. A related problem is that classification schemes may not be representative of the members in it. Some parents exhibit a blend of different traits depending on the child or situation. Also, parent trait schemes do not create separate categories for families in which the mother and father reflect different patterns (e.g., mother is authoritative, father is authoritarian).

Another pitfall of the trait approach concerns the methods used to classify parents. It is all too common for a complex trait categorization scheme to be simplified into a short questionnaire. Then, based on either parent or child reports, parents are categorized. Similarly, some studies classify parents on the basis of a short behavioral observation that is assumed to reflect a general pattern of behavior. The trait approach also reflects a static view of parents: Parents are viewed as unchanging, despite evidence to the contrary.

In sum, the trait approach has served the valuable function of establishing initial relations between parent and child behavior. However, different trait approaches have not been integrated or synthesized. With the exception of Schaefer's (1959) circumplex model of parenting traits, trait models have focused only on the researchers' favorite trait at the neglect of an integrative understanding of how different traits may cluster, covary, or be hierarchically organized.

The social learning approach has clearly demonstrated that learning principles can be a potent influence on the behavioral development of children. However, the approach can be faulted for its monolithic interpretation that the essence of parenting lies in dispensing the laws of learning. Traditionally, social learning approaches have ignored much of the complexity in parent-child relationships by interpreting interactions solely through learning principles. Explicating the origins and solutions of children's problem behaviors with reference only to learning principles (Pumroy & Pumroy, 1978) does not take into account variation in experience or between individuals. Other considerations, such as the role that attachment or cognitions may play in the relationship, have been neglected in favor of a narrow view of parents. Today, as social learning theories have gained sophistication, the problem of primacy of learning laws to the neglect of other considerations is not as great as it once was. The best example of this change is captured in the continuing development of Bandura's theoretical work. Initially, his social learning theory was based on the principles of modeling and reinforcement. In the most recent formulation of his social cognitive theory (Bandura, 1989), the roles of cognitive variables, such as expectancies and feelings of efficacy, have emerged as central.

The social address approach has been a popular one for identifying differences between groups of parents because it is both conceptually and operationally simple (Bronfenbrenner, 1986). Such studies can be implemented quickly and easily with little forethought, as exploratory techniques. The simplicity is also the chief limitation of the method, however; it cannot reveal the source of any differences identified. As Urie Bronfenbrenner and Ann Crouter (1983) pointed out, "no explicit consideration is given . . . to intervening structures or processes through which the environment might affect the course of development. One looks only at the social address—that is, the environmental label—with no attention to what the environment is like, what people are living there, what they are doing, or how the activities taking place could affect the child" (pp. 361–362).

The social address approach falls short, therefore, because it fails to examine the processes through which differences occur. Social address studies may best serve the function of initial steps, which need to be followed up with other approaches designed to reveal why relations or differences exist.

The child effects approach has served the important function of providing a check for advocates of rampant parent effects and demonstrating the role that certain child characteristics play in parent-child interactions. It is also the approach that is most readily amenable to experimental manipulations, and therein lie the dangers. Typically, these studies are designed around one brief experimental manipulation in the laboratory. Another methodological limitation lies in the choice of subjects: Generally adults and unrelated children serve as participants. The prior history and relationship between the parent and child go ignored in favor of demonstrating what is perhaps a transient effect. Such manipulations can also lead one to forget the asymmetry of power between parents and their children and the potential control the parents have over the environment (Hoffman, 1975). Overall, the child effects approach has served to correct the predominant unidirectional view of influence and remind us that in the parent-child relationship, as in any normal, close relationship, there is bidirectional influence.

The momentary process approach has revealed subtle actions that would not have been detected if a microanalytic approach had not been taken. The approach has been particularly useful for revealing the origins of dyadic interactions between mothers and infants. On the basis of this approach, some investigators have concluded that the parenting of infants requires so much automatic and apparently unlearned behavior that it must be largely intuitive and a product of our evolution (Papoušek & Papoušek, 1987; 1995).

The approach can be criticized for being essentially descriptive in nature; the impact of minute behaviors on children's development cannot readily be tested. Like the trait and social address approaches, it does not lend itself to experimental manipulation. Partly because of the lack of experimental control, these moment-to-moment processes can only be assumed to impact subsequent development; whether they do remains an open question. Nevertheless, the approach represents a unique tool for revealing interactional processes that would otherwise be overlooked.

The parental beliefs approach has created a new area of inquiry for the study of parents. It is the single best avenue for understanding the causes of parental behavior, which it does by revealing the contents of parents' minds. Furthermore, the approach holds the promise of providing a way to change child-rearing behavior through "cognitive restructuring." This restructuring may consist of providing new information about children or child-rearing techniques, revising perceptions, correcting erroneous attributions or expectations, or training in problem-solving techniques (see Chapter 7).

The central limitation of the approach concerns the importance of the cognitions being studied and their ecological validity. We now know that parents hold a wide range of beliefs about children and child rearing (e.g., Goodnow & Collins, 1990), but the degree to which these beliefs impact child-rearing behavior has not been adequately demonstrated. Given that attribution studies based on this approach are often experimental manipulations conducted in the laboratory, the ecological validity of the results is often unknown. More studies that assess naturally occurring parental beliefs while they occur are needed. Similarly, few parent belief studies have yet to make the link to child outcomes, although work toward that end is in progress (see Miller, 1988; Sigel et al., 1992).

Summary

Six approaches to the study of parent-child relationships have been identified. Each of these approaches serves a unique function in revealing part of the nature of parents and their children. Any single approach cannot adequately capture parenting or address all the key questions associated with parenting; it has been useful to have the multiple and often competing approaches.

The existence of multiple approaches makes for a disjointed empirical picture of parent-child relationships, however. Some current work is beginning to integrate several of the approaches. For example, Bronfenbrenner (1986) has advocated use of the "person-process-context" model. Such a model involves the recognition that individual characteristics of the parent (e.g., traits) and the child (e.g., temperament) can mediate the impact of a process in a particular context. The model reflects a merging of the trait, child effects, and social address approaches. Rather than conceptualizing parental behavior as a main effect, this model recognizes that behavior may be an interaction or function of parent and child variables as well as the particular context.

Together, these six approaches have helped to reveal the complex nature of parent-child relationships. These relationships are increasingly being conceptualized and studied as dynamic, reciprocal processes with contributions from each individual as well as the context in which the interaction takes place. Furthermore, the relationships are increasingly being recognized as capable of and even likely to change over time. Many of the reasons for those changes are addressed in Chapter 4, which focuses on the determinants of parental behavior.

4

The Determinants
of Parental Behavior

It is striking to note the considerable differences in child-rearing behavior observed among parents. One mother may be firm, whereas her neighbor is permissive; one father may be warm and sensitive in contrast to another, who is harsh and rejecting. What causes these differences in child-rearing behavior? This issue is one of the most fundamental parenting questions. It is inherently important to understand why parents act the way they do in order to develop and test theories about the determinants of complex behavior. In addition, it is necessary to have such knowledge when trying to predict parental behavior, change parents' behavior, or teach adults how to parent.

Systematic investigations into the etiology of parental behavior began only in the 1970s. Although some studies on the topic were conducted earlier, they are rare and disconnected. For example, one early investigation into child-rearing determinants examined the attitudes of mothers from farms, towns, and a city, under the hypothesis that place of residence has a major influence on parents' beliefs. It turned out that place of residence did not matter: No reliable differences were found between the three groups of mothers on their attitudes toward children's self-reliance (Stott, 1940).

It was not until almost thirty years later that the first extensive study on parental determinants appeared (Stolz, 1967). That study, mentioned in Chapter 3 as a pioneering effort in the parental beliefs approach, provided the first empirical evidence of some of the many competing determinants of parental behavior. Lois Stolz focused her work on four major types of influences: past experiences as children or adults; knowledge and advice received about child rearing; values and beliefs; and elements of the current situation (such as parental affect, child characteristics and behavior, and setting). Her conclusion foreshadowed current work: Parental behavior is multiply determined; of the "pluralistic pressures," the determinant that gains dominance depends on the particular situation.

That work was a precursor to numerous investigations exploring the determinants of child rearing. Currently more than thirty variables have been identified and shown to at least partially influence child-rearing behavior.

Several different models of determinants have been proposed as a way of organizing the variables.

Models of Child-Rearing Determinants

The first comprehensive statements on determinants of parental behavior were published in 1980 (Harmon & Brim, 1980). Four types of influences on parents were identified: general cultural factors (country of origin); individual factors (characteristics of the parent, unconscious influences); interpersonal factors (child behavior, family size); and the setting. That model expanded on determinants identified by Stolz (1967) but proved to be limited because it simply cataloged different potential determinants. It did not provide a way of explaining the process through which particular determinants influenced parental behavior, and it did not account for relations among determinants.

A few years later, Jay Belsky (1984) published a conceptual model of the determinants of parenting, based on ecological systems theory. That model, which has proved to be extremely influential, identified three key factors that determine parental behavior and proposed mechanisms by which the factors were interrelated. The central categories of influence according to Belsky are (1) parental psychological resources (e.g., personality, developmental history); (2) child characteristics (gender, behavior); and (3) contextual sources of stress and social support (marital relations, social network, work). These three categories combine to determine how the parent interacts with the child. The model, reproduced in Figure 4.1 indicates that parenting is multiply determined, with both direct and indirect influences.

Belsky proposed that, of the three categories of determinants, the most important influence on effective parenting is parental psychological characteristics. A psychologically strong parent is more likely than other parents to withstand contextual stresses (e.g., marital or money problems) or the challenge of difficult child characteristics (e.g., a noncompliant or physically handicapped child). The second most important determinant is social support. Parenting support most commonly comes from a spouse; secondary support figures include friends, neighbors, and relatives. For example, parents who are highly stressed by problems at work are much less likely to let that stress affect their parenting if they have adequate support from others. Belsky argues, therefore, that "the parenting system is buffered against threats to its integrity that could derive from any single weakness in any single source" (1984, p. 91).

Although one could debate the need for more bidirectional arrows to reflect mutual influences, the model nicely organizes three key influences on parental behavior. As one studies the model, however, the absence of certain determinants becomes notable. What about contextual influences (i.e., characteristics of *where* the interaction occurs) or transient parental qualities (mood) that can influence parenting? The model also does not account for more distal determinants such as cultural background or so-

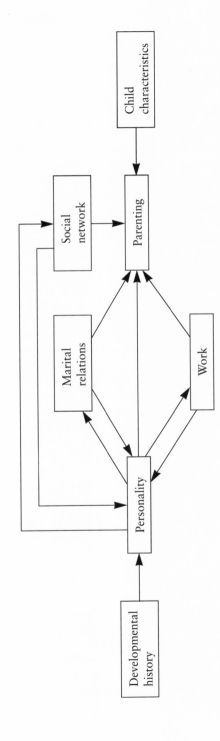

FIGURE 4.1   One Set of Determinants of Parenting. (Reprinted, with permission, from J. Belsky, 1984, *Child Development, 55,* 83–96.)

cioeconomic group. Despite those limitations, the model is useful in capturing a middle range of determinants and has helped to focus research attention on understanding determinants of parental behavior and their interrelations.

Ecological Systems Theory as an Organizing Framework

One way to include both proximal and distant determinants, along with those in the middle level, is to use Bronfenbrenner's (1989) model of ecological systems. As described in Chapter 2, this theory was intended to demonstrate the interrelations of different levels of the context on behavior. The four contextual levels provide a useful model for organizing parental determinants.

Recall that the *macrosystem* level consists of the overarching cultural institutions and beliefs. With regard to determinants of parenting, distal influences (such as normative beliefs about children shared within a culture) operate at this level. The *exosystem* refers to settings that can affect the child, but which the child does not directly participate in. The parent's workplace and social support network are two prime examples. The third contextual level, the *mesosystem,* refers to the system of relationships among the child's microsystems. Determinants that have similar effects across different settings, such as stable parent and child characteristics, are prime examples. Last, the *microsystem* includes immediate contextual variables, such as the setting, the time, and transient parent and child characteristics. A diagram of the different levels of determinants as categorized by Bronfenbrenner's model is provided in Figure 4.2 In the next section, the determinants of parenting that fit into each of the four levels are summarized.

Macrosystem Determinants

Four major macrosystem determinants have been studied to date: culture, socioeconomic status, racial or ethnic group membership, and education. These determinants represent the most general influences on parental behavior.

Culture

Cultural anthropologists were the first to note similarities and differences in parents from divergent countries. They also recognized that differing cultures could provide a natural experiment to see how parental behavior was related to children's development (Whiting & Child, 1953). Despite the considerable difficulties of conducting cross-cultural research, including the expense, language barriers, and transfer of cultural constructs, psychologists are increasingly using cross-cultural research as a way of looking at

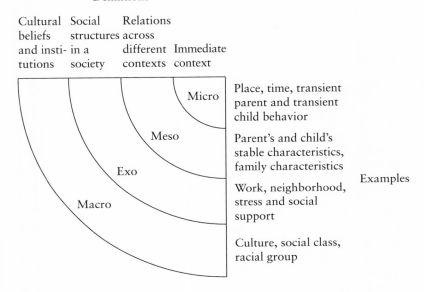

Definitions

FIGURE 4.2   An Ecological Systems Model of the Determinants of Parental Behavior.

both universals of parenting and how parents differ across cultures (Valsiner, 1989).

Cross-cultural child-rearing studies can now be found from every continent, although the majority of studies outside North America come from Western Europe, Australia, and Japan (Bornstein, 1991; LeVine, Miller, & West, 1988; Roopnarine & Carter, 1992). *Culture* refers to the way of life shared by members of a population (Ogbu, 1988); it reflects the social, economic, and psychological adaptation of a people. Concerning parents, culture influences their values and beliefs as well as norms and expectations for acceptable behavior, and it prescribes general rules of parenting conduct. Usually, *culture* is operationalized as the country where the parents are dwelling, but sometimes it is broken down more precisely. For instance, in the study of changing parental beliefs across generations mentioned in Chapter 3, Daniel Frankel and Dorit Roer-Bornstein (1982) compared two groups of mothers in Israel differing in their ethnic heritage (Kurds and Yemenites). However, that study was an exception. Most cross-cultural studies involve comparisons of parents from different countries, as is illustrated in the remainder of this section.

Exploring cultural differences in mother-infant relationships is one of the most popular topics of cross-cultural research; it is thought that impressions from a culture are stamped early in a child's development. One such study searched for cultural differences in maternal behavior toward five-month-old infants in three countries: the United States, France, and Japan (Bornstein et al., 1992). Naturally occurring mother-infant interactions were videotaped for forty-five minutes. A microanalysis of the behavior was then conducted to compare mothers' responsiveness to their infants. Overall, very few differences in maternal or infant behavior were found across the three cultures: Maternal responses to infant cues were similar, and mothers showed no differences in such caregiving practices as encouragement to explore or nurturance in response to distress. One cultural difference that was identified occurred in maternal responses to their infants' looking. Japanese mothers were significantly more responsive when their infants were looking at other people than either American or French mothers (Bornstein et al., 1992). Presumably this maternal involvement and encouragement in social looking is a reflection of the Japanese beliefs about and emphasis on close interpersonal relationships.

Cultural differences in parenting between Japan and North America can be isolated more readily after infancy, when differences emerge in the standards for acceptable child behavior and child independence. In Japan, socialization practices are designed to promote interdependence between individuals, rather than to encourage independence, as is the case in North America (Azuma, 1986). Japanese interdependence is fostered by such practices as constant and close physical relations, or "skinship" (including co-sleeping and co-bathing), and punishment based on separation (e.g., locking a misbehaving child out of the house) rather than use of authority and physical force, as is common in North America. Child-rearing practices such as these are thought to contribute to differences in adult cultural values and behavior (Weisz, Rothbaum, & Blackburn, 1984).

Socioeconomic Status

Subordinate to culture, but still a macrosystem variable, is the socioeconomic status of the parent. Within a particular culture, the social class, or socioeconomic status (SES), of the parent has been recognized as a potent determinant. Socioeconomic status is most often determined on the basis of parental occupation, but education and income are often highly correlated with occupation and sometimes are included in formulas for establishing SES. Typically, studies have contrasted parents of lower and middle SES on a range of behavioral variables, such as breast-feeding, toilet training, warmth, and disciplinary techniques (e.g., Davis & Havighurst, 1946). Because warmth has not been found to be related to SES, most attention has focused on parental use of discipline. Based on dozens of studies, it can be generalized that parents from a lower SES background (i.e., "working-class" parents) are somewhat more likely to use coercive disciplinary techniques (e.g., physical punishment) in comparison to "middle-class" parents, who rely more on psychologically-based discipline (e.g., reasoning, guilt; Erlanger, 1974; Gecas & Nye, 1974).

What might account for a relation between SES and parental behavior? The best explanation for the mechanism linking these two constructs was proposed by Melvin Kohn (1979). He theorized that parental occupation and general "life situation" lead parents to hold particular child-rearing values. Specifically, parents from higher social classes occupy jobs in which responsibility, self-direction, initiative, and independence are valued and rewarded. In turn, those parents are likely to value and promote similar values in their children (e.g., being responsible, being a good student, taking interest in how things happen). On the other hand, parents from a lower socioeconomic background, who have little freedom or responsibility in their own jobs, are more likely to value conformity to external authority (e.g., obeying parents, having self-control, acting like a boy or girl should, getting along with others). Obedience and the ability to stick to the rules are more likely to pay off in blue-collar occupations.

Kohn's model reflects the way that the requirements or demands of one's life situation affect child-rearing values, which in turn modify child-rearing practices. This can be diagrammed as follows:

Social and economic structure → Values → Child-rearing values → Child-rearing behavior.

Parental behavior, according to Kohn, is thereby strongly influenced by socioeconomic status. Support for links between SES and parental values has been found in a number of countries (e.g., Italy, Japan, Korea, Philippines, Poland, Thailand, Turkey, United States; Kohn, Naoi, Shoenbach, Schooler, & Slomczynski, 1990; Luster, Rhoades, & Haas, 1989).

Other Macrosystem Determinants

Three other macrosystem determinants of parenting have been studied: racial or ethnic group membership, religion, and education. Racial and ethnic group influences on child rearing have received relatively little attention; only recently has the empirical knowledge base expanded. However, many of the available studies have confounded ethnicity with socioeconomic status. Another problem is that, typically, researchers design their studies to determine the extent to which minority members use white-middle-class child-rearing practices. Researchers "do not study the minorities' indigenous activities, folk knowledge, and conceptual systems" and then use this knowledge to ascertain the skills and competencies the groups use in parenting (Ogbu, 1988, p. 19).

Disciplinary practices constitute one area in which reliable racial differences have been found. This is exemplified in the finding that African-Americans are more likely to be restrictive and to use physical punishment than Caucasians (e.g., Reis, Barbera-Stein, & Bennett, 1986). However, there is considerable variability within any group, and there is evidence that the disciplinary practices of African-American mothers are influenced by two other macrosystem variables: amount of education received and religious orientation. Women with more education or less strict religious beliefs were less likely to spank than other mothers (Kelley et al., 1992).

There are even fewer studies explicitly designed to investigate the two other macrosystem determinants of parenting: education and religion. The few such studies available tend to explore links with control and discipline. For example, one study found evidence that parents who attend church more frequently value conformity in their children more than parents who do not attend church (Alwin, 1986). Similarly, having more years of formal education has sometimes been associated with less restrictive and physically controlling maternal discipline (Miller & Scarr, 1989; Zussman, 1978).

With the notable exception of Kohn's work with values, most of the research into the macrosystem determinants of parenting have been confined to the social address approach. Results have been limited to correlations rather than providing an understanding of the processes by which cultural variables influence parenting beliefs and behavior. Gradually, research at this level is beginning to identify the links between cultural institutions or beliefs and parenting behavior.

Exosystem Determinants

The *exosystem* refers to social structures, settings, or phenomena that have an impact on interactions, even though the child is not directly involved. The three key exosystem determinants of child-rearing behavior are parental employment, stress, and social support.

Parental Employment

Employment is one of the most consequential determinants of parenting, because it has implications not only for children and their parents but also for the business sector and society in general. Prompting much of the attention is the dramatic increase in the proportion of working women who have young children. In 1960, only 18 percent of mothers with children under the age of six worked outside the home. By 1987, the proportion had climbed to about 57 percent (U.S. Bureau of Labor Statistics, 1988). This remarkable change in the way families lead their lives raises various questions about how work is related to parenting and children's development (to be addressed in Chapter 5).

Parental employment—or unemployment—can have a variety of obvious as well as subtle influences on parenting. But parental employment is not a dichotomous variable. Employment, as it relates to parenting, represents a complex constellation of variables, including not only objective features of the job (e.g., type of job, number of hours spent at work) but also a host of other variables such as financial need, career versus family orientation, and subjective feelings about the job (e.g., how interesting or stressful). Despite the complexity, it has been recognized since one of the earliest studies of family functioning in a place called Middletown, USA, (Lynd & Lynd, 1929) that "the long arm of the job" influences a parent's values, psychological well-being, daily moods, and availability for involvement in parenting activities (Crouter & McHale, 1993).

One variable that is emerging as an important influence on the relation between work and parenting behavior is child-rearing *commitment*. The amount of time and energy parents commit to their multiple roles (parent, worker, spouse) has implications for parental behavior, stress, and perceptions of children. A study investigating some of the relations between parenting and working illustrates one aspect of this issue. Ellen Greenberger and her colleagues found mothers to be as committed to their work as fathers were and that they shared a similar level of job satisfaction. However, mothers experienced more stress than fathers as they attempted to balance the demands of parenting along with work (Greenberger, Goldberg, Hamill, O'Neil, & Payne, 1989). Among working parents, the level of commitment to parenting apparently influences parental expectations. In a questionnaire study of almost 300 employed parents of three- to four-year-old children, parents with a stronger commitment to parenting expected more mature behavior from their children than parents who were relatively more committed to work (Greenberger & Goldberg, 1989).

Maternal employment has been found to affect the mother's emotional state. On the positive side, it can impact her general satisfaction and morale by providing stimulation, self-esteem, and relief from child care and home chores. Also, maternal employment can serve as a buffer from the stresses of marital difficulties or of interacting with a difficult child. For one or more of these reasons, maternal employment can potentially enhance the quality of parenting during the time the mother is home, particularly if the woman enjoys her job and exercises some responsibility in it (Hoffman, 1989). However, many mothers experience conflictual feelings about their desire to work and their feelings about being separated from their children. The extent of this conflict depends not only on whether or not the mothers are employed but also on the mothers' preference to be home or employed, the extent of their anxiety over separation from the infant, and the degree to which they are invested in the maternal role (DeMeis, Hock, & McBride, 1986).

In addition to causing guilt and anxiety for some mothers about being away from their young children, employment can add considerable stress to mothers' lives. Indeed, there is evidence that under some circumstances, mothers' emotional state, child-rearing practices, and perceptions of children may be negatively affected. However, a review of the research leads to the conclusion that most studies have found that maternal employment does have a positive impact on parenting (Hoffman, 1989). For example, in one observational study comparing the child rearing of homemakers and working mothers of two-year-old children, the employed women were judged to be more effective parents. Those women were more likely to be responsive but less likely to use power-assertive discipline (Crockenberg & Litman, 1991).

From a family systems perspective, one could anticipate that maternal employment also would impact paternal involvement. As might be expected, husbands of employed mothers have been found to be somewhat more involved in child care and household work than those in families with single-earner fathers (Crouter, Perry-Jenkins, Huston, & McHale, 1987). Yet the involvement is far from equal. Several different studies, including data from a variety of industrialized nations, have found major discrepancies between the number of hours worked. Fathers, on average, worked fifty hours a week in combined employment and household work, whereas mothers worked eighty to ninety hours per week at the same tasks (Scarr, Phillips, & McCartney, 1989)! The workload inequity between employed mothers and fathers is especially large when the children are under age three.

Another way in which parental employment can influence parenting has been documented in studies of unemployed fathers both during the Great Depression and during economic recessions (Elder, Nguyen, & Caspi, 1985). Vonnie McLoyd (1989, 1990) has developed a model of the process by which paternal economic loss (or poverty) can modify paternal behavior (see Figure 4.3). Although unemployed men are likely to spend more time in child care than employed men, the quality of that care is often characterized as less supportive and more negative and punitive. Such child-rearing behavior is a reflection of the men's negativeness and pessimistic outlook on life. However, several types of variables can ameliorate that association. In particular, characteristics of the father (e.g., personality or financial resources), the marital relationship (as a key social support), and the child can serve to moderate the negative paternal behavior.

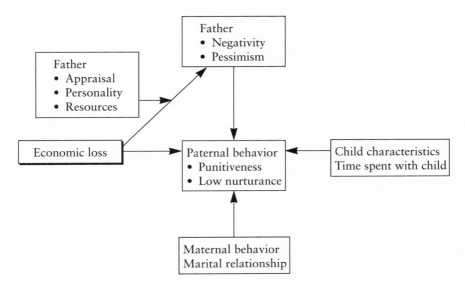

FIGURE 4.3 Conceptual Model of How Paternal Economic Loss Is Related to Changes in Parenting. (Reprinted, with permission, from V. C. McLoyd, 1989, *American Psychologist, 44,* 293–302.)

Stress and Social Support

As suggested by McLoyd's process model, stress and social support represent powerful influences on parental behavior. Stress is particularly pernicious because it can negatively influence the quality of parenting in several ways. Stressed parents are less capable of being nurturant, supportive, patient, and involved with their children (Simons, Lorenz, Conger, & Wu, 1992). Instead, stressed parents are more likely to be irritable, negative, punitive, and withdrawn and feel that they cannot deal effectively and consistently with their children (Goldberg, 1990; McLoyd, 1990). Parental perceptions about how difficult a child is as well as negative attributions about the cause of the child behavior can be exacerbated by stress (Mash & Johnston, 1990). Those, in turn, can set the stage for more difficult interactions, resulting in a self-fulfilling prophecy.

In contemporary society, stress on parents comes in a variety of manifestations. Four main classes of stressors are marital or relationship, child-related, work or financial, and personal characteristics. Examples of these stressors are listed in Table 4.1. Some of the stressors reflect acute situations, whereas others are chronic. When two or more stressors team up, it is likely that they will have an additive, or cumulative, effect.

TABLE 4.1   Examples of Possible Stressors Experienced by Parents

Marital or relationship stressors
  • Increase in marital conflict
  • Sexual difficulties
  • In-law troubles
  • Separated or divorced
  • Serious sickness or injury
  • Serious health or behavior problem with family member
  • Death of someone close

Child-related stressors
  • Pregnancy or birth of baby
  • Minor hassles with child
  • Chronic behavior problems
  • Child has handicap or developmental delay
  • Child suspended or expelled from school
  • Child caught doing something illegal

Work or financial stressors
  • Trouble with employer
  • Trouble with people at work
  • Increase in hours worked or job responsibilities
  • Got laid off or fired
  • Worse off financially or financial problems
  • Foreclosure on mortgage or loan

Personal characteristics
  • Inappropriate cognition
  • Personality problems
  • Substance abuse

Other stressors
  • Moved
  • Exposed to violence or violent environment

On the positive side, sources of social support can help counteract the effects of stress. The chief function of social support is to lead to the belief that one is cared for, loved, and valued and can turn to others for assistance. Usually, the principal support for a parent is the spouse, manifested in emotional comfort and instrumental assistance (Belsky, 1984). Social support can also come from relatives (such as grandparents), friends, neighbors, or colleagues at work.

There are now a number of studies indicating that support from a social network can mediate the effects of stress and facilitate positive parenting (Crnic, Greenberg, Ragozin, Robinson, & Basham, 1983; Crockenberg, 1981; Cutrona & Troutman, 1986). Supportive social networks enhance parents' self-perceptions of efficacy and esteem, thereby increasing parental patience and sensitivity (Cutrona & Troutman, 1986; Mash & Johnston, 1990). Evidence for this effect was found in a multimethod study of forty-four mothers of four-year-old children (Jennings, Stagg, & Connors, 1991). Using interviews and daily diaries to collect information about social networks, the authors found that mothers who had a larger "caregiving" network (including baby-sitters and advice-givers) and those who were more satisfied with their "personal" social network (including friends and neighbors) exhibited more effective child-rearing behavior during a free-play observation. In particular, supported mothers were found to be warmer and less intrusive with their children than those with little support. The authors interpreted the results as indicating that mothers with stronger social networks, in comparison with other mothers, are more likely to have their emotional needs met and, in turn, to meet their children's needs.

One other exosystem variable has received some attention by researchers: the type of *neighborhood* where the family resides also can influence parental behavior. It is not hard to picture how proximity to peers or parks, the availability of other supportive adults, or neighborhood crime can affect parenting. Consider urban poverty, the most problematic neighborhood characteristic. Although urban poverty is associated with a wide range of negative outcomes for children (crime, health problems, academic failure, substance abuse, teen pregnancy), until recently there have been few efforts to study parenting in communities where there are high levels of poverty, crime, and violence. It is telling that the places that once were labeled as "high-risk" neighborhoods are now described as "war zones" (Garbarino, Kosstelny, & Dubrow, 1991).

Given a hostile child-rearing environment, it is not surprising that parenting in high-crime inner-city neighborhoods is characterized by a distrust of nonfamily individuals, an encouragement of children's early independence and self-reliance, an emphasis on aggressive play, a competitive relationship between mother and child, and an early withdrawal of emotional support (Halpern, 1990). Some observers have argued that these patterns result from the behavior of stressed, powerless mothers whose own needs are not being met, which renders them unable to provide consistent, supportive, nonpunitive parenting. An alternative interpretation has been articulated by the anthropologist John Ogbu (1988). He does not argue that child rearing is unaffected by poverty-stricken neighborhoods. Rather, his position is that such patterns of child-rearing behavior are adaptive patterns of parenting that evolved in order to maximize the likelihood of survival and the success of children being reared in such environments. Despite the competing interpretations, both viewpoints recognize the integral role that the neighborhood, as an exosystem variable, can play in determining parental behavior.

Mesosystem Determinants

At the mesosystem level, parenting can be thought of as determined by those stable parent, child, and family characteristics that exert a similar effect across different settings.

Stable Parent Characteristics

There are several attributes that parents carry with them across different situations. The four central stable characteristics of parents that help to determine parenting are (1) experiences in their family of origin, (2) gender, (3) attitudes and beliefs, and (4) personality.

Family of Origin.   The first influence on future parental behavior, an individual's own development, has been referred to in several ways: experience in one's family of origin, intergenerational influences, or more poetically, "ghosts in the nursery" (Fraiberg, 1987). This determinant is concerned with how experiences with one's parents influence parenting. Most of the work in this area has focused on discipline and the transmission of attitudes toward child management. From a social learning theory perspective, a number of studies have found similarities between two generations of individuals in terms of the disciplinary practices they use (Van IJzendoorn, 1992). This transmission appears to start very early. In one study, children as young as five years old expressed a preference for the use of physical punishment if their mothers used it on them. Eight-year-old children showed an even stronger association between their mothers' use of physical punishment and their own preference to use it as a disciplinary response in hypothetical situations, $r = .41$, $p < .05$ (Holden & Zambarano, 1992).

Attachment experiences in one's own family constitute another domain that is beginning to reveal intergenerational effects. Based on Bowlby and Ainsworth's ethological theory of attachment (see Chapter 2), a number of investigators are discovering links between a mother's perception of her own attachment experience and her relationship with her child (Main, Kaplan, & Cassidy, 1985).

To get at this link, an interview has been developed by Mary Main and her colleagues (e.g., Main et al., 1985) to assess adults' internal model of their attachment relationship with their parents. Questions address recollections of the quality of relationships with their mothers and fathers and experiences with separation and rejection.

One prospective study used the "Strange Situation" procedure, developed by Mary Ainsworth, to illuminate the relation between mothers' internal models of attachment relations and the quality of their attachment with their infants. The Strange Situation is a laboratory research procedure comprising seven three-minute episodes that vary the presence and absence of the parent and an unfamiliar person with the infant, with the purpose of manipulating the amount of stress the infant experiences. The procedure was designed to provide a uniform assay of the quality of the attachment relationship through observing the child under stress. In this study, models of the mothers' attachment relations were assessed in an interview performed before they gave birth. Subsequently, when their infants were twelve months old, they participated in the Strange Situation. It was found that mothers' representations of attachment with their own mothers subsequently predicted attachment classification in 75 percent of the cases (Fonagy, Steele, & Steele, 1991).

In another study that assessed parent-child relationships with toddlers and preschoolers, mothers' internal working models were associated with parenting and child adjustment (Eiden, Teti, & Corns, 1995). Those studies provide strong evidence for the association between internal working models and the quality of parent-child relationships. However, the working model is not a rigid and deterministic influence on the mother's behavior. If a mother had an insecure attachment with her own mother but subsequently was able to modify her internal working model through introspection or therapy, discontinuity across generations is likely. The mother will then base her child-rearing behavior on her revised understanding of mother-child relationships and will be able to form a secure attachment with her child (Main et al., 1985).

Gender of Parent.   Some people believe that women are instinctively better at rearing children than men. They may base that belief on their observations that some fathers appear to be awkward or not particularly interested in parenting. The average mothers and fathers do indeed show various gender-related differences. The greatest contrast is typically in degree of involvement in child rearing. Despite societal changes, men on average still spend relatively little time caring for children. In 1986, the average father devoted just twenty-three minutes per day to child care, according to a study of a randomly selected, representative sample of U.S. households. That average had not changed from a decade earlier (Coverman & Sheley, 1986). The United States is not unique in the level of paternal involvement. In Israel, fathers were found to spend only about forty-five minutes each day interacting with their nine-month-old infants. In addition, they performed only one solo caregiving activity per day and took sole responsibility for the infant only once every ten days (Ninio & Rinott, 1988).

Investigations have documented that gender differences extend well beyond the extent of involvement in the parenting role. Using the microanalytic approach, researchers in several different countries have observed fathers interacting with their children differently from mothers. Fathers tend to engage less than mothers in verbal or didactic play (Power, 1985), but they are more physically stimulating and rough in their play (Lamb, 1977; Lytton, 1980; Roopnarine, Talukder, Jain, Josi, & Srivastav, 1990). Mothers tend to be more responsive to variations in their children's play (Lytton, 1979; Mulhern & Passman, 1981), more likely to enforce rules (Power & Chapieski, 1986), and more likely to communicate and play peekaboo-type games (Lytton, 1980; Roopnarine et al., 1990) than fathers. In a study of parents with both normal and hyperactive boys, mothers were found to make more demands on and be more emotionally expressive to both types of boys than fathers (Buhrmester, Camparo, Christensen, Gonzalez, & Hinshaw, 1992).

Parents also differ in their child-rearing attitudes. In a study conducted in Sweden, a number of differences were found between the child-rearing attitudes of mothers and fathers. A total of 128 couples completed a survey assessing their child-rearing attitudes and beliefs. On more than one-third of the ninety-one ratings, mothers differed significantly from fathers (Lamb, Hwang, & Broberg, 1989). Mothers placed more importance on expressive items (e.g., emotions, intimacy, enjoyment of child), whereas fathers placed more importance on items concerning instrumental issues (e.g., self-control, achievement, responsibility).

One of the potential reasons for these gender-based differences concerns the extent of previous experience with infants and children. This experiential factor is a common confound with gender. In most cultures, girls are exposed to many more child-care experiences than boys. Presumably, extensive baby-sitting experience contributes to greater competency as a parent (Fogel & Melson, 1986). There is some supporting evidence: Experienced mothers have been found to be less upset by cries of infants with difficult temperaments than less-experienced women (Lounsbury & Bates, 1982). In the study described in Chapter 3 in which a microcomputer was used for assessing individuals' ability to determine why a baby is crying, those with more child-care experience (either through parenthood or baby-sitting) performed more efficiently and accurately than those without such experience (Holden, 1988).

In summary, gender has been found to be a key determinant of parenting. Although fathers are typically not as involved as mothers and differ in some behaviors and attitudes, there is no support for the notion that fathers are inadequate parents. In the case of the 10 percent of fathers who are single parents, it is likely that they are as competent as single mothers (G. Russell, 1986). The underlying reason for much of the gender difference in parenting concerns the roles prescribed by culture. Gender reflects how one stable parent characteristic at the *mesosystem* level is nested within another level: the *macrosystem* variable of culture.

Parental Beliefs and Attitudes.   The research into parental beliefs has provided a rich documentation of many of the stable cognitive influences on parental behavior. Parents typically hold particular ideas regarding such topics as the goals they have for their children, how they want their children to turn out, how (and how fast) children develop, and how they should rear their children (Goodnow & Collins, 1990; Miller, 1988). Until recently, much of the work documenting child-rearing beliefs has been conducted with parent attitude questionnaires. Instruments have most often assessed parents' attitudes about discipline and warmth, but they also have looked at a wide range of variables, including involvement in child rearing, discipline, affection, and sex-typed behavior. However, few studies have successfully shown how child-rearing attitudes are related to parental behavior (Holden, 1995).

In one recent exception, a study demonstrated links between parental attitudes and behavior regarding mothers' use of spanking (Holden, Coleman, & Schmidt, 1995). A variety of possible determinants of spanking were tested, including mothers' attitudes toward spanking, mothers' negative emotions, children's temperament, and the type of misbehavior engaged in by the children. The participants consisted of thirty-nine mothers of three-year-old children. Each mother filled out a series of questionnaires and then for two weeks reported on nightly telephone interviews how she had handled the various disciplinary episodes of the day. The college-educated mothers reported spanking about 2.5 times a week, on average. Some evidence was found for both maternal negative affect and the type of child misbehavior as influences on the mothers' choice of disciplinary responses. However, the variable that was most implicated as a determinant was mothers' attitudes toward spanking. Those attitudes were highly correlated with reports of spanking, $r = .73$, $p < .001$. Mothers' attitudes toward spanking proved to be the best predictor of their behavior.

Many other types of attitudes and beliefs have also been implicated as helping to influence parental behavior. According to Daphne Bugental and William Shennum (1984), a parent's belief in the degree to which a child can be controlled is a key one. Parents who believe they have little power in influencing the behavior of a child are likely to be unassertive and to show negative affect when interacting with unresponsive children. Such parents, when anticipating future interactions with unresponsive children, show elevated levels of arousal (e.g., increased skin conductance and heart rate; Bugental & Cortez, 1988).

Parental attitudes and beliefs, if activated and helping to guide behavior, represent stable, across-situation behavioral influences. Such beliefs are important, therefore, not just because they influence behavior but because they provide the most readily accessible avenue for changing parental behavior; as proximal influences on parenting, they may supersede more distal influences (e.g., culture or social class). Efforts to change parental beliefs in order to influence parental behavior will be discussed further in Chapter 6.

Personality.   It is likely that individual differences in personality are associated with individual differences in parenting behavior. Recall that Belsky's (1984) model placed parental personality at the front line of parenting determinants. He argued that parental maturity and psychological well-being were fundamental ingredients for effective parental functioning. Despite the prominence of personality as a determinant of parenting in Belsky's model, relatively few studies have linked personality attributes to child-rearing behavior.

The most common finding has been at an aggregate level of analysis: Parents exhibiting a set of attributes indicating greater *psychological integration* (also called *level of personal differentiation, ego strength, or maturity*) exhibited better parenting (e.g., Brunnquell, Crichton, & Egeland, 1981). Mothers and fathers who exhibit healthy psychological functioning on a variety of indices (e.g., low anxiety, low depression, high adjustment) are more likely to express positive attitudes about their infants and exhibit sensitive parenting than other parents (Cox, Owen, Lewis, & Henderson, 1989). This cluster of personality attributes is central to effective parenting. Adults who are consumed by their own psychological problems are unlikely to provide sensitive caregiving to an infant or appropriate parenting to a young child. One dysfunctional parent revealed her lack of psychological integration when she commented, "I waited so long to have my child and when she came she never did anything for me" (Helfer & Kempe, 1988, p. 14).

Various other specific personality characteristics have been proposed to influence parenting, such as patience and calmness. However, the personality attribute that has received the most attention is the capacity for empathy. This refers to the ability to experience events from the child's point of view and therefore understand better what an infant or young child might be feeling. Parents who are high in empathy have been found to be more involved, nurturant, and positive and less negative than those who are low in empathy (Feshbach, 1987; Izard, Haynes, Chisholm, & Baak, 1991). This topic is discussed in greater depth in Chapter 6.

Other Stable Characteristics.   Although several other stable characteristics have been proposed that may influence parenting (e.g., intelligence), the age of the parent is the only other parental attribute that has received sustained attention. Two separate age-of-parent questions have been investigated. One concerns the quality of child care provided by adolescent parents, a topic to be discussed in Chapter 7. The other age-of-parent question is whether "older" parents of young children (usually defined as parents in their thirties and forties) differ in their parenting from "younger" parents. The effects of age on parenting have been of interest in part owing to the increasingly common trend for women to wait longer to bear children (Yarrow, 1991).

Few empirical studies have systematically examined the effects of parental age; the evidence available is conflicting. One study concluded that older mothers spent more time parenting, exhibited better parenting behavior, and were more satisfied than younger mothers (Ragozin, Basham, Crnic, Greenberg, & Robinson, 1982). In contrast, an observational study using three samples of mothers from two states (totaling 107 mothers) determined that older mothers were less positive in their child-rearing interactions than younger mothers (Conger, McCarty, Yang, Lahey, & Burgess, 1984). Still other investigations have found no effects for age on maternal caregiving or child-rearing attitudes (Reis, Barbera-Stein, & Bennett, 1986). With the likely exception of a decreased energy level in older mothers, there appear to be few if any systematic differences between mothers that are based solely on their age.

Stable Child Characteristics

As the child effects literature has shown, the characteristics of children can be prime determinants of parental behavior. The best documented characteristics are (1) age of child, (2) temperament, (3) gender of child, and (4) birth order.

Child's Age. Age of the child is the single most powerful influence on parental behavior. Owing to differences in their children's physical, cognitive, and socioemotional characteristics, parents show affection, communicate, discipline, and provide care in very different ways (e.g., Clifford, 1959; Crockenberg & McCluskey, 1986; Fagot & Kavanagh, 1993; Power, 1985). Age provides a "marker" variable, or index, for such characteristics as physical size, cognitive and linguistic ability, emotional maturity, and social skills competence.

As children grow older, the manifestation of parenting undergoes numerous transformations. During the first three months of infancy, the primary role for parents is to establish smooth routines by responding to the infant's basic needs (Sroufe, 1979). Parents of young infants receive some respite from the demands of caring for a baby owing to the large number of hours an infant sleeps. Over the course of an average day, a typical three-month-old infant may sleep a total of fifteen hours (Ferber, 1985). As the infant develops into a toddler and becomes more cognitively, socially, and physically competent, the parent role must change. Parents must go beyond caregiving behaviors to establish sensitive, cooperative interactions and create a safe environment (e.g., childproofing the home). By the end of the first year, the most important part of the parents' role, according to at-tachment theory, is to provide responsive availability and a secure base (Sroufe, 1979).

During their children's second year of life, parents begin to discipline and provide instruction. As children progress through their preschool years, their changing behavior elicits different parental behavior. Disciplinary techniques change; parents, on average, use more reasoning and withhold-ing of privileges but less power assertion. Parents also display less physical affection, become less protective, and spend less time with their children (Maccoby & Martin 1983). As children develop, new child-rearing behav-iors are required to complement the child's new behavioral repertoire. Ex-amples include providing firm support, setting limits, and monitoring (see Chapter 6). A time that precipitates marked change in parental behavior is the arrival of adolescence. Typically, the onset of puberty brings an increase in conflict and decrease in warmth in parent-child relationships (Paikoff & Brooks-Gunn, 1991).

Child's Temperament.   Second only to the child's age in terms of its in-fluence on parenting is the child's temperament. *Temperament* refers to the biologically rooted behavioral style of the child, involving characteris-tics such as emotional expressiveness and responsiveness to environmen-tal stimulation. There is considerable disagreement, however, about ex-actly what the core components of temperament are (Goldsmith et al., 1987). The two most prominent models of temperament are Alexander Thomas and Stella Chess's (1977) nine-dimension model (e.g., rhythmic-ity, activity level, adaptability, mood) and the more parsimonious and psychometrically defensible three-dimension model of Arnold Buss and Robert Plomin, which includes emotionality, activity, and sociability (see Bates, 1989; Goldsmith et al., 1987).

As Thomas and Chess (1977) recognized, it is not temperament itself that is most important for a child's early development but how the parents relate to that particular child's temperament. How well the parental actions relate to the children's temperament has been called *matching, congruence,* or *goodness of fit.* A questionnaire study (Sprunger, Boyce, & Gaines, 1985) demonstrated the significance of this concept by focusing on one di-mension of temperament and family life: the degree of rhythmicity between infants and the home environment. A total of 285 mothers of infants re-ported on how regular their infants were (e.g., sleep patterns) as well as the degree to which the family had a routinized lifestyle. The importance of the congruence between infants' regularity and the child-rearing practices was indexed with the mothers' perception of the overall family adjustment. Mothers who had irregular infants but who nevertheless tried to force a routine on them reported lower levels of family adjustment than mothers with regular infants who had similar routines.

Another aspect of temperament has also been linked to parental behavior. Children who are perceived by their parents to be difficult are likely to elicit less positive and responsive caregiving from mothers than easygoing children. In several different studies, it has been shown that parents of difficult children are more likely to be negative and use punitive techniques, whereas parents of easygoing children appear more authoritative and responsive (Lee & Bates, 1985; Patterson, 1986).

Child's Gender. Yet another powerful child characteristic is gender. The child's gender can influence parental behavior in various ways. First, fertility decisions are often based on children's gender. Parents may choose to keep having more children until they get the desired son or daughter. Whether the gender of the child is consistent with the parent's prior preference has been shown to have subtle repercussions for parental behavior. Parents who had wanted children of the opposite sex were more likely to perceive problems with their children and to spend less time playing with their children compared with parents who were pleased with the gender of their children (Stattin & Klackenberg-Larsson, 1991).

Many studies published since 1970 have reported reliable differences related to child gender that are independent of the congruence between preference and reality. Recall (from Chapter 3) that parental perceptions of newborns and young children were dramatically affected simply by the label of "girl" or "boy." Furthermore, many observational studies have found that parental behavior appears to be influenced by the child's gender (Fagot, 1978; Maccoby & Jacklin, 1974; Power, 1985). Boys are encouraged to play, explore, and achieve more, whereas girls are encouraged to help their mothers around the house and focus on interpersonal relationships (e.g., Fagot, 1978). Studies have also found that boys are more likely to receive power-assertive discipline, whereas girls receive more reasoning (Maccoby & Jacklin, 1974; Zussman, 1978).

Given the large number of studies in this area, two researchers (Lytton & Romney, 1991) recently set out to conduct a systematic review. They used a relatively new analytic procedure called *meta-analysis* for comparing different studies. A *meta-analysis* involves a quantitative comparison across studies by determining the strength of a particular finding in each study (Rosenthal, 1991). The meta-analytic review of 172 studies looking at whether parents systematically treat boys and girls differently arrived at a surprising conclusion: Gender effects are not as pervasive as commonly believed (Lytton & Romney, 1991). In fact, there were few significant findings. The strongest gender effects appeared to be in parental expectations or early perceptions about boys and girls, but most differences in parental treatment decreased with children's age. The authors concluded that when all the evidence is taken together, there are few robust, consistent differences in how boys and girls are treated by their parents.

Birth Order.   The order in which children are born into a family has long been considered to be a prime influence on parenting behavior. Since the 1950s, investigators have explored associations between birth order and parenting. Among the typical findings is that first-born infants receive more care, attention, and affection than later born infants because first-time parents have more enthusiasm and energy to devote to the child. However, first-born children also were reported to receive more pressure for achievement, presumably because the parents hold higher expectations for them than for later born children (Lasko, 1954; Rothbart, 1971).

More recent investigations into the topic have shown that the influence of birth order on parenting can be affected by at least three other variables: the child's gender, the spacing (time between births) of the children, and the family size. In perhaps the most careful observational study conducted to date on the topic, 193 mothers were observed interacting with their three-month-old babies (Lewis & Kreitzberg, 1979). As prior literature had found, first-born children generally received more maternal attention than later born children. However, the spacing between the children also had a significant effect: Closely and widely spaced children received more attention than moderately spaced (1.5–3.5 years) children. Presumably, mothers' perceptions and thus the attention devoted to their children were modified by the spacing of their children.

Other Stable Child Characteristics.   Two other child characteristics that have been shown to influence parenting are premature birth and physical handicaps. Extremely low-birthweight infants (e.g., born weighing only two or three pounds) are highly stressful to their parents. Premature infants born more than several weeks early are likely to be isolated from their parents in a neonatal intensive care ward at the hospital, resulting in astronomical medical bills. Beyond the question of survival, parents wonder whether the infant will develop various physical and behavior problems. In addition, the infants do not look like normal babies, have not met their parents' expectations about newborns, and do not have the physical ability to establish the reciprocal interactions that full-term infants can. Instead, premature infants have an irritating and arousing cry that elicits a stronger physiological response and more aversive reaction than the cry of a full-term neonate (Frodi, 1983). The infants may gradually catch up with their full-term peers over months and years, and the differences in evocative characteristics of the premature infant generally disappear only gradually (Barnard, Bee, & Hammond, 1984).

To an even greater extent than parents of premature infants, parents of disabled children face multiple stresses in raising their children. These stressors are compounded by the awareness that the strain is unlikely to diminish over time. Parents of such children are more likely to experience stress and disruptions in normal family functioning (e.g., concerning mealtimes, sleep, and visiting friends) and to encounter more marital difficulties than parents of children without disabilities (Bristol, Gallagher, & Schopler, 1988).

In sum, the stable child characteristics reflect individual differences across children. These and other differences among children represent a key determinant of parental behavior and therefore are a likely source of differential parental treatment (Stocker, Dunn, & Plomin, 1989). Behavioral geneticists refer to this differential behavior as *nonshared environmental influences;* such influences presumably provide an important reason that siblings in a family can be so different from one another (Plomin, 1990), as discussed in Chapter 2.

Family Characteristics

Two types of family characteristics are recognized as influencing parenting: family structure and marital relations.

Family Structure.   Family structure refers to attributes such as number of parents and children in the family. The prime family structural variable is whether it is a single- or two-parent family. Single parents (90 percent of whom are women) differ in their parenting behavior from married parents in various areas. In part as a result of the increased stress and pressure of limited time, single parents, compared with married parents, tend to spend less time with their children and engage in less supervision and monitoring. Because single parents must deal with all aspects of parenting by themselves, there is some evidence that they exhibit a "diminished" level of parenting with regard to the time and attention they are able to provide to their offspring (McLanahan, 1989). Single parents will be discussed further in Chapter 8.

A second family structural variable is the number of children in the home. Given that there is only so much time and energy parents can devote to children, it comes as no surprise that family size has been associated with differences in parental behavior. Although this characteristic has received only limited research attention, there is evidence that family size influences parental disciplinary practices. In large families (i.e., four or more children), discipline tends to be more authoritarian and more punitive than in small families (Wagner, Schubert, & Schubert, 1985; Zussman, 1978).

Marital Relations.   The recognition that the quality of the marital relationship affects child rearing was one of the major parenting "discoveries" of the 1980s. During that time, a number of studies documented links between marital relations and parenting. The majority of the empirical work on this topic examined the relation between perceived marital quality and parenting. Close, supportive, and thereby satisfying marital relationships were found to be associated with sensitive and positive parenting as well as more positive attitudes and perceptions about children (Cowan & Cowan, 1992; Cox et al., 1989; Goldberg, 1990).

Marital relations and parenting can also have negative associations. For couples experiencing marital problems, there are several ways in which the relationship might affect parenting. Parents in discordant marriages, compared with parents in happy marriages, exhibit less consistent practices and fewer of the child-rearing practices widely considered effective. It is likely that parents in unhappy marriages are less emotionally available and involved with their children (Easterbrooks & Emde, 1988). The marital discord may manifest itself in disagreements over child-rearing practices. Consequently, parents in discordant relationships may be less positive and more negative in disciplinary practices than nondiscordant parents. In addition, the interspousal conflict may "spill over" into parent-child conflict. However, poor marriages do not necessarily mean poor parent-child relationships. There is some evidence indicating that mothers in discontented marriages may compensate for the poor marital relationship by being more attentive to and involved with their children (Holden & Ritchie, 1991).

A negative spillover into parenting can most dramatically be seen in homes of battered women. Men who physically abuse their wives are frequently irritable. In one study of thirty-seven battered mothers and thirty-seven matched, comparison mothers, almost all of the battered women reported that they argued with their husbands at least every few days. In contrast, only 16 percent of the comparison women reported a similar rate of arguments. It is likely that at least some of these marital arguments spilled over into the fathers' interactions with their children. Violent men reportedly got angry at their children every few days, in contrast to the comparison fathers' rate of less than once a week (Holden & Ritchie, 1991).

Microsystem Determinants

The microsystem refers to the most proximate level of influences, in which variables in the immediate situation impact on the parent. Three types of microsystem variables have been identified: the context, transient parental characteristics, and transient child characteristics.

The Context

Relatively few studies have examined the role of context in parent-child relationships. However, it is likely that context represents a critical proximal ingredient in determining child-rearing behavior. Parents' continual assessments of the context include consideration of the setting, or location where the interaction took place; the type of activity engaged in; the presence of others; and the time of day. Although these considerations are not always at a conscious and explicit level, their presence can easily be demonstrated. Ask parents how they would respond if their children engaged in some misdeed (e.g., pushed a peer), and they are likely to protest and say, "It depends on the situation."

The most obvious contextual variable is the setting. Parenting occurs most often in the home but also in the car, supermarket, and park and in numerous other locales. If parental behavior were independent of the context, there would be a high level of cross-situational stability. Nine observational studies that compared parental behavior across two or more settings (e.g., home, laboratory, park) arrived at similar conclusions: Parental behavior can show considerable variation across different settings (Holden & O'Dell, 1996). Even within a particular setting, child-rearing behavior is affected by the ongoing activity. If a mother is given a competing task to perform while interacting with her children, her parenting will change considerably (Zussman, 1980).

Another contextual variable that can influence dyadic interactions is the presence of additional individuals. This phenomenon has been labeled a "second-order effect" (Bronfenbrenner, 1979). The presence of another child or a second parent has sometimes been shown to modify parental behavior. One of the most dramatic examples of second-order effects occurs in violent homes. In the study previously mentioned concerning child rearing in homes of battered women, the abused mothers reported they were more likely than nonbattered mothers to modify their parenting behavior (in both expression of affection and discipline) when their violent husbands were present. Presumably, the wives had learned this behavioral strategy in order to appease their violent partners and thereby avoid inciting their anger. There was not one consistent way mothers attempted to pacify their violent husbands: Some women used more strict discipline with their children, whereas others became more permissive (Holden & Ritchie, 1991).

A final contextual variable that has received some research attention is the time at which the interaction occurs. Time has been related to parenting with regard to both the time of year and the time of day. During the summer months, compared with the rest of the year, parental involvement and monitoring were found to systematically change in relation to the parents' work status (Crouter & McHale, 1993). The time of day that interactions occur is also likely to influence behaviors. If parents are in a hurry or tired, they are likely to behave differently than otherwise. Fatigue on the part of parents and children may account for the finding that mothers are twice as likely to spank their children in the evening as in the morning (Clifford, 1959; Holden et al., 1995).

Transient Parent Characteristics

Two types of parent characteristics that influence parenting can be considered transient because they are likely to change within a short period of time: beliefs and emotion. Parental beliefs, in this case referring to how individuals process information about the child in a particular interaction (e.g., perceptions, attributions, expectations, goals), have been linked to parental behavior in various ways (Bacon & Ashmore, 1986; Dix et al., 1989). Rather than attempt to cover the many links between thoughts and behavior, I describe one exemplar.

Consider the role of goals as a determinant of behavior. The particular goal the parent has in mind is potentially a strong influence on behavior. Parents often enter situations with child-centered, parent-centered, or socialization goals in mind (Dix, 1992). A child-centered goal puts the child's needs foremost, as in the case of going to the park to let the child play or taking the child on an educational outing. Parent-centered goals, in contrast, are self-centered, whereby the child's schedule and behavior are expected to fit into the parent's needs (as in taking the child to the supermarket or bringing the child along to an adult party). Socialization goals involve the intention of teaching the child to behave in a more mature fashion.

Parenting behavior is indeed affected by the particular goals the parent has in mind. In a cleverly designed study, Leon Kuczynski (1984) subtly manipulated mothers' goals by dispensing different instructions. Half of the sixty-four mothers studied were instructed that the study involved how parents achieve children's cooperation on a task while faced with distractions. The other mothers, randomly assigned to the "long-term" compliance condition, were told that their children's compliance to the task would also be observed after the mothers had left the room. The author found that mothers in the long-term child compliance condition used more reasoning, positive attributions about their children's character (e.g., "You're a hard worker."), and nurturant behavior than mothers in the "short-term" compliance condition.

Closely linked to goals is parental emotion. As Dix (1991) argued in a theoretical model of emotions and parenting, positive or negative emotions are often aroused when parental goals are met or frustrated. These emotions are essential for effective parenting, because they help to organize the parents' sensitive and responsive child-rearing behaviors. However, when emotions are too strong, too weak, or inappropriately matched to the child's behavior, they serve to undermine effective parenting.

Several empirical studies have documented how parental emotions are linked to both parental thoughts and behavior. For example, when parents are angry, their perceptions about children are likely to be affected. Theodore Dix and his colleagues documented this association using videotaped vignettes of children misbehaving (Dix, Reinhold, & Zambarano, 1990). Mothers who saw the videotapes when in an angry mood had more negative expectations about the children than emotionally neutral mothers. In another study involving observations in a laboratory setting, mothers who reported they were feeling irritable exhibited more negative parenting than other mothers (Jouriles, Murphy, & O'Leary, 1989a).

Transient Child Characteristics

Parental behavior can also be influenced by rapidly changing emotional and behavioral characteristics of the child. Children are more susceptible than their parents to changes in their physiological or emotional states. In turn, parental behavior can shift rapidly. The best evidence for how transient child characteristics influence parental behavior comes from the child effects approach, as discussed in Chapter 3. Studies examining parental responses to children's misbehavior have shown that the type of child misdeed or behavior is a powerful determinant of parental behavior. In fact, as a study by Joan Grusec and Kuczynski (1980) demonstrated, the type of misbehavior a child engages in (e.g., disobedience, harming other people, destroying property) provides a better predictor of the mother's disciplinary response than the parent's child-rearing approach or disciplinary philosophy.

Interrelations Among Determinants and Levels

As has been recognized at least since the pioneering work by Stolz (1967), parental behavior is multiply determined. Characteristics of the parent, the child, and many levels of the context all contribute to child-rearing behavior. Despite the research that typically assesses only one determinant at a time, each of the thirty or more influences on parenting do not work independently. There are two basic ways in which the determinants can be interrelated: One determinant may be nested within another, and one determinant may have impact on another.

When examining the many different determinants organized into the four levels of the ecological systems model, it is apparent that variables at one level may have corresponding variables at another level. Thus, some determinants are embedded within others. For example, all of the macrosystem determinants discussed, particularly culture and socioeconomic status, have corresponding variables nested at each of the lower levels of the system.

The role of culture in parenting provides, perhaps, the clearest example. The way that culture influences parenting can be found embedded in all three lower levels of the model. It is not hard to visualize how cultural influences are manifested in the exosystem levels of work, support, and neighborhoods. Culture is even more evident in the mesosystem-level variable of parents' stable characteristics. Parenting ethnotheories (including values, attitudes, and expectations) are the primary vehicle in which culture is exemplified and passed on (Harkness & Super, 1995). Even at the microsystem level, the types of child-rearing contexts the parents find themselves in, as well as the transient characteristics permitted in the culture, reveal the nested nature of culture.

In a similar way, the exosystem variables that influence parenting (work, stress and social support, neighborhoods) are also manifested at the more immediate contextual levels of the mesosystem and microsystem. As a consequence of stress, parents may take on stable parenting characteristics that reflect chronic exposure to stress. In turn, those characteristics are likely to impact interactions in the microsystem.

A second way to consider how the determinants of child rearing interrelate is by examining their influence on each other. Three ways in which particular variables influence each other include additive effects, moderating variables, and mediating variables, as depicted in Figure 4.4.

Additive, or cumulative, effects result from variables combining to form a stronger influence on behavior than any single variable. A parent with an explosive temper and a temperamentally difficult child add up to a dangerous combination. If the parent also loses a job, the risk of negative or even abusive parenting is considerably higher than if only one or even two variables are present. One study that demonstrated such additive effects was conducted by Kristi Hannan and Tom Luster (1991). They reasoned that the more risk factors there were on parental behavior, the greater the likelihood of a poor child-rearing environment. To assess the environment, they used the Home Observation for the Measurement of the Environment (HOME), a combined interview and observation procedure that measures different aspects of the child's environment such as the amount of cognitive stimulation, parental warmth, and use of physical punishment (Bradley & Caldwell, 1984). Data from 602 families with one-year-old children were collected. Six potentially detrimental influences on child rearing were assessed: three contextual factors (absence of a partner, three or more children, and low income); two maternal characteristics (low IQ score, adolescent mother), and one child characteristic (difficult temperament). The risk factors were then added to form a risk index. The relation between risk index and HOME assessment was then computed. The results revealed a strong relation between risk index and low HOME environment score. Only 22 percent of families with one risk factor had low HOME scores, in contrast to 88 percent of families with six risk factors.

A second way that determinants can be related is by one variable moderating another. A moderating variable affects the impact of another variable. For parenting, the most important moderating variable is the marital relationship. Supportive spouses can reduce the effects of stress by providing assistance, advice, and encouragement to their mate. A close, supportive marital relationship can help to moderate the negative effects of financial hardship as well (Simons et al., 1992). Similarly, a close marital relationship can reduce the negative influences on parenting of a parent's psychologically painful childhood by the partners recognizing those effects and one spouse suggesting behavioral alternatives for the other.

A third type of interrelation involves one variable mediating the effect of another. As depicted in Figure 4.4, the variables that are mediated must pass through the mediator. For example, economic hardship is mediated by the feelings of economic strain on the part of the parent. If parents fail to recognize or ignore their financial problems, it is unlikely that economic hardship will influence parenting. But when the financial problems are recognized and experienced in the form of strain, parenting will likely be negatively impacted (Simons et al., 1992).

The most important mediator is parental beliefs; several studies have demonstrated that beliefs can mediate child rearing. Susan Crockenberg and Karen McCluskey (1986) assessed infant irritability and maternal sensitivity at twelve months using the Strange Situation procedure. They found that mothers with irritable infants provided less-supportive care if they believed that responsive care would reinforce the demandingness of their infants. Thus, maternal beliefs mediated the extent to which infant irritability was predictive of maternal sensitivity. Similarly, parental beliefs mediate attributions about child behavior. Mothers with authoritarian disciplinary attitudes interpreted children's misconduct differently from authoritative mothers (Dix et al., 1989).

A fourth relation among parenting determinants, which is not graphed in Figure 4.4 is an interaction. Interactions occur when relations or functions between two types of variables differ depending on the particular exemplar of each variable. A common interaction found in parent-child relationships is between the gender of the parent and the gender of the child. Fathers, for example, are sometimes observed to behave differently toward their sons than toward their daughters (Power & Chapieski, 1986; Simons, Whitbeck, Conger, & Melby, 1990). In an observational study of sex-typed play, for example, it was found that fathers were more likely to reward their daughters but punish their sons for cross-sex play (Langlois & Downs, 1980). Evidently, for identifying the determinants of parental behavior,

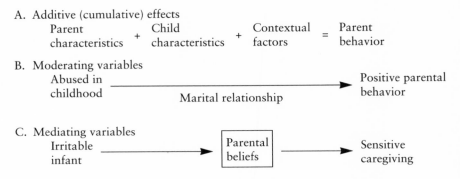

A. Additive (cumulative) effects

Parent characteristics + Child characteristics + Contextual factors = Parent behavior

B. Moderating variables

Abused in childhood ──── Marital relationship ────▸ Positive parental behavior

C. Mediating variables

Irritable infant ────▸ Parental beliefs ────▸ Sensitive caregiving

FIGURE 4.4   Three Types of Interrelations Among Determinants.

knowledge about each variable that contributes to the interaction is necessary. Interactions between parents' gender and children's gender and other variables, such as parental beliefs about gender-role socialization, may provide a partial explanation for the fact that consistent differences in parental behavior toward boys and girls have only occasionally been found (Lytton & Romney, 1991).

The description of interrelations among influences has focused on contemporaneous influences; the dimension of time has been ignored. However, the passage of time provides another influence on parenting. Parents, like children, are changing, and as a consequence, the impact of particular determinants may also change (Maccoby, 1984). Perhaps the best illustration of this point is in the area of attachment. As discussed earlier in the chapter, researchers working on the role of internal models of attachment have concluded that it is the individuals' current internal representation of their attachment relationship, not the historically accurate relationship, that plays a determining role in close relationships (Main et al., 1985).

Developmental and contemporaneous influences on parenting operate in a complex manner. As Stolz recognized in 1967, "the multiple determinants of parent behavior result in child rearing that is organically human rather than mechanistically automatic. . . . The variety of causes of parental behavior that have been described should serve as an antidote to oversimplification in research, and as a warning that an intricate network of influence operates to determine parent practices" (Stolz, 1967, p. 280). This complexity makes understanding and predicting parental behavior difficult to achieve with any accuracy. A complete understanding of parental influences must take a dynamic perspective that appreciates the complex interrelations of variables on parenting.

Summary

Parenting behavior is determined by more than thirty types of influences. These range from global cultural traditions to subtle cognitive or affective variables. The ecological systems theory was used to organize the influences and show how some determinants were nested within each other. Much of the current knowledge about how the influences work remains at the level of main effects. Developing a more complex and multivariate understanding of the determinants of parenting remains an important objective of parenting research. This goal can be achieved only by taking a dynamic, process-oriented approach to understanding how one determinant is related to another. The next chapter addresses a different goal, that of summarizing the evidence concerning how parents affect their children's development.

5

Associations Between Parenting and Children's Outcomes

Recent psychological studies indicate that personality is very largely a product of the interactions between parents and child.
—Percival Symonds (1949, p. 3)

Ordinary differences between families have little effect on children's development, unless the family is outside of a normal, developmental range.
—Sandra Scarr (1992, p. 15)

This chapter concerns the most important issue of parent-child relationships: What effects do parents have on their children? To be more precise, no one doubts that parents have a substantial effect on their children (see Figure 5.1); rather, the issue is *how* parents influence their offspring. Is it simply through passing on their genes to their children, as some behavioral geneticists would argue? Or, at the other extreme, is the way children turn out exclusively the result of the child-rearing environment that parents create, independent of biological predispositions? As the quotations introducing this chapter illustrate, there are sharply divergent views reflecting differences in theoretical positions, research orientations, and the kinds of data collected. Unfortunately, to dichotomize these two sources of influence is a simplistic approach to understanding how they influence development. Both genetic material and the environment are constantly interacting and impacting development. Efforts to tease one apart from the other are ultimately unproductive. A more productive focus would be on how individual differences in children and parents interact with basic developmental processes to produce particular outcomes.

The fact that there is considerable variation in how parents rear their children and in children's outcomes makes this a fertile area of inquiry. Early family experience has long been thought to lay the foundation for childhood and adult characteristics. Theories about development have often emphasized the role of parents, given parents' importance in determining children's early physical and social environment. Most of the major personality and behavioral theorists, including Sigmund Freud, Alfred

Calvin and **Hobbes** by **Bill Watterson**

FIGURE 5.1   Parents—and Maybe Even Children—Wonder and Worry About the Effects of Child-Rearing Practices. "Calvin and Hobbes" copyright 11/93 Watterson. Reprinted with permission of Universal Press Syndicate. All rights reserved.

Adler, Erik Erickson, B. F. Skinner, and Albert Bandura, believed that parental behavior leads children to develop generalized behavioral tendencies that have some durability (Rowe, 1994).

Since the 1960s, numerous studies have examined those theoretical orientations in an effort to identify links between parenting and child outcomes. It should be remembered that results from the studies reflect scientific interpretations made by researchers. These interpretations are certainly a considerable improvement over the unsubstantiated opinions of the ministers, philosophers, and physicians described in Chapter 1, because they are empirically derived. Yet the interpretations are scientific constructions, susceptible to the prevailing paradigms, the scientific zeitgeist ("spirit of the times") dictating what should be studied and how results are to be interpreted, as well as the individual orientations or biases of the researchers (Scarr, 1985). Those qualifications hold for all types of research; the study of parental effects on children presents additional, unique problems.

Hazards to Identifying Parental Effects

Discovering how parents affect their children's development is vital, not only for parents and scientific inquiry but also for addressing many contemporary social problems. Parents want—and need—to know whether picking up a crying infant will create a spoiled child or how they can promote their children's academic success. Developmental psychologists seek to discover how variations in the child-rearing environment are linked to differing child outcomes. Society in general needs to know whether changes in child-rearing practices are accountable for such problems as the increasing rates of teenage pregnancy or delinquent behavior (to be discussed in Chapters 7 and 8).

Unfortunately, it is difficult to make definitive statements about the effects of parents on children for several conceptual reasons. Foremost, human development is considerably more complex than depicted by early notions of how children develop. If ontogeny were governed by the principles of unidirectional influence (instead of being bidirectional or transactional), determinism of early experience (over later experience), relative fixity (instead of plasticity), and the preeminence of parental impact (over other influences), scientists by now would have accrued a cookbook of knowledge concerning how parents affect their children. For at least five specific reasons, parental effects cannot be readily and conclusively isolated.

First, just as parenting is multiply determined, so too is human development. Children are influenced by many different socialization agents, including siblings, peers, substitute caregivers, teachers, and grandparents. Although parents may mediate the effects of others and provide a constant source of environmental input, healthy children cannot be isolated from many other sources of influence. Second, children influence parents. The direction of effect does not always proceed from parent to child, as the child effects literature has clearly demonstrated. Third, children contribute to their own development. They are not simply pawns of parents but take an active role in directing their own future. They do this in several ways. Children help to select their developmental environment, as a consequence of their interests, talents, and personality. Children also evoke responses from others that reinforce (either positively or negatively) their behavior (Scarr & McCartney, 1983). Although children's input and role in influencing parents should not be forgotten, that does not mean that the main effect is from child to parent; parents ultimately have more power than children and exert more constraints on children's behavior than children do on parents' behavior.

A fourth problem in identifying parental effects is that individuals change over time. This discontinuity in both parents and children may be the result of new influences or experiences. When behavior changes, attempts to determine which prior behavior is causally linked to which outcome can resemble a guessing game. A final reason that identifying parent effects is difficult is that associations between child rearing and child outcomes are not always uniform across families. As will be discussed toward the end of this chapter, certain characteristics of a parent or a child (e.g., sex of individual) may modify the associations between particular parents and children.

From a scientific viewpoint, the only definitive way to identify parental effects is to use the experimental method. The ideal study would involve randomly assigning newborn babies to different parents. To further enhance the scientific value of the study, the newborn infants would all be genetically identical, cloned from one embryo. Parents would be carefully trained and monitored to use different child-rearing practices, only some of which would be beneficial. Of course such a proposal is immoral, unethical, and technically unfeasible. Instead, evidence has to be culled and extracted from such sources as animal studies, "natural experiment" studies (involving unusual experiences), correlational studies, short-term experimental manipulations, twin studies, and adoption studies. However, each of these approaches has its own methodological limitations.

The most commonly used approach to identify parental effects is the correlational study. Besides being unable to reveal information about causation, correlational studies often contain significant confounds. For example, when one tries to assess the effects of maternal depression on children, the findings are often confounded with other problems including paternal psychiatric status, marital discord, or marital status (Goodman, Brogan, Lynch, & Fielding, 1993). Therefore, attempts to pinpoint one specific characteristic (such as depression) with a particular outcome are problematic. An additional problem is that studies of parental effects have had inconsistent results. Some studies find support, other studies find no support, and still others report a complex interaction with other variables. The technique of meta-analysis represents a promising approach for integrating the results of studies of child-rearing effects. To date, however, not one meta-analysis has been conducted on studies of parental influence.

Yet another methodological hazard lies in looking only for direct parent-to-child dyadic effects (e.g., P → C). An effect might be found in only one parent or the other (M → C or F → C), or there could be a sequential, triadic effect (F → M → C). In some cases, effects may emerge only when there is a combination of mother and father effects (M + F → C). An apparent parent-to-child effect could also be due to a third variable, such as poverty. Or a parent effect could arise only as an indirect effect, such as will be discussed with regard to peer relations.

A final hazard is making an inaccurate attribution that the parents caused a problem. Since the early 1900s, mothers in particular have been blamed for whatever goes wrong with their offspring. One literature review of 125 clinical articles found that mothers were blamed for causing seventy-two different types of psychopathology; fathers were generally ignored and thus rarely blamed (Caplan & Hall-McCorquodale, 1985). At one time, mothers were accused of being "schizophrenogenic," or causing schizophrenia, as well as causing autism in their offspring; these problems have subsequently been discovered to have biological rather than social origins.

One way to avoid false attributions of blame—or success—is to attribute no effects to parents, as some behavioral geneticists argue. Child outcomes are not due to acts of commission or of omission, according to these researchers; rather, a parent's impact is limited to contributing half of the genetic material (Rowe, 1994). Such a view is in stark contrast to the orientation of most parent researchers, who focus on child-rearing practices. Those contrasting positions serve as a reminder that the most complete conceptualization of parental effects must reflect the transactions among children's genotype, their biological systems, and the environment they experience.

Despite the hazards of identifying effects, there are a number of sources of evidence indicating that the child-rearing environment can have a significant effect on children. Before reviewing that literature, I present a brief review of some of the early research that has contributed to our understanding of the effects of parents.

Early Research into Parental Effects

Two types of early but influential research will be summarized: animal studies and natural experiments. Both types of studies have contributed to the prevailing view that the environment children are raised in can have a profound effect on their development.

Animal Studies

Some of the most dramatic examples of parental effects on development do not come from human research but rather from animal research. Here there is greater latitude in using the experimental method, which allows for well-controlled manipulations to study the effects of environmental deprivation or enrichment. One of the first and most provocative psychologists to use animals for addressing questions about development was the American-trained Chinese researcher Zing-Yang Kuo. Kuo investigated such questions as the nature of animal instincts, the role of the environment in development, and the relation between nature and nurture. A number of his animal studies challenged the prevailing views about the nature of development by demonstrating that animals could be trained to behave in ways that appeared unnatural or even anti-instinctual. For example, he trained rats to rear cats, and he modified the fighting, eating, and sexual behavior of pugnacious chow dogs (Kuo, 1967). Through his environmental manipulations, Kuo created extraordinary demonstrations of the variability of behavior and the role that experience can play in subsequent behavior.

Another early influential animal behavior scientist was Konrad Lorenz, one of the founders of the field of ethology. He is best known for his discovery of the phenomenon of *imprinting* in birds and the concept of an irreversible *critical period* in development. Both concepts have influenced subsequent thinking about the role of parents and early experience in children's development.

The most sensational example of the application of these two notions to parent-child relationships occurred in the 1970s with the concept of *bonding*. According to the pediatricians Klaus, Kennell, and their colleagues (Klaus et al., 1972), there is a period shortly after birth in which a mother can bond with her newborn child if she is given the opportunity. If the newborn was unavailable because of medical interventions or hospital practices, however, the mother's opportunity to bond with her infant could be irretrievably lost. Klaus and his colleagues backed up their claim with an experimental study that purported to show that women who had opportunities to interact with their newborns right after birth and across the next few days would develop a more loving relationship with their infants. That original study was problematic for a variety of reasons (e.g., small sample size, few significant findings, lack of validity of the measures), not to mention fundamental flaws in the concept of bonding (Eyer, 1992). Most independent efforts to replicate the findings were unsuccessful, and the concept has fallen out of scientific favor.

Since the work of Kuo, Lorenz, and others, a large number of studies have examined the effects of early sensory deprivation or stimulation on subsequent intellectual and social performance. Studies of a wide assortment of animals have reported a number of links between sensory experience early in life and mental as well as social development. One of the most influential laboratories in the area of environmental deprivation and social development was run by Harry Harlow in Wisconsin. Among his most famous findings was that rhesus monkeys raised in isolation without mothers developed extreme pathological behavior, including stereotyped behaviors (rocking, sucking fingers), antisocial behavior, and sexual abnormalities as adults (Harlow, Dodsworth, & Harlow, 1965). Subsequently, studies documenting the dramatic effects of early social deprivation have been done with other species of animals (see Cairns, 1979). These studies have served to highlight the importance of early parent-child relationships. Although the animal work reflects an indirect source of evidence about human development and is limited by issues of generalizability, it has played a prominent role in developmental psychology and in conceptions of parental impact on children's development (Clarke-Stewart, 1978a).

Natural Experiments

"Natural experiments," referring to incidents in which children were raised without parents or deprived of a normal environment, have provided a second indirect source of information about the effects of parents. The oldest of these experiments occurred with the so-called feral children: children supposedly raised by animals and thus in the absence of language, human social interaction, and culture. Throughout history, at least fifty-four cases of such children have been reported. After a careful analysis of each case, however, it was concluded that most of the supposed feral children were in fact recently abandoned children who were mentally ill or in some way handicapped (Clarke & Clarke, 1976). Only in a few of the cases does it appear that a child was actually reared by an animal, such as the famous case of the "wild boy of Aveyron," who was discovered in France in 1799 (Itard, 1962). Even in that case, because there is no information about the state of the child before his unusual experience or about the duration or quality of that experience, any conclusions are scientifically invalid.

More recent manifestations of the effects of parent deprivation can be found in cases of child abuse in which children are left alone in severe isolation. The best-documented example is that of Genie, a girl who was isolated from almost all social interaction from the age of eighteen months until thirteen and one-half years. She had spent most of her life strapped to a potty by her abusive father. When she and her blind mother finally escaped, she weighed fifty-nine pounds and was mute. Over the next few years she showed remarkable development, as is described by the linguist who worked with the adolescent. Genie eventually learned to talk and developed some of the sensory, motor, and social skills she was missing, but she was unable to fully recover from her long-term neglect. One of the most obvious deficits she had concerned syntax; despite the fact that she developed a large vocabulary, her linguistic ability continued to be impaired because she never mastered the rules of grammar (Curtis, 1977; Rymer, 1993).

A better source of natural experiments concerning the effects of not having parents is children raised in orphanages and residential institutions. In the 1940s, the alarm was sounded that children deprived of mothers were developing abnormally and were at risk for a variety of emotional, intellectual, and health problems (Spitz, 1945). Later it was recognized that those children were deprived of many things besides mothers, including social interaction and intellectual stimulation. Although studies of children in institutions suffered from various methodological problems (Pinneau, 1955), they provided sufficient evidence to confirm the obvious: The absence of appropriate social contact early in life is deleterious to development (Rutter, 1979).

The animal research and natural experiments set the stage for investigations into the effects of normal child-rearing environments on children's development. The early classical studies of parent effects were conducted by Alfred Baldwin, Sears, Baumrind, and their colleagues, as introduced previously. I now turn to contemporary research findings that address the issue of associations between parental characteristics and child-rearing practices and children's outcomes.

Contemporary Research Findings

Because the vast majority of findings purportedly showing parental effects on children consist of correlations between parental characteristics or behavior and child outcomes, it is more accurate to describe the results of such research as reflecting *associations* between characteristics of parents and children. The literature on parent-child associations is voluminous; a thorough review could fill up several books. Several comprehensive reviews of the literature published before the mid-1980s are available (Clarke-Stewart, 1978b; Clarke-Stewart, 1988; Maccoby & Martin, 1983; Martin, 1975; Rollins & Thomas, 1979); it is likely that the prodigious amount of literature has precluded more recent attempts to summarize it.

With that caveat stated, I intend the work described in the following sections to provide a representative sampling of some of the best work in the area. The research cited has relied on a variety of theoretical approaches (Chapter 2) and reflects work from all six approaches to the study of parents (Chapter 3). A summary of the major findings will be presented in three groupings: beneficial associations, detrimental associations, and no apparent associations.

Beneficial Child-Rearing Associations

Conceptions about what are beneficial, substantive, and empirically verifiable outcomes in children have changed over time. For example, children's resistance to temptation in laboratory settings was a prominent outcome variable in the 1960s, considered an index of conscience development (Parke, 1974). That outcome measure has been largely discarded in favor of more ecologically valid and direct indices of children's functioning. Currently, the key domains in which parent variables have been linked with beneficial child outcomes include (1) general competence, (2) peer relations, (3) internalization and prosocial behavior, and (4) cognitive development and school achievement.

General Competence.   Child competence is often used as an index of positive child outcomes. A competent child can be defined as "one who is able to make use of environmental and personal resources to achieve a good developmental outcome" (Waters & Sroufe, 1983). Parenting has been related to children's competence through (1) investigations into parent-child attachment, (2) linkages with patterns of parenting, and (3) assessments of specific parenting behaviors.

The central significance of attachment theory lies in its power to predict developmental outcomes. Advocates of the approach, such as Alan Sroufe and June Fleeson (1986), have argued that infants who are securely attached at twelve months of age will develop an internal working model of that relationship and then carry it forward to other relationships, such as with teachers and peers. Consequently, a number of studies have examined relations between attachment classification and subsequent functioning.

To date, the evidence is mixed. Some studies have found support for the theory: Children securely attached to their mothers at twelve or eighteen months of age are indeed more compliant, enthusiastic, persistent, and cooperative and better at problem solving than insecurely attached children (e.g., Arend, Gove, & Sroufe, 1979; Frankel & Bates, 1990; Matas, Arend, & Sroufe, 1978). However, the predictive validity of the attachment classification association is not always strong (Lamb, Thompson, Gardner, & Charnov, 1985). For example, although securely attached preschool-aged girls were found to be more socially competent than insecurely attached girls on several different indices (e.g., teacher and peer ratings; LaFreniere & Sroufe, 1985), the relations did not hold for boys. In another example, using a modification of the Strange Situation for older children, it was found that boys who were classified as insecurely attached at age six were less well liked by peers and rated as less competent by teachers. However, no comparable associations held for girls (Cohn, 1990).

There are several explanations for these mixed results. First, there may be discontinuity in the relationship. A child who is securely attached at one age may subsequently form an insecure attachment owing to changes in the family structure or level of stress (Pianta, Sroufe, & Egeland, 1989). Children also develop multiple attachments, so that even though they may have an insecure one with one individual, they can profit from a secure relationship with someone else. Furthermore, there are various other plausible influences or life experiences independent of the caregiver that could affect children's competence (e.g., parental divorce, impact of a peer group).

Rather than making predictions about children's outcomes based on their attachment classification at twelve months of age, a more developmentally appropriate way to understand the effects of early parent-child relationships is to investigate correlates of individuals' internal working models of attachment. This mental model, one that develops from an individual's previous history of close relationships, provides a representation of both the self and others. As such, it influences an individual's likelihood to seek close relationships as well as give support to others.

Using the Adult Attachment Interview (AAI) or a questionnaire to assess current attachment style (e.g., Collins & Read, 1990), a number of developmental and social psychologists are finding links between how people think about their early attachment relationships and how they are currently functioning. Persons who hold secure representations of attachment with their parents are classified as *autonomous*. Such a classification is made when individuals give an objective and balanced description of their childhood. People categorized as *dismissing* provide autobiographical accounts that reflect being cut off from the emotional nature of their childhood relationships. Such individuals may idolize, derogate, or be unable to recall their early experiences. *Preoccupied* individuals continue to be overinvolved with some traumatic childhood experience; they tend to exhibit incoherence, anger, or passivity in recalling their childhood.

Individuals classified into these categories have been found to have systematic personality and behavioral differences. Autonomous college students exhibited more physical contact, provided more emotional support to others, were less anxious, and in general were functioning better than others (Kobak & Sceery, 1988; Simpson, Rholes, & Nelligan, 1992). An even more impressive finding came from the study previously mentioned: Women's attachment representation, assessed with the AAI during their pregnancy, accurately predicted their Strange Situation attachment classification with their twelve-month-old infants in 75 percent of the cases (Fonagy et al., 1991). Mothers who expressed autonomous views of their own relationships were likely to develop a secure attachment with their infant, but women who were dismissing or preoccupied were likely to have an insecure attachment, as assessed by the Strange Situation.

A different approach to linking parenting to subsequent child competence is evident in using the trait approach to parents. A number of investigators have found connections between parental style and child competence. The most careful and prominent work finding such an association has been the longitudinal study by Diana Baumrind (1971). In a series of studies, she found evidence indicating that different parental patterns of child rearing are associated with particular outcomes in their children. *Authoritative* parenting was generally found to be correlated with a variety of positive outcomes in children at several different ages. She found that children of such parents were more competent, as exhibited by greater social responsibility (e.g., cooperative behavior, friendliness toward peers) and independence. Baumrind has written that the outcome associated with the authoritative pattern "is uniformly positive for both sexes at all ages studied, unlike any other child rearing pattern" (Baumrind, 1983, p. 138).

The two other major patterns of child rearing were associated with lower levels of child competence. *Authoritarian* parents discouraged independence, often in a harsh and punitive way. Consequently, according to Baumrind, children of such parents were less independent, assertive, and achievement-oriented than children of *authoritative* parents (Baumrind, 1973). *Permissive* parents, who failed to provide firm control, had children who were neither independent nor oriented toward achievement. However, the effects are not always as robust as Baumrind portrays. A close reading of her work indicates that the associations between parenting types and child outcomes are complex. For example, some of the associations are qualified by the gender of the child.

Catherine Lewis (1981) has proposed that Baumrind's data could be interpreted in a different way. She argued that the influence could occur in the opposite direction: Competent children may elicit authoritative parenting from their parents. Although Baumrind (1983) has taken issue with that interpretation, it is likely that the competence of both parents and children is the product of a reciprocal process.

Baumrind's differentiation of parental styles has continued to provide a fruitful approach for studying parent-child associations. In a review of the literature, Maccoby and Martin (1983) found that by extending Baumrind's classification scheme into the four patterns (authoritative, authoritarian, permissive, and uninvolved) discussed in Chapter 3, they were better able to summarize the existing literature. A large number of studies concerning associations between parents and the functioning of preschoolers, elementary school–aged children, and preadolescents can fit into such a categorization. Foremost is the finding that authoritative parenting is frequently linked with a variety of positive outcomes, including social responsibility and high self-esteem, independence, cognitive competence, and facility with language (Grusec & Lytton, 1988).

Recently, Baumrind's typology has proved its usefulness again in accounting for relations between parenting and child outcomes in adolescence. Based on the self-reports and school records of teenagers from about four thousand families, youth from authoritative families were found to be best adjusted according to a variety of indices tapping psychosocial development (self-reliance, work orientation, self-esteem, and personal competence), problem behaviors (substance use, delinquency, antisocial behavior), psychological distress (anxiety, depression), and school achievement. Children from neglectful homes fared the worst (Lamborn, Mounts, Steinberg, & Dornbusch, 1991). In a one-year follow-up study with 2,353 of the adolescents, the earlier results were replicated and extended (Steinberg, Lamborn, Darling, Mounts, & Dornbusch, 1994). Differences in adjustment that were associated with parenting style were maintained or had even widened (e.g., academic competence, delinquency) one year later. These studies have provided renewed support for the trait approach as a way of revealing associations between parents and children.

A third approach intended to link child rearing with child competence has focused on correlates of particular parental practices. For example, in both North America and Egypt, maternal vocal stimulation has been positively related to toddler behavioral competence (Wachs et al., 1993;

Wachs & Gruen, 1982). Other investigators have found that parental encouragement of emotional expressiveness is related to teacher-rated competence in preschoolers (Roberts & Strayer, 1987). With older children (preadolescents and adolescents), parental support, low rates of punishment, and assigning children household responsibilities have been connected with child competence (Amato, 1989). Reviews of the literature indicate that other specific parental practices associated with high levels of competence in children include consistent enforcement of demands and rules, high expectations and training to meet them, warmth, use of reasoning, and open communication patterns (see Grusec & Lytton, 1988; Maccoby & Martin, 1983).

Relations with Peers.   One central ingredient of social competence is how well a child gets along with peers. Not only are positive peer interactions important for functioning in the present, but the quality of peer friendships has been found to be a good indicator of later adjustment (Hartup, 1989). Linking parent-child relationships with peer interaction was a popular area of investigation in the 1980s. Sufficient empirical evidence now exists to confirm that parents exert both indirect and direct influence over their children's peer relationships (Parke & Ladd, 1992; Putallaz & Heflin, 1990).

Researchers who subscribe to the indirect effects perspective believe that the way children act toward others is based on their history of interactions with their parents. Two hypotheses have been investigated. One hypothesis holds that a secure attachment provides children with the emotional security to enable them to venture from the mother and interact with peers. There has been some evidence to support this indirect effect of mothers' influence. Securely attached preschool girls (but not boys) were found to be more popular (LaFreniere & Sroufe, 1985), and five-year-old children who were securely attached at twelve months were more likely to enjoy positive, close friendships than insecurely attached children (Youngblade & Belsky, 1992). However, reviewers of these and other studies have concluded that the relation between attachment classification and peer competence is far from clear; the studies are "riddled with ambiguous findings and failures to replicate" (Lamb & Nash, 1989, p. 234).

The second hypothesis posits that children learn to interact with other social beings based on their experiences with their parents or siblings; the social interaction skills developed in those relationships are used when interacting with peers. Support for this association has been found by Deborah Vandell and Kathy Wilson (1987). Using a Vygotskian approach and a microanalytic methodology, they videotaped twenty-six infants when they were six and nine months old. The infants were filmed for ten minutes in each of three types of interactions: with their mothers, with their older siblings, and with a same-age peer. The researchers found that infants who had more frequent turn-taking experiences with their mothers at six months, indicating that their mothers were *scaffolding* their interactions, engaged in more turn-taking interactions with siblings and peers at nine months. This study, although it cannot prove causality, at least provided some evidence that one type of maternal behavior preceded a positive child outcome.

In studies of contemporaneous relations, there is evidence that children may model their interaction styles after their relationship with their parents. Using the trait approach, investigators have discovered that democratic and authoritative parents are more likely to have popular children than are *authoritarian* parents (Dekovic & Janssens, 1992; Hart, Ladd, & Burleson, 1990). Similarly, parents who used intrusive and controlling styles of child supervision had children who were less well liked than the children of parents who were indirect and unintrusive in their supervision (Ladd & Golter, 1988). Children raised in environments containing parental warmth, open verbal communication, and emotional expressiveness were more likely to be skilled in peer interaction than other children (MacDonald & Parke, 1984; Putallaz, 1987). Fathers' behavior may also play a role in the development of peer competence. Fathers who were engaged in child rearing and played more with their sons had boys who were more popular with their age-mates (MacDonald, 1987).

Parents can also directly influence the quality of their children's peer relations by coaching and structuring the child's environment (Ladd, Profilet, & Hart, 1992; Lollis, Ross, & Tate, 1992). Parental planning of social contacts, transporting of children, and supervising of peer interactions have been related to the quality of peer relations (Ladd et al., 1992). One study designed to test the relation between child-rearing variations and the quality of preschool children's peer relationships in and out of school was conducted by Gary Ladd and Beckie Golter (1988). The researchers focused on two types of parental management practices: initiating peer contact for their children and monitoring the quality of play. Using a multimethod design, including parental telephone interviews, behavioral observations, teacher reports, and peer reports, they found several systematic relations between parental behavior and peer relations. Parents who initiated peer contact had children with a greater number of and more consistent playmates. For boys this initiation was also associated with greater peer acceptance. In addition, parental monitoring of children was found to relate to functioning in school. Parents who used an intrusive monitoring style had children who were rated as less socially competent by teachers.

There is other evidence indicating that less intrusive monitoring is associated with greater social competence. Parents who practiced a more indirect form of monitoring and supervising their children's peer relations, such as providing advice before the interaction, only occasionally coaching during interactions, but maintaining awareness of the child's activities, tended to have children who were more popular than children of intrusive parents (e.g., Lollis et al., 1992).

Beyond early childhood, there is evidence that parents continue to influence their children's peer relations. Adolescents who perceived their parents to be *authoritative* were better adjusted in their peer relations than other teenagers (Fuligni & Eccles, 1993). One way authoritative parents influence their adolescents is by providing a positive influence in the area of peer relations. More specifically, three parental practices have been found to relate to involvement in different types of peer groups. Parental monitoring of the whereabouts of their children, encouragement of achievement, and engaging in joint decisionmaking have been linked to membership in different adolescent peer groups. Parents who engaged in these practices had children who were more likely to be in a peer group of high achievers. In contrast, parents who engaged in none of the three practices were likely to have children who joined the drug crowd (Brown, Mounts, Lamborn, & Steinberg, 1993).

Internalization and Promotion of Prosocial Behavior.   The single most important way that parents attempt to influence their children is to *socialize* them to behave in ways that are acceptable in their cultural context. In our society, children are not permitted to go around hitting other people or parading naked in public. Parents educate their children concerning what is and is not acceptable through such techniques as modeling, instructing, and disciplining. But parents cannot always be around to monitor their children's behavior; children need to "internalize" society's standards of conduct so that they behave appropriately in the parent's absence. Thus, children must develop a conscience to police their own behavior.

Vygotsky, Freud, Bandura, and other theorists have discussed the instrumental role parents take in promoting this process (Lawrence & Valsiner, 1993). Socialization necessitates that children develop an internal motivation to control their behavior and act in a socially acceptable way. During the toddler and preschool years, children require a considerable amount of parental direction, supervision, and discipline in order to behave appropriately. Children gradually begin to exercise self-regulation, however, so that constant parental supervision is not needed (Kopp, 1982). Parents then must promote a motivational shift in their children whereby the children behave appropriately because of their own internal controls rather than a fear of punishment.

Early efforts at associating parenting with internalization used the trait approach to link parenting styles with a variety of measures of child internalization (e.g., greater self-control, resistance to temptation, compliance, guilt over transgressions, responsibility for their actions). A number of studies have found that parental qualities of nurturance and warmth, in conjunction with some control, were associated with indices of internalization (Grusec & Goodnow, 1994).

An alternative approach to the investigation of child-rearing traits as precursors to internalization has been to associate specific child-rearing techniques with particular child behaviors. This approach has resulted in the finding that parents frequently attempt to elicit prosocial behavior (e.g., helping, caring, sharing) and to inhibit antisocial or selfish acts. The child-rearing techniques used toward these ends are thought to be critical. Hoffman (1975) argued and subsequently found evidence that parental use of power-assertive behavior (e.g., physical punishment, threats) results in a decreased likelihood of internalization because it arouses anger and hostility in children. Consequently, children are less willing to comply. Instead, parents who use reasoning (possibly along with some power assertion) about the negative consequences of the child's misbehavior had children who exhibited greater internalization.

Recently, Grazyna Kochanska (1993; Kochanska, DeVet, Goldman, Murray, & Putnam, 1994) has argued and subsequently found some support for the view that parents must do at least two things to promote conscience development. First, parents need to arouse, to an appropriate level, a child's anxiety in response to a misdeed so that the child experiences some emotional discomfort. Then, the child must be allowed to exercise self-regulation in order to refrain from committing the misdeed or to control an impulse. On the basis of this work and that of others, it is clear that self-regulation develops through multiple child-rearing efforts, including prohibiting misbehavior, teaching acceptable behavior, expressing appropriate expectations, and allowing children enough freedom to practice regulating themselves.

It is likely that parents promote the shift from external adult regulation to internal child control by an important attributional process. Some investigators have argued that power-assertive parenting results in children making external attributions about why they behaved appropriately (e.g., "I didn't hit him because I would have gotten spanked"). If the child learns to behave appropriately only to avoid punishment rather than because he or she wanted to act in a socially acceptable way, internalization will not take place. But if a parent teaches a child to attribute the cause of the socially acceptable behavior to the child's own personality attributes, the child is more likely subsequently to regulate him- or herself in that way (Lepper, 1983).

In addition to making correct attributions, disciplining, providing affection, and modeling moral behavior, parents can promote the development of conscience by selectively and appropriately arousing the child's anxiety level, reading fairy tales and other books containing moral messages, and teaching religion as a way to help their children internalize parental standards of conduct (Brody & Shaffer, 1982; Kochanska, 1993).

The parent's role in the process of internalization is complicated by the child's temperament, according to Kochanska (1995). For children who are more fearful and anxious, mothers who use gentle discipline techniques and thus are able to evoke in their children an optimal level of arousal have children who show greater internalization. In contrast, children who are relatively fearless seem to take a different pathway for developing internalization. For those children, a secure attachment and a positive, cooperative relationship with their mothers was associated with enhanced self-control. This study indicates that there are at least two diverse routes to internalization and that the route taken appears to be determined by the child's temperament.

Researchers have also investigated how parental behavior is associated with children's socially desirable actions, such as prosocial behavior. Similar to the research on internalization, evidence indicates that parents play three major roles: (1) as disciplinarians when the child fails to be prosocial or is antisocial, (2) as suppliers of affection, and (3) as models of appropriate behavior (Hoffman, 1975; Radke-Yarrow, Zahn-Waxler, & Chapman, 1983).

When disciplining children, parents try to influence their children's prosocial behavior by discouraging morally unacceptable thoughts, feelings, and actions while inculcating their children with moral standards and values. Parental power-assertive disciplinary techniques (e.g., physical punishment, prohibitions) are unrelated to or negatively related to children's moral reasoning and behavior (Brody & Shaffer, 1982). In contrast, use of reasoning has been positively associated with prosocial actions (Hoffman & Saltzstein, 1967; Radke-Yarrow et al., 1983). Another effective maternal practice is including an affective tone of empathy along with an explanation of the acceptability of the behavior. Mothers who used this technique as a way of teaching their toddlers and preschoolers how to respond to someone in distress had children who exhibited more prosocial behavior than other children (Zahn-Waxler, Radke-Yarrow, & King, 1979).

Closely related to prosocial behavior is expressing empathic reactions to others. Supportive, empathic parents are likely to model and encourage empathic expressions in their children (Dix, 1992; Eisenberg et al., 1992; Feshbach, 1987). Parental warmth alone is probably insufficient to foster empathy. Rather, it is most likely to develop under three conditions, according to Mark Barnett (1986). Children will most likely develop empathy if their own emotional needs are satisfied, they are encouraged to experience and express a range of emotions, and they observe and interact with others who encourage emotional sensitivity.

Cognitive Development and School Achievement. Several different aspects of child rearing have been associated with cognitive development and school achievement. The parental characteristics most commonly linked to positive outcomes are (1) parental involvement, (2) the quality of parent-child interaction, (3) verbal communication and instruction, and most recently, (4) parental expectations and beliefs.

Numerous studies have found associations between the extent of parental involvement with the child or the child's school and cognitive development or academic achievement. Using a variety of indices, researchers have found that parents who are more involved have children who perform at a higher level (Grolnick & Ryan, 1989). What is not understood is what is behind that association. For example, it could be that the involvement is one index of the parental efforts to maximize the child's positive outcomes. Alternatively, the involvement could be causally unrelated to academic success and it is a third variable, such as intelligence, that is driving the association between involvement and performance.

The quality of the parent-child relationship has also been related to positive performance on academic measures. In particular, quality of discipline and quality of affective relations have been implicated as important variables. Scores on the HOME subscales have been found to be significantly related to school achievement as well as predictive of school achievement and classroom behavior at age ten years (Bradley & Caldwell, 1984; Bradley, Caldwell, & Rock, 1988). Furthermore, parental warmth, support, and authoritative control have been found to be associated with positive performance in elementary school (Grolnick & Ryan, 1989). In high school, authoritative parenting has repeatedly been positively related to grades (Steinberg, Elmer, & Mounts, 1989; Steinberg, Lamborn, Dornbusch, & Darling, 1992).

Several studies have found evidence for links between parenting practices and young children's cognitive development. There is some evidence that the rate of vocabulary growth in young children is a consequence of the amount of maternal speech they are exposed to and whether their parents read books to them (Huttenlocher, Haight, Bryk, Seltzer, & Lyons, 1991). Furthermore, a rare experimental study in the area of child rearing and child outcomes has demonstrated that parents can accelerate language development through reading stories to their two-year-old children (Whitehurst et al., 1988). Thirty children were randomly assigned to a control or experimental group. In the experimental group, mothers were instructed to read books in an interactive fashion (e.g., asking questions, elaborating on the pictures, providing feedback to child's comments). After one month, the two groups of children were compared. The children in the experimental group scored significantly higher in their expressive language abilities than the control group children. Furthermore, in a nine-month follow-up study, the experimental group of children continued to perform better than the control group.

Other researchers have found maternal stimulation to be predictive of subsequent cognitive competence (MacPhee, Ramey, & Yeates, 1984) and to make a contribution that is independent of the child's characteristics (Bornstein & Tamis-LeMonda, 1989). However, it is likely that some aspects of language and cognitive development are environmentally "fragile," or sensitive to variations in parenting practices or other forms of environmental stimulation, whereas other aspects are "resilient" in that they develop almost independently of the quality of the environment (Wachs, 1992).

Yet another way in which verbal stimulation has been related to cognitive development is with the verbal strategy of *distancing*. Distancing involves putting a cognitive demand on the child to separate the child mentally from the present moment (e.g., "Do you remember where we saw one of those?"). In a series of studies, Sigel and his colleagues have found evidence that parental use of distancing positively relates to academic achievement and overall intellectual ability (Sigel, Stinson, & Flaugher, 1991).

Maternal instructional techniques have also been linked to children's cognitive development in a number of studies (Clarke-Stewart, 1988). Mothers who use a didactic interaction style that is verbally and cognitively demanding have children with higher intelligence test scores than mothers whose teaching style is directive, dominating, and cognitively undemanding (Bornstein, 1985).

Many studies have found positive associations between some aspect of verbal stimulation or communication and cognitive development or school achievement (Hess & Holloway, 1984; Wachs & Gruen, 1982). Mothers who were observed to be responsive and attentive to their children's needs both in infancy and when their children were twelve years old had children with higher IQ and math achievement scores (Beckwith, Rodning, & Cohen, 1992).

One other association between parenting and children's cognitive outcomes is found regarding parental expectations and beliefs about children's performance. Parental educational expectations have been repeatedly correlated with children's academic achievement (Seginer, 1983). Parents have also been regarded as "expectancy socializers" for school achievement. That is, they teach their children what level of performance is expected from them. Support for this proposition comes from the finding that parents' beliefs about their daughters' math aptitude are more strongly related to their children's self-concepts and expectancies than are the children's own past performances in math (Parsons, Adler, & Kaczala, 1982). More generally, parents' values and beliefs about their children have been linked to children's intellectual abilities (Miller, 1988). For instance, across six cultural groups in the United States, parents who value children's conformity to external standards of behavior rather than independence have children who perform less well in school (Okagaki & Sternberg, 1993).

Evidently, child-rearing practices do play a significant role in children's cognitive development. In reviewing parental effects on cognitive achievement, some researchers have gone as far as saying that parents play three fundamental roles: They determine which skills children learn, when children learn them, and the level of expertise achieved by children (Okagaki & Sternberg, 1991).

Detrimental Child-Rearing Associations

The flip side of the parent-association coin concerns the negative outcomes that have been associated with parenting practices and parental characteristics. These negative effects are manifested in behavioral or developmental problems. Five areas of negative outcomes will be summarized here: (1) childhood behavior problems; (2) psychiatric disorders; (3) adolescent problems (delinquency, substance abuse, and promiscuous sex and teenage pregnancy); (4) problems associated with marital conflict and divorce; and (5) problems associated with maltreatment.

Behavior Problems. When children experience chronic stress or difficulties in their lives, they are likely to respond by exhibiting some type of behavior problem. Problems can range from chronic noncompliance and acting out to serious mental health problems, such as depression or suicide attempts. Behavior problems are important indicators of current child functioning, but they also can be predictive of negative outcomes in the future. Experiencing peer rejection, performing poorly at school, exhibiting antisocial behavior, abusing substances, and developing a police record have been identified as sequelae of prior behavior problems (Miller & Scarr, 1989; Patterson, DeBaryshe, & Ramsey, 1989).

The types of problems children exhibit are typically divided into two categories: *internalizing* and *externalizing*. Internalizing problems are associated with emotional overcontrol: inhibition, shyness, anxiety, and depression. In contrast, externalizing problems are directed outward and include noncompliance, aggression, or more generally, the syndrome labeled *conduct disorder*. Conduct disorder is the umbrella term that refers to children who exhibit a wide range of behaviors that are to some degree antisocial. Noncompliance, oppositional behavior, aggression, temper tantrums, disobedience, lying, destructiveness, defiance, and rudeness are examples. Behavior problems often have a number of causes that may interact, including genetic determinants, family influences, peer pressure, and school factors. But there is now considerable evidence indicating that parents play a major role. However, evidence for parents' role is affected by the methodology used as well as characteristics of the parents and children. In a meta-analysis of forty-seven studies linking parental caregiving with externalizing behavior, it was found that observation and interview studies that looked at patterns of child-rearing behavior had stronger results than other studies using only questionnaires (Rothbaum & Weisz, 1994).

The earliest link between child rearing and behavior problems has been identified in those with an insecure attachment classification (Lyons-Ruth, Alpern, & Repacholi, 1993). Similarly, a lack of maternal responsivity during infancy has been related to subsequent behavioral and emotional problems (Beckwith et al., 1992), although there are some conflicting results (e.g., Fagot & Kavanagh, 1990).

Even stronger evidence has been found to connect particular child-rearing practices with child behavior problems. A constellation of child-rearing behaviors have been linked to childhood aggression. Parental rejection, permissiveness of aggression, inconsistent discipline, and punitive, power-assertive disciplinary practices have all been associated with childhood aggression (Martin, 1975; Parke & Slaby, 1983). A recent and thorough documentation of this effect can be found in a large, prospective study involving 584 children. A consistent relation was found between parental use of harsh, physical discipline when their children were preschoolers and subsequent child aggression in kindergarten (Weiss, Dodge, Bates, & Pettit, 1992). Ineffective discipline and a lack of rules or supervision have also been associated with behavior problems (Patterson & Stouthamer-Loeber, 1984; Wahler & Dumas, 1989).

Certain familial characteristics have been tied to behavior problems. Children from families that are disadvantaged, disorganized, discordant, or deviant in some way are more likely to exhibit conduct problems than other children (Rutter, 1985). For example, maternal drug use has been associated with child behavior problems, especially in boys (Stein, Newcomb, & Bentler, 1993).

This work indicates that parents, by the way they interact with their children, can indeed play a major role in establishment and maintenance of behavior problems. However, the particular mechanisms that produce the behavior problems are not yet clearly understood. At the same time, the child effects approach reminds us that parents are not the sole cause of the behavior problems. In fact, the temperament quality of irritability in children has been found to be an important precursor to behavior problems (Lee & Bates, 1985). Similarly, temperamentally more difficult children are more likely to be more aggressive when they are older (Zahn-Waxler, McKnew, Cummings, Davenport, & Radke-Yarrow, 1984). A third example concerns preadolescent boys. Using structural equation modeling techniques, it was found that the boys' antisocial behavior negatively impacted the quality of parental discipline and peer relationships. The difficult behavior of the boys (e.g., arguing, shouting at parents, hurting siblings, stealing items) was likely to result in ineffective disciplinary practices, as assessed from home observations (Vuchinich, Bank, & Patterson, 1992).

Child Psychiatric Disorders.   One of the most striking examples of detrimental child-rearing effects occurs in children who manifest *failure to thrive* (FTT). FTT usually appears during the first year of life, and its major symptom is sudden cessation of growth in infants who appeared to be developing normally. These infants are extremely thin for their height because they generally have feeding disturbances. In addition, they have characteristics such as unusual watchfulness, a lack of cuddliness, and a high degree of passivity. It appears that the etiology is a combination of factors that may include biological factors (abnormalities, disorders, or diseases), environmental stress, and dysfunctional mother-child interactions (Stevenson, 1992).

The poor quality of interactions can often be attributed to factors in the parent (e.g., depression, substance abuse) or in the quality of the parent-child relationship (e.g., neglecting or rejecting). If the parent can change the quality of interactions with the help of counseling before too much time passes, most FTT children can resume a normal growth path. If the child's growth is stunted for too long, however, there are irreversible effects on development (Sturm & Drotar, 1989).

Other child psychiatric disorders have also been linked to parents' mental health problems. Parents' psychiatric problems put their children at risk for a variety of cognitive, social, and emotional problems (Baldwin, Cole, & Baldwin, 1982; Cutrona & Troutman, 1986). Although there is now strong evidence for the genetic transmission of certain psychiatric disorders, such as schizophrenia (Gottesman & Shields, 1982), there is also evidence for the co-occurrence of abnormalities in the parent-child relationship. Children of parents with schizophrenia are also at risk environmentally. In fact, one study determined that parenting practices of people with mental illnesses are more predictive of child outcome (intelligence and social competence) than is the diagnostic label the parent was given (Goodman & Brumley, 1990).

Considerable evidence has accumulated concerning the consequences of being reared by a parent experiencing an affective disorder such as depression. As early as infancy, children of depressed mothers show a variety of adjustment problems and early signs of depression (Gardner, 1992). Children of depressed mothers are more likely to form insecure attachments, experience problems in regulating and controlling emotion, develop behavior problems and unfavorable self-concepts, have intellectual impairments, exhibit ADHD, and be viewed by peers as abrasive, withdrawn, and unhappy (Downey & Coyne, 1990; Gelfand & Teti, 1990).

Although most investigations have focused on mothers with mental illnesses, there is evidence that fathers also contribute to their children's psychopathology. Paternal mental illness has been related to children's externalizing problems, such as ADHD and conduct disorder, and to internalizing problems, including depression and anxiety (Phares & Compas, 1992). Similarly, paternal alcoholism has been linked to an increase in child psychopathology (West & Prinz, 1987).

In general, the offspring of parents with psychiatric disorders experience a significantly greater risk for mental health problems than children in the general population. Although genetic and biological vulnerabilities play an important role, so do environmental influences. Beyond the parental variables indicated previously, higher risk is also associated with mental illness in siblings, number of siblings, stress, and socioeconomic status (Goldstein, 1988).

Adolescent Problems.   The three major problems experienced by adolescents (and increasingly, preadolescents) are delinquency, promiscuous sexual behavior and teenage pregnancy, and substance abuse. Delinquency is the most obvious problem: Each year more than 2 million adolescents are arrested for various crimes. A number of parental variables have been implicated in the onset of delinquency. Besides the parents' socioeconomic status, variables include a lack of parental monitoring and inconsistent discipline in early childhood; parental marital discord and divorce; and a criminal, antisocial, or mentally ill parent (Loeber & Dishion, 1983; Patterson, DeBaryshe, & Ramsey, 1989; Patterson & Stouthamer-Loeber, 1984; Patterson et al., 1989).

A leading expert in this area, Gerald Patterson, has described a model of the developmental sequence of key experiences that lead to delinquent behavior in boys (Patterson, DeBaryshe, & Ramsey, 1989). Recall that his social learning coercion theory was described in Chapter 3; he has built on that theory and linked it to the development of delinquency, as indicated in Figure 5.2. Patterson's data indicate that boys as young as age two or three are receiving "basic training" for later behavior problems. Parents who use poor disciplinary practices (e.g., coercive, punitive, inconsistent methods) and who fail to monitor their young children are likely to have boys who develop conduct problems, such as frequent aggressive behavior. Because of such behavior, these children are likely to be rejected by their normal peers. Poor academic performance is also a common concomitant in these children. The combination of rejection by normal peers and academic failure contributes to the boys' joining a deviant

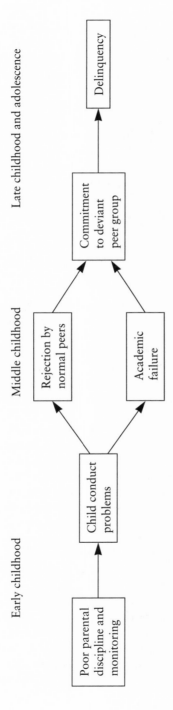

Early childhood   Middle childhood   Late childhood and adolescence

FIGURE 5.2   One Theory of Parents' Early Role in the Development of Delinquent Behavior. (Reprinted, with permission, from G. R. Patterson, B. D. DeBaryshe, and E. Ramsey, 1989, *American Psychologist, 44,* 329–335.)

peer group in late childhood. It is a short step then to engaging in delinquent behavior.

Another type of problem behavior that emerges at about the same time as delinquency is promiscuous sexual behavior and its consequence, teenage pregnancy. Various parent variables have been associated with the onset and frequency of sexual behavior in teenagers. Poor parent-adolescent communication, divorce, and father absence have been linked to early sexual activity in teenagers (Feldman & Brown, 1993). Part of the cause can be attributed to lack of parental supervision, particularly in single-parent homes. Additionally, rejecting fathers and unsupportive or indulgent parents have been associated with sexual behavior in boys (Feldman & Brown, 1993).

Although early sexual activity is associated with various health hazards, many more problems occur if the teenager becomes pregnant. Besides health effects for the mother and her child, teenage mothers experience lost opportunities for education and adequate employment, increased likelihood of being involved in an unstable marriage, increased stress and depression, and greater probability of providing inadequate parenting (Angel & Angel, 1993; Furstenberg, Brooks-Gunn, & Chase-Lansdale, 1989). Several family characteristics and child-rearing variables have been associated with an increased likelihood of having an adolescent bear a child. In addition to the risk variables associated with promiscuous sexual behavior, whether the adolescent's mother had a child when she was an adolescent has proved to be an important predictor of teenage parenthood (Furstenberg et al., 1989; Holden, Nelson, Velasquez, & Ritchie, 1993).

A third type of adolescent problem behavior is alcohol or drug use. Although it is now recognized that the etiology of substance abuse includes environmental, behavioral, psychological, and social factors, a number of studies have found associations between parental variables and children's substance use and abuse. Parents who provide firm control have adolescent children with low rates of drug use, whereas nondirective, absent, or unengaged parents have children with the highest rates of drug use (Baumrind, 1991; Block, Block, & Keyes, 1988). Similarly, adolescents who had close relationships with their fathers and received advice and guidance from their mothers were less likely to drink or use drugs than other teenagers (Coombs & Landsverk, 1988).

Another type of parental influence occurs in the modeling of drug use. Parents' use of alcohol and marijuana is associated with their children's drug use (Barnes, Farrell, & Cairns, 1986). This modeling influence may start early: It has been discovered that preschool children of heavy drinkers can distinguish the smell of different alcoholic beverages (Noll, Zucker, & Greenberg, 1990). Such evidence suggests that children may be inadvertently socialized into developing cognitive schemes and expectations about drugs and their use.

Problems Associated With Marital Conflict and Divorce. Another area that has received extensive attention since the early 1980s concerns the detrimental effects associated with marital conflict and divorce. Children, particularly boys, from discordant marriages experience various forms of maladjustment, including behavioral and academic problems (Emery, 1982; Grych & Fincham, 1990). Marital conflict affects child functioning through direct and indirect processes such as disrupted child-rearing practices, modeling, changes in the parent-child relationship, or even co-occurring changes in the environment (Easterbrooks & Emde, 1988; Emery, Fincham, & Cummings, 1992). However, those processes may be mediated by such factors as the child's interpretations or attributions of the conflict or the child's affective responses (Cummings & Davies, 1994; Grych & Fincham, 1990).

When there is severe marital discord, as in the case of battered women, the likelihood that the children will develop problems is even greater. Given the conservative estimate of occasional wife abuse at about 16 percent of all U.S. families (Straus & Gelles, 1988), a substantial number of children are involved. These "unintended victims" typically exhibit internalizing and externalizing problems, cognitive and academic skill deficits, and several other problems (Jaffe, Wolfe, & Wilson, 1990). On average, 25 to 75 percent of the children of battered women residing at shelters exhibit problems at the clinical level, compared with about 10 percent of comparison samples (Holden & Ritchie, 1991; Jouriles, Murphy, & O'Leary, 1989b).

These data reveal some of the effects experienced by children of highly discordant couples. However, there are also a number of risks for the children of parents who choose to divorce. Children of divorced parents are much more likely to exhibit behavioral and emotional problems than peers from two-parent homes (Amato & Keith, 1991; Emery, 1988; Hetherington & Clingempeel, 1992). Divorced mothers report that almost 30 percent of their children have problems at or above the clinical level; in comparison, children from intact families have a 10 percent rate of clinical problems (Hetherington & Clingempeel, 1992). Unfortunately, it is difficult to isolate the factors causing the problems because so many changes are inherent in the process of parental divorce (e.g., marital discord, separation, parent absence, economic changes, changes in child-rearing practices). Consequences of divorce are influenced by a host of variables, including the age and sex of the child, the child's age when the parents separated, the current age of the child, and the degree of continuing acrimony between the parents (Emery, 1988).

Problems associated with parental divorce are not left behind in childhood. There is now evidence that adults who had divorced parents are somewhat less well adjusted than adults who grew up in intact families (Amato & Keith, 1991). Furthermore, there is evidence for the intergenerational transmission of divorce. Adults from divorced homes have higher rates of divorce than their peers from intact marriages (Amato & Keith, 1991; Glenn, 1987).

There are several possible explanations for the fact that adults of divorced parents are more likely to divorce than their peers. Children growing up without the model of a two-parent home may fail to learn how to act appropriately in their role as husband or wife. Another explanation is that children from single-parent families engage in sexual behavior sooner and thus may enter into a marriage at an earlier age than individuals from two-parent families. A third, competing explanation is that children with divorced parents, compared with their peers from intact homes, may develop different attitudes toward, expectations about, and commitments to marriage. These individuals may be more prone to resort to divorce when marital problems emerge. Using a sample of about fifteen hundred adults, one researcher reported that the explanation that best accounted for the interview data was that individuals from divorced families were less committed to marriage. Because children of divorced couples are more apprehensive about marriage, they enter into marriage less invested in its success than others and consequently may be quicker to dissolve it (Glenn, 1987).

Problems Associated with Child Maltreatment.   A wide range of problems are associated with the maltreatment of children. The types of negative outcomes depend on the type of maltreatment, its duration, and a host of other variables. In the case of physical abuse, the type of abuse that has been studied most extensively, there is a range of potential physical, emotional, behavioral, and cognitive consequences (Wolfe, 1987).

The most serious physical effects are death; intracranial hemorrhage (from shaking or throwing infants), which can result in mental retardation, visual impairment, or blindness; and spinal cord injury. More common but less serious consequences include broken bones, scars, and burns. Emotional and behavioral repercussions from the abuse may appear as developmental delays, externalizing problems (most commonly seen as aggressive, hostile, and noncompliant behavior), low self-esteem, and changes in sleeping or eating patterns (e.g., Starr, 1988; Wolfe, 1987). Concerning social issues, day-care teachers report that children who have been battered are more aggressive, are less positive and socially competent, interact less with peers or adults, and are less popular than their nonabused peers (George & Main, 1979; Salzinger, Feldman, Hammer, & Rosario, 1993).

The effects of neglect and sexual abuse have also been investigated. Children who have been neglected are likely to exhibit behavior problems. Neglected children have been observed to be withdrawn and less sociable with peers and to perform poorly in school or on achievement tests (e.g., Eckenrode, Laird, & Doris, 1993). Sexual abuse has been associated with a variety of both initial and long-term effects, including depression, anxiety, hostility, aggression, delinquency, problems with sexual adjustment, prostitution, symptoms similar to those of post-traumatic stress disorder, and most dramatically, multiple personality disorder (Kendall-Tackett, Williams, & Finkelhor, 1993).

To summarize, a wide range of studies have found associations between familial characteristics and negative child outcomes. The five major areas of evidence that have been reviewed do not exhaust the evidence of detrimental parental effects. For instance, the appearance of racial prejudice in grade school children is sometimes a consequence of parental attitudes and behavior (Aboud, 1988). But the five areas of influence presented illustrate the potent role that parents can play in the development of negative child outcomes.

Other Areas of Child-Rearing Associations

Some associations between child rearing and child outcomes that have been identified in other areas cannot readily be classified as either beneficial or detrimental. These domains include developing appropriate sex roles, learning to be parents, acquiring healthy habits, and succeeding to high levels of accomplishment. In the area of sex-role development, children's acquisition of sex-appropriate behavior and schemas has been related to parental warmth and appropriate use of control (e.g., Fagot, Leinbach, & O'Boyle, 1992). Another way that parents influence their children's sex role development and social competence is through modeling and encouraging particular characteristics; however, the evidence is conflicting as to the best type of parental behavior. In one questionnaire study, high school students who were more socially competent perceived their parents to be androgynous (both expressive and instrumental; Spence & Helmreich, 1978). In contrast, another study found that sex-typed parents, rather than androgynous parents, had better adjusted nine-year-old children (Baumrind, 1982). Although the issue is unresolved, the two conflicting studies indicate there is indeed a relation between parents' sex-role orientation and the social functioning of their offspring.

Parents also have a significant, if unintended, impact on their children's knowledge of parenting. The research into this topic has focused on the intergenerational transmission of parental attitudes, disciplinary practices, and attachment classification, as discussed in the description of the family-of-origin determinants of parenting in Chapter 4.

Another domain in which parents have a direct and indirect impact on their children is in the acquisition and socialization of health attitudes and behavior. Parents influence children's eating habits, health attitudes (use of medical care, refraining from smoking), and health behavior (brushing teeth, exercising, use of vitamins and seat belts, compliance with immunization schedules; Tinsley, 1992). For example, parents play a role in development of healthy eating habits by such practices as prohibiting consumption of nonnutritious foods, monitoring food consumption away from home, and allowing the child to make decisions about food (Olvera-Ezzell, Power, & Cousins, 1990).

Evidence exists indicating that parents can also have a significant impact, which could be beneficial or detrimental, on the attainment of high levels of accomplishment. Based mostly on case studies, it is clear that parents are essential catalysts and orchestrators of the talent in their offspring. Child prodigies, such as Mozart or Yehudi Menuhin, result from a unique blend of the individual, the environment, and the contemporary culture and era (Feldman & Goldsmith, 1986). Nevertheless, parents must provide considerable stimulation, extraordinary attention, and a childhood largely isolated from peers if the child's talent is to develop (Radford, 1990).

Parents of individuals who attain a high level of accomplishment share a number of characteristics. According to a study of highly accomplished individuals in each of six fields (e.g., world-class concert pianists, tennis champions, research mathematicians), parents played a critical role in their children's achievement (Bloom, 1985). The central characteristics and behaviors shared by many of the parents were (1) valuing and encouraging development in one particular domain, (2) setting standards of achievement and excellence, (3) instilling the habit of hard work and trying to do one's best, (4) providing support and encouragement, and (5) organizing and managing their children's time.

The influence of child rearing can be seen in a variety of other domains. For example, studies of intergenerational transmission have shown correspondence between parents and children in domains of political and religious beliefs and of values and attitudes (Acock & Bengtson, 1980; Smith, 1982). Curiosity in preschool children has been found in families in which there is more positive maternal involvement and less authoritarian control (Endsley, Hutcherson, Garner, & Martin, 1979). More generally, the development of an optimistic (or pessimistic) outlook on life has been related to parental behavior. The way in which mothers account for the causal determinants of everyday events (their "explanatory style") and the types of attributions mothers use when criticizing their children are two of the prime ingredients in children's development of their orientation to life, according to Martin Seligman (1991).

Areas of Little or No Child-Rearing Association

Studies sometimes have come up empty-handed when looking for expected parent-child associations. Perhaps most astonishing to many people has been the lack of association between child rearing and children's temperament or personality. Studies employing the behavior genetics approach, using data from twin studies and adoption studies, find surprisingly little evidence of parental environmental effect on at least four of the Big Five personality traits of extroversion, conscientiousness, emotional stability, openness to experience, and agreeableness (Loehlin, 1992; Rowe, 1990). According to John Loehlin's (1992) computations, the effects of child rearing (shared family environment) on different personality dimensions averaged from 0 to 11 percent of the variance. Genetic effects had considerably more influence, accounting for an average of 22 to 46 percent of the variance. However the remaining and majority of the variance, between 44 and 55 percent, was attributable to environmental effects unique to the individual (nonshared family environment), genotype-environment interactions, or measurement error.

To some extent, one can account for the lack of shared environmental effects found in behavioral genetics research on a variety of methodological and conceptual grounds. For instance, (1) the environment has not been adequately or extensively assessed, (2) different environments have been assumed to be equal when they likely are not, and (3) the lack of similarities between siblings may be overestimated by the methodologies employed and variables assessed (Hoffman, 1991).

One exception to the claims of the behavioral genetics researchers may be in the area of agreeableness. One researcher has marshaled evidence indicating that child-rearing practices may indeed impact the expression of agreeableness, perhaps the personality variable most amenable to environmental influence (Graziano, 1994). Nevertheless, in contrast to the quotation by Symonds (1949) at the beginning of the chapter, recent empirical work indicates that child rearing has far less impact on children's personality than many suppose.

The evidence collected from behavioral geneticists with regard to intelligence also points to a limited impact of child rearing. Researchers have shown that children's IQ scores most closely resemble the scores of those with whom they share genetic material. In one study, children who were adopted at birth had IQs that correlated more highly with those of their biological parents ($r = .30$) than those of their adoptive parents ($r = .15$; Horn, Loehlin, & Willerman, 1979). However, such indicators of genetic influence do not negate the effect of the environment. There is also evidence that the quality of the home environment predicts children's IQ at ages three and four, even when the mother's IQ is partialed out (Yeates,

MacPhee, Campbell, & Ramey, 1983). Evidently, heredity and the environment interact to contribute to the development of intelligence.

Two other areas in which few associations have been found bear mentioning. Despite the Freudian view that fathers must play a critical role in their son's psychological development, a meta-analytic review discovered very few reliable differences between father-absent and father-present children in the very area in which differences would be most expected: that of sex-role development (Stevenson & Black, 1988). And one alternative lifestyle of parents does not appear to have systematic effects on children: Recent studies have concluded that being reared by homosexual or lesbian parents does not result in any consistent effect, either negative or positive, on any of a variety of children's outcomes (Flaks, Ficher, Masterpasqua, & Joseph, 1995; Patterson, 1995).

Moderators of Parent-Child Associations

It is tempting to try to account for development with simple causal relations between parents and children. For instance, mothers of newborns might want to know how soon they can return to their job without negatively affecting their infants. However, maternal employment is not such a robust variable that it results in consistent effects on children. Instead, whether returning to work will have an effect on the family and what kind of effect it exerts depend on a number of variables including the mother's and father's attitudes, the type of work engaged in, the number of hours worked, available social support (e.g., father's involvement), the quality of nonmaternal child care, and the child's gender (Hoffman, 1989).

Similarly, no single parenting practice results in a universal child outcome; if that were the case, the effects of child rearing would be much better understood by now. For a variety of reasons, particular parental practices may have no effect or any of several effects on children. There are multiple variables that appear to modify the associations between child-rearing practices and child outcomes. Some of these modifying variables have been identified in studies of children who were at risk for negative outcomes owing to poverty or exposure to risk factors associated with psychiatric disorders. These variables that can moderate the negative effects are labeled "protective" or "resiliency" factors (Rutter, 1987; Werner & Smith, 1989). Moderators can be grouped into three categories: child, parent, and family characteristics.

Child characteristics are the most important moderators. The child's age, as a marker of the child's cognitive development, has frequently been implicated as moderating the effects of certain child-rearing practices, such as discipline, or major events, such as divorce. The child's gender is also a key variable that can moderate the effects of some parental influences or char-

TABLE 5.1   Potential Moderators of Child Outcomes

Child characteristics
- Age
- Attractiveness
- Autonomy
- Birth order
- Ego development
- Gender
- Intelligence
- Locus of control and attributional style
- Self-esteem
- Social skills and coping abilities
- Temperament

Parent characteristics
- Beliefs, attitudes, and perceptions about child
- Coping abilities and social support
- Gender
- Psychological well-being

Family and other characteristics
- Physical crowding
- Marital relations
- Family size and presence of siblings
- Family cohesion and warmth
- Social support, availability of relatives
- Ethnic group and socioeconomic status

acteristics. It is not surprising that boys tend to show greater initial reactions to their parents' divorce and their fathers' departure, given the special relationship that many fathers and sons experience.

Investigations into child resiliency and vulnerability have helped to identify many other child characteristics, besides age and gender, that can function as moderator variables. For example, during the Great Depression, one study found economic hardship resulted in paternal rejection of unattractive but not attractive daughters (Elder et al., 1985). Examples of the child characteristics that may influence parental associations are listed in Table 5.1.

In addition to child characteristics, several types of *parental characteristics* have been identified as moderating child outcomes. Parental gender, psychological well-being, beliefs and perceptions, and social support are most commonly identified as key variables (Conger et al., 1984; Crockenberg & McCluskey, 1986; Sameroff & Seifer, 1983). In Chapter 4, McLoyd's process model of the modification in paternal behavior after economic loss was discussed. Her work has demonstrated several moderator variables, including social support, strong psychological characteristics, and negative attitudes toward physical punishment. Consequently, unemployed men with one or more of these attributes are considerably less likely than their peers to engage in harsh parenting.

The third category of variables that can moderate associations between parents and children are *family characteristics*. The most frequently studied exemplars are the quality of marital relationship, the family's social support, and the family's socioeconomic status. In families in which the parents enjoy a warm and close relationship, the negative consequences of economic strain on parenting are partially moderated (Simons et al., 1992). Similarly, a good marital relationship can help to protect children from the negative behavioral effects of parental depression (Miller, Cowan, Cowan, Hetherington, & Clingempeel, 1993).

Predicting outcomes is both enhanced and made more complicated by the recognition that moderator variables may interact or be additive with other variables. Interactions with child gender are most commonly recognized; for example, boys are more likely than girls to develop behavior problems in response to marital discord. Variables may be additive as well; the presence of two or more moderator variables is likely to help a child against negative outcomes, whereas the presence of two or more of the risk factors (comorbidity) can serve to exacerbate the negative outcomes. It follows that schizophrenic parents who were also maltreating their children were found to have offspring with more behavior problems than children whose schizophrenic parents did not maltreat them (Walker, Downey, & Bergman, 1989). Similarly, when parental depression and alcoholism team up, the effects are worse than when there is just one problem (Fitzgerald et al., 1993).

Moderator variables generally "work" to influence an association in one of three ways. Some moderator variables (e.g., physical attractiveness or high intelligence) serve to buffer or protect an individual from an otherwise negative association. Other moderator variables can serve to compensate for or replace something missing in the environment. A close, supportive relationship with a grandparent or other individual can serve to fill in a social vacuum for a child of an uninvolved parent. The third way that moderators can work is to influence an individual's behavior; for example, unemployed men with good social support are able to maintain adequate parenting. The existence of moderator variables further attests to the complex dynamic operating among the characteristics of parents, characteristics of children, and other variables in the environment.

Mediating variables are not understood as well as moderators. *Mediators* are intermediary variables that change the relation between other variables. With regard to parent-child associations, mediating variables are most often cognitive, affective, or personality characteristics in children. For example, children's interpretations of and attributions about marital conflict can have a critical impact on how they react to the conflict (Grych & Fincham, 1990). The existence of moderators and mediators once again argues for the need to examine the processes involved in child-rearing associations.

The Five Fundamental Arenas of Child-Rearing Influence

Given the intricate interplay among multiple variables, it is difficult to isolate a specific and uniform set of child-rearing influences on children's development. At the same time, in reviewing the beneficial and detrimental associations linked to child rearing, it is clear that parental influences occur primarily in five arenas. These centers of influence will be briefly summarized.

The constellation of parent-child interactions that combine to form the *attachment process* represents one of the major arenas in which parents influence their offspring. Parents who provide warm and sensitive caregiving have offspring with secure attachments at twelve months. The quality of attachment that develops during the child's infancy and childhood appears to have a lasting influence through the development of an internal working model of the self and others. The quality of relationships that individuals develop with others is, in large part, a function of that working model.

The second major arena of parental influence is that of *social learning* experiences. The key role parents play in this arena is serving as models and dispensing rewards and punishments. Parents are often unaware of the contingencies they are teaching through their own behavior. The central child outcomes associated with this domain include prosocial and antisocial behavior, moral development, and internalization.

Parents also influence their children during social interactions in ways that are not necessarily linked to attachment or social learning outcomes. *Interactional processes* that arise during social interactions include the Vygotskian notion of scaffolding and communication patterns such as "distancing" that have been related to cognitive development. Parents may be unaware of these interactional processes and use them unintentionally. Cognitive development and patterns of social interaction have most commonly been linked to this arena of parental influence.

A fourth arena in which child-rearing influence occurs results from the *explicit teaching* and instruction parents provide. Included here are the expectations and standards parents hold for children's behavior. Social competence, maturity, and achievement are representative outcomes linked to this area of influence.

The fifth major arena of parental influence reflects what the parents do or fail to do related to the quality of a child's *environment*. In this arena of influence, parents may promote exposure to positive influences such as organizing contact with peers, limiting TV viewing, or attending religious services. Alternatively, parents may fail to limit exposure to negative influences or even provide experiences that can corrupt children. Areas of outcomes that may be affected through this form of influence include the quality of peer relations, cognitive development, and substance abuse.

It should be kept in mind that a parent effects model does not accurately explain *how* parental influence occurs in these arenas of influence. Instead, parental influence is mediated by characteristics of the child. A recent model in the social learning arena illustrates this. Children's internalization is mediated by the child in at least three ways, according to Joan Grusec and Jacqueline Goodnow (1994). First, the parental disciplinary behavior depends on the type of misbehavior the child engages is. Second, after the parent has disciplined the child, the child needs to perceive accurately the parental message (e.g., "Do not hit your brother; it is not okay to hit someone"). Third, if the message is going to become internalized, the child needs to accept it as one worthy of following. At multiple steps in the process of influence, therefore, the child plays an active role.

Summary and Reappraisal of Parental Influence

This chapter has summarized data concerning associations between parental characteristics or behavior and child outcomes. It is clear that parent effects are not simple, one-sided, or inevitable. Extreme views from either environmentalists or human behavioral geneticists are inaccurate. There is ample evidence that the considerable variation in child rearing among parents can affect children's development in both positive and negative ways. On the other hand, current evidence indicates that parental behavior has little association with most of the variables studied under the rubric of personality.

Perhaps the central conclusion about parental influence is that it depends on the particular domain. Parental impact is not monolithic across all areas of child functioning. One can propose a continuum of child-rearing effects: At one end, parental practices may have a substantial impact on children's development, whereas at the other end, parental behavior may have virtually no impact on children. For some outcomes, this lack of impact may be due to a strong genetic influence; for others, it may be due to a strong peer influence. This domain-specific influence helps to explain the apparent conflict between the quotation from Scarr (1992) that opened the chapter and information on parent-child associations presented in this chapter.

Five key arenas in which parents influence their children were identified. Within these arenas, parental influence occurs through recurrent patterns of interaction. With the possible exception of maltreatment, it is likely that parental effects occur only with repeated or chronic exposure to that influence.

Parental influence on development is also subject to development itself. That means several things. First, how children respond to child-rearing variations is dependent on the children's developmental level. One must always bear in mind the child's level of functioning and particular characteristics in order to understand how the family environment may be having an influence. It also means that as children grow, it is likely that they will continue to be influenced by new experiences.

These new experiences represent continuing sources of influence on a child's development. Other social forces may include siblings, peers, teachers, relatives, and clergy. In addition, the developmental context, ranging from culture to a specific neighborhood, is increasingly being recognized as a subtle yet important influence on development. Yet another competing influence is the "wild card." Idiosyncratic experiences or chance events, such as accidents or unusual incidents, can have lingering effects on individuals (Hoffman, 1991).

The most important competing source of influence on children's development is the children themselves. Children affect how others behave or the impact of others by such processes as evoking responses, selecting their own niche, and perceiving or interpreting events in a particular way (Grusec & Goodnow, 1994; Scarr & McCartney, 1983). Each of these potential influences may contribute to the complex interplay of variables that combine in largely idiosyncratic equations to compose an individual's development.

In sum, extreme views—either advocating the almost limitless power of parents over their children's development or maintaining that parents are inconsequential—are misguided. A balanced view of familial influence must recognize that parents are indeed responsible for some outcomes in their children, but not for all. Chapter 6 builds on the information in this chapter by focusing on child-rearing processes and characteristics that help make parents more effective at producing positive child-rearing outcomes.

6

The Attributes
of Effective Parents

*All happy families resemble one another; every unhappy family is unhappy in
its own way.*

—Tolstoy, *Anna Karenina*

What distinguishes effective parents from ineffective ones? This chapter summarizes what are considered to be the qualities and skills of parents that create happy families and competent children. Parents with these characteristics can be described as "effective." The synonyms *competent, good, intelligent,* or even *optimal* all refer to the ability of a parent to exhibit the appropriate characteristics and skills that contribute to positive outcomes in a child's life.

At the onset, it should be pointed out that the classification of effective and ineffective parents is not an altogether appropriate one. Dichotomies rarely provide an accurate depiction of reality, and that is especially the case with parenting. Most parents cannot readily be classified as good or bad, effective or not. In concert with the point made in Chapter 5, it is more useful to look at how well a parent functions in a particular domain or arena of influence. One parent may be particularly warm and nurturant and thus fare well in the attachment arena but be inept at planning and managing the child's environment.

Within a particular arena, one can think of the quality of parenting as representing a continuum. At one extreme is highly pathological parenting, comprising extensive and continuous child maltreatment. The other end of the continuum represents the (unattainable) ideal of consistently excellent parenting (see Figure 6.1). This chapter explicates the top third of that continuum; Chapter 7 will consider the bottom third.

Not everyone accepts the notion of a continuum of parenting or at least its usefulness. The British psychiatrist Donald Winnicott (1967) argued that parents only needed to be *good enough;* such parents provide all the necessary parental ingredients for successful development. Others similarly have endorsed the view that "good enough" parenting is adequate, because chil-

117

FIGURE 6.1   The Continuum of Parenting.

dren's internal genetic endowment governs much of development (Bettelheim, 1987; Scarr, 1992).

There is at least one empirical study, however, that suggests good enough is not enough. Recently Baumrind (1991) published results concerning adolescent functioning from her longitudinal investigation into the development of competence. She divided the 116 parents of fifteen-year-old children into six groups: directive (24 percent of the sample), democratic (22 percent), unengaged (19 percent), authoritarian (18 percent), good enough (11 percent), and nondirective (6 percent). These patterns were based on measures of parental control, support, and restrictiveness. The good enough families exhibited a moderate—but not high—level of positive parental qualities (providing control and support). Adolescents from those homes were found to be somewhat less competent on various personality, academic, and social behavior indices than the children from homes of authoritative and democratic parents.

Indeed, as this chapter will indicate, there is evidence for a payoff for effective parents: They are more likely to have competent children, to live in a happier home, and to experience enhanced satisfaction themselves. Toward that end, three topics will be considered. First, the characteristics attributed to effective parents will be described. Second, an alternative approach to thinking about effective parents will be presented. Rather than identifying static characteristics of capable parents, a model describing the process of child-rearing inherent in effective parenting will be presented. Third, educational programs designed to make parents more competent will be discussed.

Issues in Identifying Effective Parents

It is not difficult to generate a long list of the presumed characteristics of effective parents. Child-rearing advice found in books, magazines, newspapers, and research articles is replete with what parents should and should not do (Clarke-Stewart, 1978a; Young, 1990). However, identifying the essential and enduring ingredients of such parenting is difficult for various reasons. Even if one limits the search to the judgment of "experts" (meaning those who work with or conduct research with parents), there are three potential problems: Experts disagree, they change their minds, and their advice is often based on laboratory studies or small samples of children or behavior.

Consider the comments from an early parenting expert. He recognized that "the oldest profession of the race is facing failure. This profession is parenthood. . . . The rearing of children is the most difficult of all professions, more difficult than engineering, than law, or even than medicine itself" (Watson, 1928, pp. 11–12). But his solution was far too limited. He believed that all parents could be transformed into effective caregivers simply by teaching them learning principles. John B. Watson was particularly alarmed about what he saw as the dangers of giving too much "mother love." Among other errant pieces of advice, he wrote the following:

> There is a sensible way of treating children. Treat them as though they were young adults. Dress them, bathe them with care and circumspection. Let your behavior always be objective and kindly firm. Never hug or kiss them, never let them sit in your lap. If you must, kiss them once on the forehead when they say good night. Shake hands with them in the morning. Give them a pat on the head if they have made an extraordinarily good job of a difficult task. Try it out. . . . You will be utterly ashamed of the mawkish, sentimental way you have been handling it (1928, pp. 81–82).

Fortunately, few of Watson's contemporaries agreed with him, and his advice was not widely accepted. However, there continue to be conflicts among child-rearing experts. Experts disagree concerning such topics as disciplinary practices and the use of physical punishment, how much stimulation infants should be given, the effects of day care, and as Chapter 5 illustrated, even how much influence child rearing has on children's development.

Parenting advice has changed dramatically over the past century. Although contemporary experts are now more likely to base their advice on the results of empirical studies, all too often that empirical foundation is limited. A related problem is the issue of cultural relativity. The characteristics of effective parents must be evaluated in relation to the specific culture, socioeconomic status, and environment in which the child is raised (Harkness & Super, 1995; Ogbu, 1981). Parents who raise their children in dangerous inner-city neighborhoods adopt different parenting practices than families living in the suburbs. In violent environments, parents cannot afford the luxury of negotiating with a child, giving choices, or having a child disobey a parental command (see Garbarino et al., 1991).

What determines the effectiveness of a parent is, ultimately, how the child turns out. Some desired outcomes are universal, but others are specific to a culture or subculture. The most fundamental universal goal of parenting is to raise a child to become a physically and mentally healthy adult who is a contributing member of society (Whiting & Edwards, 1988). Toward that end, parents must instill in children self-esteem as well as respect for others, an ability to solve problems, and a degree of psychological health sufficient to withstand adversity.

The socialization goals of parents can vary across cultures. The contrast between Eastern socialization practices and Western ones is a good exemplar. Japanese parents raise their children differently from U.S. parents owing to differing outcome values. Japanese value cooperation and close group affiliation. Mothers promote these outcomes through providing close physical contact ("skinship") and developing a relationship based on interdependence. Many Japanese infants, toddlers, and preschoolers spend virtually all of their waking and sleeping time in direct physical contact with their mother.

In contrast, U.S. parents rear their children to become independent, autonomous, and instrumental (Weisz et al., 1984). Consequently, parents from the United States typically do not sleep with their infants, and by the end of the first year of life, they spend a considerable amount of time away from them. A mother who is effective in Japan would likely be viewed as permissive and indulgent through U.S. eyes. Conversely, effective U.S. mothers would be viewed by Japanese as callous and insensitive for leaving their infants with other caregivers or forcing them to sleep alone.

Cultural values and constraints help to determine what constitutes effectiveness in parents. Similarly, within a culture, different social groups may have differing values that result in different characteristics leading to parental effectiveness. With the exception of the work by Kohn (e.g., 1979) on socioeconomic influences on socialization, described in Chapter 4, there is not enough information to address the issue of the socialization goals of subgroups. Consequently, the summary of attributes of effective parents is mostly based on research concerning Caucasian, middle- and upper-middle-class U.S. parents.

Attributes of Effective Parents in the Five Arenas of Influence

The attributes of effective parents can be organized under the five arenas of parental influence, as identified at the end of Chapter 5. A prerequisite of effectiveness in each arena is a certain level of involvement. *Involvement* means commitment to a child's welfare and therefore motivation to meet the child's needs. At the most basic level, this involvement means providing for the physical needs of the child (e.g., food, clothing, shelter, and protection). Beyond those necessities, parental involvement requires devoting a substantial amount of time to providing care and attention to the child. It is unlikely that short periods of "quality time" are sufficient for effective involvement.

Underlying involvement is an attitude of commitment and interest in the child's welfare and development. Given the large variability in the degree to which parents are committed to and active in their role as parents, this variable provides an initial criterion for identifying parental effectiveness (Greenberger & Goldberg, 1989; Pulkkinen, 1982). Like each of the parental attributes to be discussed, the ways in which parental involvement is manifested are highly dependent on the age of the child. Nevertheless, effective parents display age-appropriate involvement at least through adolescence; in contrast, many ineffective parents become disengaged sometime after early childhood (Hetherington & Clingempeel, 1992).

The Attachment Arena

During the first year of a child's life, parents of infants must perform a series of recurrent tasks that include feeding, clothing, diapering, comforting, and stimulating the infant. What is important is how parents perform many of those tasks. The "how" of parenting is captured by the construct of parental sensitivity. *Sensitivity* (sometimes called *responsivity*) refers to being attuned to a child's cues. A more explicit definition is "the appropriate, consistent, and contingent responses" of the parent to the child's needs (Lamb & Easterbrooks, 1981, p. 127). Parental sensitivity or its absence can most readily be observed in early infancy when a child becomes distressed. Key indicators of sensitivity are how rapidly and dependably the parent comes to the child's aid as well as how successful the parent is at comforting the child and meeting the child's needs.

The very act of being sensitive requires a number of underlying characteristics. These include attentiveness, empathy, correct interpretation of the infant's cues, and nonintrusiveness combined with emotional availability (Biringen & Robinson, 1990; Martin, 1989). Sensitive parents are able to quickly relieve their children's anxiety and fears by offering emotional comfort.

Several other aspects of sensitivity have been identified in the psychiatric and psychological literature. The psychiatrists Donald Winnicott and Heinz Kohut both have written that parental *mirroring* of the child's emotions (i.e., reflecting back to the child what the child is feeling) is essential for early development (Baker & Baker, 1987; Winnicott, 1967). Closely related to mirroring is "empathic awareness" (Feshbach, 1987), which refers to the ability to recognize the emotions experienced by a child and respond appropriately to those emotions.

Yet another ingredient of sensitive parenting involves balancing the needs and desires of the child with the needs of the parent and others. Empathic goals are those that are child-centered and provide outcomes that children experience as desirable (Dix, 1992). However, sensitive parents must also balance the child's desires with socialization goals (ones that teach or constrain) and with the goals associated with the needs of other family members. All too often, these goals conflict. When an empathic goal of letting the child continue to watch TV conflicts with the socialization goal of getting the child to clean up the playroom, the sensitive parent must evaluate what is in the short- and long-term best interest of the child and family. This judgment process is fundamental to sensitivity.

A characteristic of effective parents related to sensitivity but encompassing a broader array of behavior is parental *warmth*. Warmth, or what is colloquially called "love," has long been recognized as a key dimension of parental behavior (e.g., Schaefer, 1959; Maccoby & Martin, 1983). As a psychological construct, warmth has been operationalized and measured in various ways. Acceptance, appreciation, physical affection, giving approval for good behavior, playful joking, sharing mutually rewarding activities, and responding to the child in a positive and accepting way have all been used as indices of warmth (Russell & Russell, 1989). Parental warmth not only is positively associated with various indices of child adjustment, as discussed in the last chapter, but also can help to buffer a child from adverse events such as peer rejection (Patterson, Cohn, & Kao, 1989).

The Social Learning Arena

Within the social learning arena, parents influence their children through modeling and dispensing reinforcements and punishments. Effective parents must model desired behaviors and avoid modeling undesired ones. In the area of prosocial and moral development, effective parents model responsive and cooperative behavior with their children (rather than domination and control) to establish a reciprocal relationship based on the spirit of cooperation, mutual support, and compliance (Parpal & Maccoby, 1985). Parents need to be models of controlled and planned behavior if the child is expected to act similarly. Parents also need to model how to cope with stress and crises as well as demonstrate how to resolve interpersonal conflict (Cummings & Davies, 1994). Alternatively, parents who model aggressive behavior, premarital pregnancy, or inability to control their appetites are more likely to have children who do the same, as indicated in Chapter 5.

Effective child rearing also requires judicious use of operant learning principles. Parents frequently must respond to children's transgressions with a wide array of disciplinary actions. Across a number of observational studies, parents of normal young children have been observed to attempt to control their children once every three or four minutes (Wahler & Dumas, 1989). Furthermore, children disobey their parents in about 25 percent of the cases. Evidently, some disciplinary practices are more effective than others. At a global level, there is widespread agreement that the central attribute of effective discipline is a reliance on *reasoning*, the hallmark of authoritative parenting (Baumrind, 1971). The parental act of reasoning represents a mixed bag of verbalizations. It may be a discourse on the nature of the misdeed, a rationale for why the behavior is not acceptable, a lecture in normative behavior, a discussion of consequences or feelings, or a recommendation for future behavior. Some discussion of the transgression, whereby the child's point of view can be heard, is also a common attribute of skillful reasoning. Of course, the level of discourse needs to be developmentally appropriate, such that it does not exceed the child's linguistic abilities (Grusec & Goodnow, 1994).

Effective use of reasoning typically co-occurs with other disciplinary responses (e.g., power assertion or withdrawal of love) and is dependent on the type of child transgression. For example, Judith Smetana (1989) found that the type of reasoning provided was a function of the misdeed: Children who broke a social convention (arbitrary parental rule, such as to pick up toys) received a different message than children engaged in a moral transgression (such as hitting someone else). Grusec and Goodnow (1994) have argued that disciplinary effectiveness depends on a host of factors, including the nature of the misdeed, the nature of the child (e.g., temperament, mood), and features of the actual disciplinary response (e.g., content of message, how it is said). An effective parent must take into account a variety of considerations before determining the appropriate response.

There is some disagreement in the parenting literature about the extent to which power assertion is necessary. Although researchers agree that competent parents avoid unnecessary or extreme uses of power assertion as well as arbitrary demands, unnecessary restrictions, and reliance on power, some power assertion in conjunction with reasoning may be necessary to gain the child's attention or maintain control (Maccoby & Martin, 1983). Independent of the degree of power assertion they exhibit, effective parents have been observed to maintain a certain degree of warmth toward their young children while disciplining (Baumrind, 1971; Grusec & Lytton, 1988; Maccoby & Martin, 1983).

Social learning theory would predict that *consistency* in discipline is important. The meaning of consistency is ambiguous, but it surely does not mean responding in the exact same way to each and every child behavior (Lytton, 1979; Grusec & Goodnow, 1994). Rather, consistent parenting involves setting rules, responding similarly in similar situations, monitoring the child for compliance, and following up on stated consequences of misbehavior. According to Patterson (1982), the key point of consistency is giving the child the message that the parent will win a conflict and not capitulate to the child. When parents do give in to a child's demands or misbehavior ("Okay, you can have a piece of candy"), they fall into a negative reinforcement trap whereby short-term gains (e.g., stopping the whining) are won at the expense of rewarding the child's difficult behavior. There is some evidence that parents who are inconsistent have children who are more likely to exhibit conduct problems and experience more parent-child conflict than consistent parents (e.g., Patterson, 1982).

Less effective parents are also less likely to use operant conditioning principles appropriately. A common parental error is to give attention to, and therefore reinforce, undesired behavior (Wierson & Forehand, 1994). Home observations have determined that mothers in families with normal children use more rewards for positive behavior and use more negative consequences for deviant behavior than mothers of children with behavior problems (Snyder, 1977).

Parents frequently get angry with their children, because negative emotion is a by-product occurring when a child has violated a parental standard or goal (Dix, 1991). That negative emotion can easily result in an escalation of negative behaviors (e.g., yelling, hitting). Children then reciprocate the negative, escalating behaviors, and the interaction escalates into a *coercive cycle* (as discussed in Chapters 3 and 5). This cycle often ends when one of the participants gives in (usually the parent) and thereby reinforces the escalated, noxious behavior (Patterson, 1982). Effective discipline requires patience and the ability to *inhibit negative emotion* and behavior.

If parents are to effectively socialize their children, they frequently must *set limits* on the children's behavior and desires that are inappropriate, dangerous, unhealthy, or incompatible with parental values, goals, or needs. One example of parental limit setting was found in a study of preschoolers and their television viewing practices (St. Peters, Fitch, Huston, Wright, & Eakins, 1991). The parents who set the most limits were labeled *restrictive* parents; they closely regulated TV viewing and did not encourage it. *Selective* parents encouraged viewing but regulated the types of shows watched; *laissez-faire* parents neither encouraged nor regulated viewing; and *promotive* parents encouraged viewing. Given the problems associated with extensive television viewing in children (e.g., increased aggression, family conflict, passivity, consumerism), the restrictive parents could be called the most effective because they limited not only the type of programs watched but also the total amount of viewing time.

The Social Interaction Arena

There are other ways that effective parents promote their children's development, outside of the attachment and social learning arenas. Microanalytic studies have shown that parents engage in subtle and fleeting actions with their infants that are designed to promote interactions.

Mothers use *attention-getting, stage-setting,* and *scaffolding behaviors* while interacting or playing games such as peekaboo and roll the ball (Hodapp, Goldfield, & Boyatzis, 1984; Trevarthen, 1977). As infants get older, mothers who are effective in engaging their children's attention modify their behavior by increasing reinforcements (clapping, saying "good") and altering the type of scaffolding to encourage more interaction (Hodapp et al., 1984). Effective parents create this zone of proximal development by regulating their children's behavior and erecting appropriate scaffolding for children that enables them to perform at more advanced levels.

These types of early interactions, which occur more often during interactions with effective parents, have also been recognized as important in social learning and attachment theories. Infants learn the fundamental principles of social interactions—including synchrony, reciprocity, and complementarity—through such interactions. At the same time, the quality of these types of interactions has been linked to the formation of secure and insecure attachments (Isabella, 1993).

As children get older, parents must exert more control and seek more compliance. How mothers effectively coordinate their controlling efforts has also been investigated using the microanalytic approach. Rudolf Schaffer and Charles Crook (1979) found that effective mothers of preschoolers used a sequential strategy of first gaining their children's attention before directing them to do something. Another subtle interactional skill of mothers of preschoolers was identified by Michael Westerman (1990), who observed effective mothers (in contrast to mothers who had children with compliance problems) to follow an unstated *homing* rule of interaction. When their children were in need of help in completing a block task, these mothers homed in with specific directives. However, when the children were doing well at the task, the mothers homed out, as inferred from the less specific nature of their instructions. This coordination between the children's success or failure and the mothers' level of instruction or intrusiveness differentiated mothers with normal children from those with children with compliance problems. Although this study does not speak to whether this ability to coordinate is causally related to behavior problems, it does reveal another skill of effective parents.

Taken together, studies of social interactions have identified several attributes of parents that are linked to more positive outcomes in their children. The types of behaviors the parent engages in are closely tied to the child's developmental level (Rogoff, Ellis, & Gardner, 1984). These results fit into Vygotsky's theory that highlights the central role that parents or others play in facilitating the child's cognitive and social development. Parents do this by being sensitive to the "zone" between what the child has already mastered and what the child can do with assistance. Effective parents then structure the task and direct a child's behavior in such a way that makes it relatively easy for the child to succeed (Pratt, Kerig, Cowan, & Cowan, 1988).

The Teaching Arena

In the teaching and instruction arena of influence, effective parents must be capable mentors. The socialization process involves teaching a range of lessons, including mundane habits (e.g., sphincter control and hygiene), normative behavior (e.g., appropriate behavior in public settings), the values held by the parent as well as the culture, and the skills needed for future survival and functioning. Effective parents therefore must be adept at teaching.

The way parents teach even rudimentary skills has been found to differentiate the effectiveness of parents. More effective parents have been found to use more *positive reinforcement, questions,* and *feedback* with young children than less effective parents (Laosa, 1978). Competent parents are also more likely to *openly communicate* with their children on a wide range of topics, including feelings, needs of individuals, reasons for rules, and behavioral expectations (Saarni, 1985). During conversations, effective parents are more likely than other parents to stimulate their children's intellectual development by use of certain cognitive distancing techniques. These techniques, including placing demands on the child to remember past events, to use their imagination, and to anticipate future actions, are all attributes of the speech of parents who are more cognitively challenging and competent (Sigel et al., 1991).

One of the first ways that parents teach their children to have a sense of responsibility, the "work ethic," and the value of money (through allowance) is by assigning chores. Although children as young as eighteen months often spontaneously join in helping with housekeeping chores (Rheingold, 1982), it is sometime during the preschool or early grade school years that parents begin to give their children household work to do. The chores of younger children typically involve "self-care" (e.g., making bed, cleaning room, putting away clothes), as opposed to the "family work" chores that get assigned to older children (setting or clearing table, washing dishes, vacuuming, taking care of pets). Presumably, effective parents are more likely to assign and require the completion of household chores, but given the limited empirical work on the topic, the data supporting a link between assignment of chores and positive child outcomes are equivocal (Goodnow, 1988a; McHale et al., 1990).

Parents also recognize the importance of their teaching role. In an interview study of parents' beliefs concerning how they socialize their children, Thomas Power and Josephine Shanks (1989) found that parents of children from the fifth, eighth, and eleventh grades believed that they influenced their children the most by telling, reasoning, and persuading. The parents were much less likely to mention such influence techniques as rewards and punishments or structuring the environment. Although the use of techniques changed to some degree with the age of the child and the gender of the parent, the central finding was that parents believed they were having the greatest impact on their children's socialization through direct instruction and teaching.

The Structuring of the Environment Arena

Parents, at least while their children are young, act as executive directors of their children's daily schedule and environment. In this capacity, parents who structure their children's lives so they consist of reasonably regular schedules and activities are thought to be more effective than other parents. In turn, children feel more secure and function better in environments where the daily activities are consistent, predictable, and routinized (Boyce, Jensen, James, & Peacock, 1983).

In their capacity to structure the environment, parents plan and manage the types of experiences and interactions the child engages in. This is sometimes called *situational management*. By effective planning, anticipation, and management, the ratio of positive to negative (i.e., disciplinary) interactions can be maximized. This can be accomplished, in part, by creating different "zones" for child behavior. Following Vygotsky's theoretical lead, Jaan Valsiner (e.g., 1985) has identified three zones of child behavior that parents construct: (1) the zone of free movement (consisting of the area, persons, and objects available to a child); (2) the zone of promoted actions (the behaviors encouraged or demanded by caregivers); and (3) the zone of forbidden behavior (actions that are off-bounds to the child). Competent parents, compared with less competent ones, probably maintain relatively larger zones of free movement and promoted actions and a smaller zone of forbidden behavior.

Consider how an effective parent structures the environment to manage a challenging task: taking a young child shopping. I observed twenty-four mothers and their two-and-one-half-year-old children during their trips to the supermarket to discover how competent mothers managed the task (Holden, 1983). It did not take long to see that effective mothers were highly strategic: They anticipated their children's behavior and directed their children to positive activities before they misbehaved. The activities ranged from engaging them in the shopping task to giving them an object to play with or something to eat. Mothers also avoided certain problematic aisles in the supermarket or pushed their cart down the center of aisles so their children could not reach tempting objects. Mothers who used such *proactive* techniques more frequently, rather than relying on reactive management techniques (e.g., prohibiting, reasoning, diverting), had children with lower rates of misbehavior in the supermarket. The efficacy of such proactive management behavior has also been related to a lower rate of behavior problems (Pettit & Bates, 1989); such behavior is also likely to decrease the risk of childhood injuries through childproofing of the home (Holden, 1985).

One parenting skill that underlies the effective structuring of a child's environment is maintaining an awareness about the child and what the child is currently engaged in. This attribute, known as *monitoring,* involves far more than simply knowing the child's whereabouts. Effective monitoring involves being aware of the child's physical and emotional health, who the child is with, and whether the child has completed his or her chores. For older children, it may also include awareness of the status of homework and school performance that day, what the child is reading, what activities the child is involved in, who the child is talking with on the phone, and what the child purchases (Crouter et al., 1990).

Effective monitoring reflects parental involvement and interest but also requires good parent-child communication. At least two studies have found that there is an inverse association between monitoring and child behavior problems. Parents who reported they monitored their preadolescent children more (as indexed by their knowledge of the child's daily experiences) had sons with higher school grades and, in dual-earner families, had sons with fewer conduct problems (Crouter et al., 1990). In another study assessing parenting and adolescent male behavior, a lack of parental monitoring was the child-rearing variable most highly correlated with delinquent behavior and contacts with police (Patterson & Stouthamer-Loeber, 1984).

In addition to structuring and monitoring children's activities, competent parents are also able to provide their children with a *sense of control* (Finkelstein & Ramey, 1977; St. Peters et al., 1991; Steinberg et al., 1989). The ways parents do this are highly dependent on their children's ages. For the parent of an infant, this means responding quickly to the child's cry so that the infant learns that the environment is responsive (Ainsworth & Bell, 1977). The parent of a preschooler might let the child choose between two different outfits to wear to school. Providing some degree of "democratic choice" for older children and allowing them to make decisions and solve at least some of their own problems affords older children a sense of psychological control and autonomy (e.g., Steinberg et al., 1989).

Giving control does not mean conferring unlimited power, because that would conflict with limit setting and be incompatible with efficient family functioning. Through attaining an appropriate sense of control, however, children are thought to gain an internal sense of control and to become more instrumental and psychologically autonomous.

Social Cognition in Effective Parents

Since the mid-1980s, researchers in increasing numbers have been using the parental beliefs approach to investigate the cognitive attributes inherent in competent parenting (e.g., Bacon & Ashmore, 1986). In contrast to the parental attitude research, this new approach looks at the ongoing processes and adjustments involved in parental social cognition. Four aspects of parental social cognition have received attention: (1) accurate perceptions and attributions, (2) appropriate knowledge and expectations, (3) effective problem solving, and (4) healthy parenting self-perceptions.

Developing accurate perceptions about a child is a crucial ability of effective parents. Being able to "read" an infant's needs is considered an important requisite for effective interaction (Martin, 1989). Similarly, accurately perceiving a child's temperament is believed to be necessary for matching appropriate parental behavior (Thomas & Chess, 1977). It is not surprising that depressed mothers have sometimes been found to hold negative and inaccurate perceptions about their children's behavior (Webster-Stratton & Hammond, 1988).

A common parental perceptual chore is identifying the cause of child behavior. When a child misbehaves, such as fighting with a sibling, parents make assessments about the cause of that behavior. Is the child misbehaving because of a situational factor—maybe he is tired or hungry—or is the child misbehaving intentionally as a way of gaining attention? Judgments of children's behavior may involve multiple determinations, including whether the child understood the effects the behavior would have, whether the child had the ability to produce those effects, and whether the child was free from external control (Dix & Grusec, 1985).

Based on the determinations of the child's intentions, parents make attributions about whether the behavior was caused by the child's personality disposition or by environmental circumstances (Dix et al., 1986). There is some evidence that less effective parents make inaccurate attributions. For instance, a group of physically abusive mothers were much more likely than a comparison group of mothers to attribute the cause of a child's misbehavior to the child's personality (Larrance & Twentyman, 1983). Those mothers appeared to have a bias in their attributional assessments.

Closely related to perceptions and attributions are parental beliefs and expectations. Parental beliefs about child development and child rearing form a key basis for parenting behavior. The appropriateness of those beliefs are subject to wide fluctuations even within a particular culture (Goodnow & Collins, 1990). Some studies of abusive parents (as an example of ineffective parents) have found that those parents hold inappropriate expectations about what their children are developmentally capable of doing, as will be discussed in Chapter 7.

In contrast, positive expectations about children and current circumstances can help to overcome some of the problems associated with an impoverished environment. Empirical support was provided by a multimethod study of 267 mothers who were at high risk for inadequate parenting owing to low income (Brunnquell et al., 1981). The mothers filled out a variety of questionnaires both during pregnancy and when their children were three months old. In addition, the mothers were observed and rated on the quality of their child care. The mothers who were rated as providing better quality care to their infants had more positive expectations about their children and parenting than mothers providing inadequate care.

If parents are to be effective in nurturing a child's development, they must also be adept at solving child-rearing problems. Parents frequently deal with problems, ranging from immediate and mundane issues such as determining why their baby is crying (Holden, 1988) to long-term planning such as resolving what to do with children during summer vacation. The way the parents go about solving problems is important not only for efficaciously resolving issues but also for promoting respect among family members and modeling how to deal with problems.

Some work has been conducted concerning the characteristics of effective family problem solving. In one observational study of families jointly solving problems given to them by the experimenters (e.g., building a tower, planning a vacation), it was found that families that successfully completed the tasks, in comparison to the other families, spent more time planning, used more strategies of problem solving, and were better able to reach joint agreements (Bleckman & McEnroe, 1985).

A final area of parental social cognition that has received attention involves parents' perceptions about themselves as parents. In particular, feelings of efficacy, competence, and satisfaction as a parent have been associated with effective parenting (Johnston & Mash, 1989). It is now thought that to be effective, parents must develop a sense that they have some control over their interactions with their children and that they are able to accurately perceive their children, predict their behavior, and be responsive to them (Teti & Gelfand, 1991). The degree to which parents feel competent and confident in controlling children has been shown to have implications for their interactions with the children. Mothers who believe they have little control over a child are more likely to feel sad and experience irritation and annoyance when interacting with the child than those who feel they are in control (Bugental et al., 1989, 1990). Alternatively, having the illusion of great control over a child can have negative ramifications. Mothers who entertained such illusions, as assessed in a laboratory simulation task, were likely to be depressed and at risk for insecure attachments with their infants (Donovan & Leavitt, 1989). Achieving a balance in one's perception of control appears to be important for effective child rearing.

Although considerable progress has been made in identifying characteristics and skills of effective parents compared to less effective parents, there are several questions that remain. To date, little systematic work has been done in identifying the key variables within individuals that promote effective parenting. Such an individual-difference approach could reveal how personality and cognitive variables are related to, or interact with, parenting skills. Intelligence and personality are two such variables that have received little systematic attention.

Several studies provide examples of the usefulness of assessing individual-difference variables for identifying effective parents. In the study mentioned previously concerning high-risk mothers and their infants, it was the mothers who scored higher on an intelligence test who were more likely to be observed as providing excellent care to their infants (Brunnquell et al., 1981). Maternal intelligence scores were also found to be modest but significant correlates of positive disciplinary techniques (Scarr, 1985).

A personality variable that appears to be more important than intelligence is the level of personal integration, more commonly called "maturity." As mentioned in Chapter 4, several studies have found that indices of maturity provide the best differentiation of the quality of parenting.

Influences on Parent Effectiveness

The previous section has identified more than a dozen characteristics and skills associated with effective parents. Effectiveness does not lie completely in the hands of the parent, however; parental competence is multiply determined. Ecological systems theory reveals that, in addition to the parent's own child-rearing abilities, two subsystems help to determine effectiveness: the child's characteristics and the social support system (Belsky, 1984).

Child characteristics, most notably child age, temperament, and physical or mental disabilities, can have a determining influence on parental effectiveness (Mash & Johnston, 1990). A child who is difficult to understand, noncompliant, or unpredictable can make an otherwise effective parent feel incompetent. Alternatively, a compliant or easy-natured child who wants to please a parent can give the illusion that the parent is effective (Lewis, 1981). The role that child characteristics play in influencing parental effectiveness, as the child effects literature reminds us, should not be underestimated.

The other key subsystem that influences parental effectiveness is the degree of social support received. Social support from a spouse or friend has been linked to effectiveness in several ways. Parents in close, supportive marriages were found to exhibit more warmth, sensitivity, and positive attitudes than parents without such support (Cox et al., 1989). In another study, mothers of infants who had little social support were observed to be less responsive than mothers who were receiving support (Crockenberg, 1981).

As this systems approach has shown, child-rearing effectiveness does not reside completely within each parent. In fact, the difficulty inherent in attempts to isolate the independent contributions of the parent, the child, and their unique relationship represents one of the thorniest problems in the study of parent-child relationships (Martin, 1989; Kenny, 1988).

A Process Model of Parent Effectiveness

Despite the progress that has been made in revealing the attributes of effective parents, for the most part research has focused on static parental characteristics. Although this approach to cataloging the characteristics that are associated with effective parenting is useful, it implies that a good parent simply has more positive qualities and more skills than an ineffective parent.

More is not always better. For instance, one investigator discovered that parental warmth was not related to child competence in a linear fashion. Although increased parental warmth was indeed associated with increased child competence, after a certain point, additional warmth did not further contribute to competence. In fact, too much warmth was linked to a decrease in child competence (Roberts, 1986).

Evidently, competent parenting consists of more than a set of skills; it involves using them appropriately during interactions within an enduring and unique relationship. The way parents adapt and adjust to a changing child, changes in themselves, or changing life situations is not captured by a static approach. To understand how effective parents operate, the ongoing interaction process must be the focus of attention.

There are other sources of evidence pointing to the importance of the process by which parenting is conducted. In a review of studies of ineffective and dysfunctional parents, it was concluded that the major child-rearing deficiency was a stress-induced lack of attention that resulted in an *inability to adapt* to children's cues (Wahler & Dumas, 1989). Similarly, Grusec and Goodnow (1994), in their discussion of child internalization and parental use of discipline, argued that "parents [must] be flexible in their disciplinary reactions, matching them to the child's perception of and reactions to the conflict situation: Effective parenting involves sensitivity to the child's emotional state and cognitions" (p. 17).

Within the previous description of attributes of effective parents, several of the characteristics are potentially in conflict. To cite a few examples, effective parents must be involved but not too intrusive. They must be warm but also firm. Empathic and child-centered goals need to be balanced with socialization and adult-centered goals. Parents need to impart a sense of control but not let the child become a little dictator. Parents also need to be consistent but flexible in their disciplining.

Many other examples of this conflict can be found in the family research literature. Effective families avoid both enmeshment (there is no individuality) and disengagement (members are so separate they have little effect on each other; Cooper, Grotevant, & Condon, 1983). Achieving a balance between individuality and connectedness is essential. Boys develop self-reliance and resistance to peer pressure when family relations are neither too close nor too distant (Steinberg & Silverberg, 1986). Too little or too much monitoring may impede a child's development of autonomy (Crouter et al., 1990). Some separation anxiety but not too much appears to be best for mothers to develop secure attachments with their infants (McBride & Belsky, 1988). Parents help children develop a conscience by inducing some affective discomfort (guilt or anxiety) but not too much (Kochanska, 1993). Similarly, parents want their children to be compliant to them but at the same time self-reliant and independent.

How does one capture this dynamic but delicate balancing act that effective parents must engage in? One solution is to think about effectiveness in a different way. Competent parents must be effective at balancing competing concerns of child rearing. It can be argued that parents' effectiveness lies more in the way they go about handling the ongoing parent-child interactions than in the number of positive attributes they possess.

There is a theoretical model that captures such an approach. The philosopher Georg Wilhelm Friedrich Hegel proposed that the development of knowledge proceeds through the process of developing a thesis (i.e., idea, behavior), to which an antithesis (counteridea, alternative action) then emerges. Subsequently, a synthesis of the thesis and antithesis is arrived at. This synthesis then forms a new thesis, which is followed by the development of a new antithesis, and so on. Klaus Riegel (1976) and others have advocated the use of this *dialectic* model for capturing the nature of development. Such a model assumes that individuals are changing in a changing world. The focus of study is not on particular characteristics or traits but on "interactive changes in common activities and everyday situations" (Riegel, 1976, p. 691).

According to a process model, an effective parent is one who can arrive at an appropriate synthesis out of a thesis and antithesis (Holden & Ritchie, 1988). Sometimes it involves a conscious, intentional decision. More often than not, the parents are unaware of the process, and the resolution is accomplished unknowingly and unintentionally. Any one particular parenting response may or may not be appropriate, depending on the context, the child, and the parent. Competent parents are constantly adjusting their child-rearing behavior based on their appraisal of the situation and individuals involved.

There are various implications of this approach for the consideration of competent parenting. It suggests that parenting cannot be characterized by a cookbook approach. Although certain skills and attributes are obviously necessary for competent parents, the core of effective parenting lies in how the parent appraises the child and situation and then resolves competing needs or notions.

In summary, there is wide agreement among parenting experts on the basic ingredients of effective parenting, albeit from a limited cultural and ethnic point of view. What is not well understood is how these ingredients are combined during interactions to form the parenting behavior. Appreciation of these manifold interactions is important not only for understanding the basis of effective parenting but also for teaching individuals how to parent. The last section of this chapter provides an overview of contemporary efforts at parent education.

Making Parents More Effective: Parent Education

History and Approaches to Parent Education

Parent education is not a new educational fad; it has a long history. As discussed in Chapter 1, philosophers, physicians, and others have dispensed child-rearing advice in an effort to tell parents how to rear their children. In the United States, the first organized parent education programs began in about the year 1806. By the early part of the 1900s, parent education became an increasingly common form of social activism, but it was not until the 1930s that it became a widespread movement. During the 1970s, there was a resurgence of interest in parent training owing to increasing awareness of (1) parents' influential role in their children's development; (2) problems many parents were having in child rearing, caused in part by increasing societal stress; (3) the inability of schools to take the place of parents; and (4) new scientific knowledge accumulating on child rearing (Clarke-Stewart, 1978a).

Also during the 1970s, two of the better known contemporary parenting programs were developed: Parent Effectiveness Training (PET) (Gordon, 1976) and the Systematic Training for Effective Parenting, or STEP (Dinkmeyer & McKay, 1976). PET is perhaps the best-known program. The course not only teaches fundamental parenting skills (e.g., active and passive listening, identifying the "ownership" of the problem) but also focuses on awareness of the child's and parent's role in interactions. To do this, PET teaches parents about implicit models of parenting through the *Inconsistency Principle*. In contrast to social learning approaches, which would advocate consistency in parenting, Thomas Gordon argued that it is impossible to be consistent. Depending on the parent's mood and what else is going on in the environment, a child behavior (e.g., making a request, pounding on a piano) might be acceptable at one time but unacceptable at another. Gordon argued, therefore, that a central part of parenting is recognizing and accepting that fluctuating nature of acceptable and unacceptable behaviors. Although not labeled as such, his Inconsistency Principle is yet another example of a dialectic that parents must negotiate.

Contemporary parent education programs fall into one of two approaches: preventive or remedial. The preventive approach is designed to educate parents or future parents about child rearing before problems emerge. These programs are sometimes found in high schools. The second approach, which is considerably more common, is to use parent education to remedy problems of the child, the parent, or the parent-child relationship (Schaefer & Briesmeister, 1989). Parent training programs have been developed for a wide variety of problems, including habit disorders (e.g., sleep, bedwetting, stuttering), conduct disorders (e.g., hyperactivity), anxieties and depression, developmental disorders (e.g., autism, physical or mental disability, and parent-child relationship disorders (e.g., failure to thrive, child abuse). Indeed, training parents to become "cotherapists" by teaching them new parenting skills is considered to be the single most promising treatment for reducing conduct problems in young children (Kazdin, 1987).

Parent education consists of one or more of four types of activities: (1) gaining information (through lecture, group discussion, or readings); (2) changing beliefs (through discussion, use of diary, self-analysis activities); (3) acquiring new skills (through demonstrations, role playing, readings, discussion); and (4) solving problems (through homework, observations, discussions; Fine & Henry, 1989). The format of parent education also varies widely, including group treatment programs, work with individual parent-child dyads, and parent self-help programs.

Parent Education Models

Although a variety of educational approaches exist, there are three major types of parent education: reflective, Adlerian, and behavioral (Medway, 1989). The reflective model is exemplified by Gordon's PET program. The emphasis is on teaching the parents to become more aware of, to understand, and to accept the child's feelings. In addition, it is designed to get parents to become more cognizant of their own feelings during interactions with their children. This approach is sometimes called the "communication model."

The Adlerian model, based on the theories of Alfred Adler, emphasizes understanding why a child is misbehaving, promotes cooperative family interactions, and recommends control through such disciplinary techniques as teaching logical consequences. This technique involves letting children learn for themselves. For example, if a child refuses to wear a coat when it is cold outside, one lets her go without it so she will get cold and want to wear one on similar days in the future. The STEP program is a prime example of this approach (Dinkmeyer & McKay, 1976).

The third parenting approach involves behavioral training. Such training focuses on observable behavior and reveals to the parent those actions that are maintaining the child's negative behavior. Behavioral training programs rely heavily on social learning principles in general and operant conditioning specifically. Parents are taught new skills such as how to avoid reinforcing undesired behaviors and how to effectively reinforce desired behaviors (Wierson & Forehand, 1994). Behavior modification–based programs typically teach the use of such skills as differential social reinforcement (providing attention contingent on child compliance and withdrawing attention if the child is noncompliant) and how to use certain disciplinary techniques (e.g., ignoring, commands, time-out).

Social learning–based family intervention programs expand on behavior modification principles by including as their basic elements (1) the accurate identification and labeling of problematic child behavior, (2) refocusing from preoccupation on negative behavior to emphasis on positive behavior, (3) administering effective social reinforcement, (4) enhancing parent-child communication, (5) learning to anticipate and solve new problems, and (6) teaching alternatives to physical punishment (Miller & Prinz, 1990).

Discouragement of the use of physical punishment is a particular challenge in parent education programs because it is used so widely and parents often have strong positive attitudes about using it. Approximately 80 to 90 percent of all parents of young children in the United States at least occasionally spank their children (Wauchope & Straus, 1990). To reduce its use, parent educators often cite a litany of problems associated with spanking, including the fact that it models and is associated with subsequent aggression, causes resentment, does not teach the child how to behave, and in rare cases, can lead to child abuse. Parent training programs often teach that there are more effective techniques that are less punitive and authoritarian, such as reasoning, using time-out, or teaching natural consequences.

Today, the behavioral parent-training programs commonly used in most clinical practices are similar, although they were developed independently by psychologists Rex Forehand, Gerald Patterson, and Robert Wahler. Covering the ages from about three until eight or ten, each of the programs is designed to provide parents with a social learning approach to changing child behavior. Parents are taught to attend to positive behavior either by providing social reinforcement or awarding points for good behavior and to use time-out or ignoring to punish undesired behavior. Training for parent-child dyads or family units typically involves from five to ten or more sessions.

One such program, based on the Wahler model, is the Early Intervention Project (EIP) originating in Chicago. The EIP is designed for parents of children with a range of behavioral and developmental problems. The most common presenting complaints are noncompliant or aggressive behavior and problems with eating, toilet training, or dressing. The program involves two components: teaching the use of differential social reinforcement and a supportive discussion group for mothers. Parents are referred to the program by pediatricians and other professionals and come from a wide range of racial and SES groups. Thousands of families have been successfully trained by the program.

Like all parent education programs, the training is not universally successful. The central procedure for evaluating the effectiveness of the program consisted of observing mothers and their children during twenty-minute play sessions, both before and during the behavioral training. The only instruction given during the play sessions was that every two minutes mothers must direct their children to play with a different toy. The first three observations provided baseline information about the level of child compliance and noncompliance. Subsequently, the mothers were instructed in the use of differential social reinforcement. Intervention 1 sessions then began and continued until children attained the criterion of 85 percent compliance to maternal commands. At that point there was one "reversal" session in which mothers were instructed to attend only to noncompliance (to demonstrate what would happen if they lapsed into their former ways). Finally, Intervention 2 sessions consisted of reinstating the use of differential social reinforcement until the children once again attained an 85 percent compliance rate.

In a study of the program's effectiveness, 32 percent dropped out before completing it (Holden, Lavigne, & Cameron, 1990); the 68 percent completion rate is similar to that of many other programs (Medway, 1989). For those who completed the training, it took an average of twenty-five sessions until their children attained the criterion of 85 percent compliance to maternal commands. The dramatic increase in the rate of cooperative behavior, coupled with a complementary decrease in oppositional behavior, is shown in Figure 6.2.

Just as the EIP program was successful at changing children's rate of compliance, parent education has repeatedly been found to be an effective technique to reduce child behavior problems and change parental attitudes and behavior (Medway, 1989; Wahler & Dumas, 1989). The core premise is that parents play a central role in the acquisition and maintenance of certain problematic child behaviors such as conduct disorders. Behavioral par-

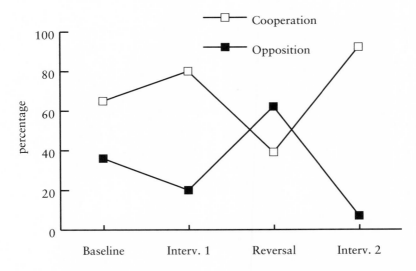

FIGURE 6.2   Mean Percentage of Cooperative and Oppositional Behavior Across the Four Phases in Children Whose Parents Completed a Parent Training Program. (Reprinted, with permission, from G. W. Holden, V. V. Lavigne, and A. M. Cameron, 1990, *Journal of Clinical Child Psychology, 19*, 2–8.)

ent-training programs have been found to be effective in producing immediate behavioral changes in children (Kazdin, 1987). Although most evaluation studies follow the parent-child dyad for only a short time after treatment, some parent training programs have been found to be effective several years after treatment (Medway, 1989). A side benefit is that there are sometimes positive changes in nontargeted behavior or sibling behavior. In the case of children with severe conduct disorders, however, or in multistressed families, the outcome is typically not so favorable (Miller & Prinz, 1990; Wahler & Dumas, 1989).

Summary

Researchers have identified more than a dozen key characteristics associated with effective parenting. In addition to being involved and having such attributes as warmth and sensitivity, effective parenting requires a keen ability to make appropriate behavioral adjustments in ongoing interactions. Indeed, effectiveness in parenting often involves the dynamic process of balancing alternative concerns. This process is captured by the concept of dialectics. Despite the importance of key parental attributes and the flexibility to make appropriate behavioral adjustments, child-rearing effectiveness also depends on child characteristics and the support of others.

Parent education programs have a long history of assisting parents. The underlying assumption of such programs is that parents are capable of modifying their behavior. Different types of parent education program attempt to make parents more competent by teaching new behaviors, child-rearing skills, or interactional styles. If more individuals received such training, either before they became parents or after, it is likely that there would be a reduction in the rate of problematic parent-child relationships and dysfunctional parenting, which is the focus of the next chapter.

7

When Parenting Goes Awry: Child Maltreatment

Father is charged in death of infant son.
Mother gets eighty years for holding child in scalding water.
Ex-husband beat boy to death, woman says.
Parent charged with sexual abuse.

Newspaper headlines such as these appear all too frequently in communities around the country. To some observers, especially nonparents, the phenomenon of child abuse may appear to be an anomaly: Why would parents or other adults willfully harm children? Child maltreatment is the most visible indicator of flagrant dysfunctional parenting, and it is a phenomenon that is becoming increasingly common in our society. On the basis of research conducted mostly since the 1970s, researchers now have a much better understanding of why some parents maltreat their children, which in turn has provided a better understanding of what is involved in healthy parenting.

Child Maltreatment Through the Ages

Child maltreatment is not a new phenomenon, and it is not localized to particular geographic or cultural regions. Historians and anthropologists agree that children have been maltreated since antiquity (Ariès, 1962; deMause, 1974; Sommerville, 1982). Societies have tolerated or even sanctioned a wide range of atrocities to children that parents—and others—have committed for thousands of years. A few examples of widespread practices serve to illustrate the nature and prevalence of child maltreatment.

Infanticide, as a method of culling out unwanted or undesired children, is a practice that has been and continues to be practiced widely. The Bible has references to a variety of forms of infanticide and murder of children, including ritual sacrifice, interment of live newborns in the foundations of buildings and bridges, and the widespread massacre of children both at the time of Moses' birth and later when Jesus' birth was prophesied. Infanticide was routinely practiced in ancient Greece, Rome, Arabia, and China

(Zigler & Hall, 1989). Both Plato and Aristotle advocated the destruction of defective newborns, and the Greek physician Sonorus, in his second-century A.D. book, included a section entitled, "How to recognize the newborn that is worth rearing" (Ruhrah, 1925, p. 6).

Various other documents allude to common practices of the physical abuse of children. A Persian physician named Rhazes wrote in A.D. 900 that many children who lived in the harems of Baghdad had been intentionally struck. Sonorus wrote of the need to carefully choose wet nurses, not just on the basis of health, age, and breast size but also on the basis of their personality. He recommended finding an even-tempered woman so she would be less likely to drop or roughly handle the baby. In 1684, a guidebook for physicians warned that swelling in infants' heads "may be due to the nurse's fault in letting the child fall and dashing it against a thing." The Dowager Countess Mountcastell included in her 1823 manual for mothers the advice, "Blows on the head from harsh instruction have been suspected to produce water on the brain, and the mode in which some people gratify their anger towards children by shaking them violently might also lead to serious consequences."

Rough handling was not unusual in American homes during the colonial days, as suggested in Chapter 1. Harsh discipline and physical punishment were commonly practiced for the purpose of instructing children. Parents spanked in order to "drive the devil out" and teach the child to behave appropriately. Maltreatment in the name of educating the young has been widely practiced for centuries in many countries. Ariès (1962) recounted many of the disciplinary techniques commonly used in European schools beginning in the fifteenth century. Use of the birch rod, whippings, and other bodily assaults were frequent occurrences as punishment for behavioral and scholastic infractions.

Sexual child abuse, primarily of females, also has a long history. During the Roman Republic, the doctrine of *ius primae noctis* gave the father of the family the right to have sexual intercourse with any female member of his household who was socially his inferior. That was similar to the eighteenth-century French principle of *droit du seigneur*, or "right of the senior," which allowed the head of the household to sleep with whomever he desired. That right was immortalized in Mozart's opera *The Marriage of Figaro*. In that opera, Figaro, on the eve of his wedding, outsmarted his master's attempts to seduce his fiancee. The opera was banned for a time because it was considered too subversive.

Operas not only portrayed maltreatment, they also caused it. An institutionalized form of maltreatment occurred with the creation of *castrati*: males who were emasculated prior to puberty to preserve their high-pitched voices. Although males have been castrated for centuries as eunuchs or for penal, military, religious, or medical reasons, it is estimated that thousands of boys became castrati in Italy solely for musical reasons. This surgery was conducted from the early seventeenth century until the end of the eighteenth century (Peschel & Peschel, 1987). Besides the creation of voices recognized for their brilliance and lyricism, the effects of the castration included various physiological and physical abnormalities, not to mention psychological problems.

When it comes to bodily mutilation, females have been targets far more often than males. This is most dramatically evidenced in the religious and cultural practice of clitoridectomy, euphemistically called "female circumcision." The procedure involves removing part or all of the clitoris sometime between infancy and puberty. The operation has been, and continues to be, practiced in many parts of Africa and the Middle East. Because the operation is often performed in unsterile conditions without anesthesia, it is painful and can result in a variety of health problems, including infection, infertility, or even death. When these "circumcised" women later engage in sexual intercourse, they experience considerable pain. Despite the obvious cruelty and frequent calls for abolishing it, the practice has proved difficult to end because it is deeply enmeshed in the culture. Many men will not marry a woman unless she is circumcised, because the clitoridectomy is thought to ensure faithfulness and family stability by eliminating all sexual pleasure for the woman (Hosken, 1978).

Child labor is yet another example of culturally sanctioned child maltreatment that continues today in many parts of the world. This practice first became widespread in the latter part of the eighteenth century during what has been called the Industrial Revolution. Children as young as five years old were forced to work in factories and other settings. In the nineteenth and the early part of the twentieth century, children in the United States labored on farms as well as factories (sweatshops), restaurants, and mines. Textile mills received the most attention from children's rights activists, because children as young as five years old toiled long hours in dangerous conditions. Although U.S. laws have long prohibited child labor, the practice continues, most commonly in the form of migrant labor. In many other parts of the world, especially developing nations, child labor continues to be widely practiced.

As these examples indicate, children have been maltreated throughout history by familial, cultural, religious, and economic institutions (deMause, 1974; Sommerville, 1982). It is only during the twentieth century that there has been a dramatic shift toward empathy for the welfare of children and an awareness of the problem of child maltreatment (Sears, 1975; Starr, 1988). The remainder of this chapter will focus on the narrower question of why some parents maltreat their children.

The Four Faces of Child Maltreatment

The study of child maltreatment is a relatively new area of scientific inquiry. Although there were occasional medical reports of fractured bones and subdural hematomas (bruises) in children published in the 1940s and 1950s, professional attention to the topic began to coalesce only in 1962 when the problem was given the label of *battered child syndrome* (Kempe, Silverman, Steele, Droegemueller, & Silver, 1962). Kempe advocated for that term because, as a pediatrician, he was alarmed at the relatively high incidence of nonaccidental fractures and other outcomes of battery. However, as more attention was devoted to the problem, it became increasingly clear that battering, or *physical abuse* as it came to be called, represented only the most obvious form of child maltreatment. The term *maltreatment* is preferable to the more commonly used term *child abuse* because it includes both acts of commission (e.g., hitting) and acts of omission (e.g., failing to protect the child), both of which could result in injury or trauma to a child. Three other major forms of maltreatment have also been recognized to be widespread: sexual abuse, neglect, and psychological maltreatment.

Largely because physical abuse is the form of maltreatment most likely to leave observable signs, it is the best understood and most extensively researched type of maltreatment. It is typically defined as "an act of commission where a parent or other caregiver does something injurious to a child" (Starr, 1988, p. 122); however, the terms *injury*, *substantial*, and *harm* are ambiguous. The major indicators of abuse include bruises, fractures, and burns. These injuries are mostly caused by three types of actions: hitting with an object (belt, strap, switch, stick, or paddle); hitting with a hand; or propelling (throwing, dropping, pushing; Johnson & Showers, 1985). Other common forms of physical abuse include violently shaking a baby or child (the "shaken baby syndrome") and burning a child with a cigarette, stove, iron, or hot water.

In comparison to physical abuse, child neglect sounds more benign. It is not. Because it refers to the failure of a caregiver to provide the necessary physical and social ingredients for normal, healthy development, it can result in pervasive, long-term problems. Neglect occurs in three domains. Some parents are derelict in attending to the physical needs of their children by failing to provide for nutrition, clothing, or shelter. Nutritional neglect may involve providing inadequate caloric intake for a child or adhering to bizarre diets. A second form of neglect is ignoring the child's medical or health needs. Parents who refuse, for religious reasons, to provide their children with medical attention when it is obviously needed are a prime example. The third manifestation of neglect is a disregard of the supervisory role parents must play to ensure their children's safety. Neglecting to use car seats for infants and young children is perhaps the most common form of failure to protect a child from potential harm.

Sexual abuse has only received sustained research attention since the late 1970s. Given the nature of the act, it is extremely difficult to study. Sexual abuse is commonly defined as either (1) forced or coerced sexual behavior imposed on a child by an adult or (2) sexual activity between a child and a significantly older person (e.g., three years). A wide range of actions constitute sexual abuse. Sexual abuse includes actions involving contact as well as actions that do not. Contact can range from a single touch to some form of repeated penetration. Noncontact abuse includes adults exposing themselves to children or stimulating children with pornography. Consequently, determining whether sexual abuse has occurred depends on the age of the child, the age of the perpetrator, and the actions involved.

Psychological maltreatment is the most recent form of maltreatment to be identified. The essence of this form of abuse is degradation of the self-worth of a child resulting in long-term negative consequences for that child. The first international conference on the topic, held in 1983, developed a "working generic" definition:

> Psychological maltreatment of children and youth consists of acts of omission and commission which are judged by community standards and professional expertise to be psychologically damaging. Such acts are committed by individuals, singly or collectively, who by their characteristics (e.g., age, status) are in a position of differential power that renders a child vulnerable. Such acts damage immediately or ultimately the behavioral, cognitive, affective, or physical functioning of the child (Brassard, Germain, & Hart, 1987, p. 6).

The nature of psychological maltreatment makes it especially hard to study. Physical evidence, such as can be found with physical abuse, sexual abuse, or neglect, is missing. As the definition suggests, the phenomenon has no clear boundaries, it can change over time and cultures, and its effects are not necessarily observed immediately; the future harmful results are probabilistic rather than certain. For these reasons, as well as the inherent problems of collecting accurate data, there exist few empirical investigations (Clausen & Crittenden, 1991; Egeland, Sroufe, & Erickson, 1983). Currently, psychological maltreatment is thought to be manifested in five fundamental ways (Hart & Brassard, 1994); these are listed and defined in Table 7.1.

One of the most revealing accounts of psychological maltreatment comes from the autobiography of Pulitzer prize winner Richard Rhodes (1990). According to Rhodes, he and his brother were victims of psychological maltreatment in addition to being neglected and physically abused by their stepmother. The school-aged boys were most often victimized by being degraded and terrorized, but they were also ignored and exploited financially by their stepmother. After more than two years of the maltreatment, the malnourished boys escaped to the police.

Until recently, different manifestations of maltreatment were studied separately, because most child abuse experts did not recognize their interrelations. Today, the predominant view of researchers in the area is that

TABLE 7.1   Five Basic Types of Psychological Maltreatment

Type	*Definition*	*Examples*
Spurning	Rejecting or degrading child	Labeling as inferior, shaming, ridiculing, humiliating, or singling child out for criticism
Terrorizing	Verbally assaulting, bullying, creating a climate of fear	Threatening to hurt or abandon child; leaving child in unsafe setting
Isolating	Keeping child away from normal social experiences	Locking child in room after school to avoid peers
Denying emotional responsiveness	Ignoring child's attempts and need for interaction; showing no emotion in interactions	Failing to express affection; being detached and uninvolved
Exploiting or corrupting	Teaching child a socially deviant pattern of behavior	Promoting aggression, sex, delinquency, or substance abuse; degrading those racially or ethnically different

SOURCE: S. N. Hart and M. Brassard, 1994. *Draft guidelines for psychosocial evaluation of suspected psychological maltreatment in children and adolescents*. American Professional Society on the Abuse of Children. Reprinted by permission.

psychological maltreatment is inherent in the other three forms of maltreatment (Hart & Brassard, 1987). The actions that constitute neglect as well as physical or sexual abuse are psychologically damaging in themselves. Moreover, it is suspected that many doses of psychological maltreatment compound the trauma associated with any single incident of physical abuse or neglect. The relations among the forms of maltreatment are further complicated by the suspicion that two or even all three of the types of maltreatment co-occur. Although there is no reliable empirical evidence of the rates of co-occurrence, there is plenty of anecdotal support. Rhodes (1990) provided a firsthand account of how his stepmother engaged in multiple expressions of psychological maltreatment, along with periodic physical abuse and nutritional neglect.

Statistics

For a variety of reasons, determining accurate rates of child maltreatment is almost impossible. Neither offenders nor victims are likely to be forthright in reporting the maltreatment; available estimates of maltreatment can be faulted on definitional or methodological grounds. Current estimates are based on three types of sources: (1) national surveys; (2) reports from schools, social service agencies, neighbors, relatives, medical personnel, police, or victims; and (3) extrapolation from small samples. The fact that different sources typically use different definitions and criteria for maltreatment as well as different sampling techniques means that few estimates are similar. The National Center on Child Abuse and Neglect (NCCAN) and the National Committee for the Prevention of Child Abuse (NCPCA) are two of the leading child abuse centers in the United States, and their data provide the best approximations of the scope of the problem in this country. However, it is likely that the incidence of maltreatment is greatly underestimated owing to failure to report incidents, lack of awareness that maltreatment has occurred, inaccurate recall, and untruthful reports. The one exception to this tendency of underreporting may occur in the case of child custody disputes, an area in which there is indication that fathers are sometimes falsely accused of sexual abuse (Ceci & Bruck, 1993).

The Incidence of Maltreatment

Three types of data are provided concerning the incidence of maltreatment: reports of maltreatment, confirmed cases, and estimates of abuse. In 1991, there were almost 1.8 million reports of child maltreatment, involving an estimated 2.7 million children. This represents about 4 percent of the child population (NCCAN, 1993). Typically, about one-third of child abuse reports are substantiated, resulting in about 862,000 confirmed child victims in 1991 (NCCAN, 1993). However, other sources estimate the rate to be considerably higher. Some estimates of physical abuse alone put the rate at 15 percent of U.S. children. A midfigure estimate of 11 percent means almost seven million children are physically abused each year (Straus & Gelles, 1988).

The statistics that are available indicate that of the four types of maltreatment, child neglect is the most prevalent. In 1991, 44 percent of the substantiated child victims had been neglected, compared with 24 percent who were physically abused and 15 percent who had been sexually abused. Only 6 percent of the children were victims of psychological maltreatment, according to NCCAN statistics (1993); this low rate reflects the difficulties in reporting, recognizing, and confirming psychological maltreatment. Similarly, it is likely that a great many cases of neglected and sexually abused children do not get reported. Many children and adults do not disclose their victimization for a variety of reasons such as fear, shame, or lack of understanding of the wrongfulness. Depending on the study, from 6 to 62 percent of adult females and 3 to 31 percent of adult males have reported that at some point in their childhood they were sexually abused (Finkelhor, 1987). These widely divergent estimates are due to differing definitions of sexual abuse, methods of inquiry, sample size and characteristics, and location.

One statistic that is frequently replicated is the relation between SES and child maltreatment. Although people in all SES groups maltreat and abuse their children, the rates are significantly higher in groups with low SES (e.g., NCCAN, 1993). Extrapolations from studies with small samples provide alarming implications. In one study of 161 women with lower SES, 29 percent reported they were abused as children (Egeland, Jacobvitz, & Sroufe, 1988). In another study of 102 poor adolescent mothers, 15 percent reported being severely beaten as a child, 12 percent reported physical neglect, and 17 percent reported being sexually abused (Zuravin, 1988). It is estimated that in poor families, compared with more affluent ones, children are 3.5 times more likely to be physically abused and 6 times more likely to be sexually abused (Sedlak, 1988, cited in National Research Council, 1993). Although these studies are subject to sample selectivity and self-report biases, they are suggestive of the widespread problem in low-income communities.

The statistic that is most alarming is a relative one: The rate of maltreatment is increasing. In 1970, it was estimated that some forty thousand children were being physically abused (Steele, 1970). Twenty years later, the number of confirmed cases was 205,000. Between 1985 and 1990, the number of reports of maltreatment rose between 3 and 8 percent each year. The increase is due to at least four factors: (1) new laws, (2) heightened public awareness, (3) expanded social service agencies, and (4) increased rates of maltreatment. It is difficult to tease out just how much of the increase in reporting is due to a real increase in the rate of maltreatment. One piece of evidence is the number of fatalities in children attributed to physical maltreatment. Over the five-year period from 1986 to 1990, there was an increase each year in the number of child fatalities attributed to abuse (NCPCA, 1991). Although some of the increase may well be due to greater awareness and more accurate attributions concerning the cause of death, these data provide the best evidence to suggest there may be a real increase in rates of abuse. The increase in rates of reports of child maltreatment and child fatalities from 1985 to 1990 is depicted in Figure 7.1.

There is evidence that maltreatment is also rampant around the world, although it is difficult to estimate the incidence because few nations have adequately researched the problem (Daro, 1992). Despite the dearth of data, there is evidence that infants, children, and adolescents around the world are victims of many forms of abuse and neglect. Several examples will suffice. Systematic infanticide is commonly practiced in such countries as India and China, where amniocentesis and ultrasound scanners are used for the purpose of identifying female fetuses, which are undesirable. In

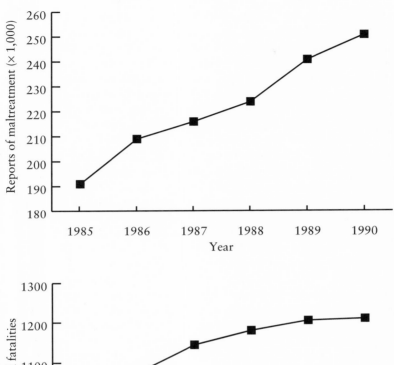

FIGURE 7.1 Changes in Rates of Reports of Child Maltreatment and Maltreatment Fatalities. (Reprinted, with permission, from National Center for the Prevention of Child Abuse, 1993.)

China alone it is estimated that up to 1.7 million female fetuses are aborted each year (Kristof, 1993).

Harsh physical punishment and other forms of physical child abuse are widespread in many countries (Daro, 1992). For instance, in some Asian countries, such as Hong Kong and Malaysia, physical punishment of children by caning is practiced both by parents and by the judicial system. Sexual abuse and child prostitution are also widespread around the globe (Campagna & Poffenberger, 1988). Child neglect can be readily found among children raised in poverty and, more dramatically, in the estimated 100 million children who grow up on the streets. Street children are particularly endemic in Latin American countries: Brazil alone may have up to 17 million such children (Campos et al., 1994).

Victims and Perpetrators

Who are the victims? The child's age is an important determinant. A majority of the victims are young children, although teenagers are not immune. In 1991 about 40 percent of the victims of maltreatment were younger than six years old; a total of 63 percent of the victims were less than ten years old (NCCAN, 1993). However, about 20 percent were from ten to thirteen years of age, and 16 percent were fourteen or older. In the case of physical abuse, young children between three months and six years are most at risk (Wolfner & Gelles, 1993). Boys and girls are about equally likely to be victimized by all forms of maltreatment except in the case of sexual abuse. Incidence reports indicate that females are victimized in 80 to 90 percent of sexual abuse cases (NCCAN, 1993). When all forms of abuse are combined, females represent 54 percent of the victims, and males, 46 percent. With regard to race or ethnic group of the victim, white children were victims in 55 percent of the confirmed cases, African-Americans in 26 percent, and Hispanics in 9 percent (NCCAN, 1993).

About 80 percent of the perpetrators of child maltreatment are parents; other relatives compose the next most common category, with 11 percent of the cases (NCCAN, 1993). Mothers are more likely to maltreat their children than fathers, but there is a simple explanation for this: Mothers are far more likely to be the primary caregivers and thus spend considerably more time with the children than do fathers. The exception is sexual abuse; males commit the crime in about 95 percent of cases involving female victims and 80 percent of cases involving male victims. Stepfathers are also overrepresented as perpetrators of sexual abuse in proportion to their incidence in society. One study found that 17 percent of women who lived with stepfathers had been abused, compared to only 2 percent of women who lived with their biological fathers (Russell, 1984).

The Etiology of Child Maltreatment

What causes a parent to maltreat a child? If a child is unwanted or rejected, it is not hard to understand why that child is at risk. However, such a simple explanation does not account for most of the cases. Various theories about the etiology of maltreatment have been developed. Because most of the available evidence concerns physical abuse, most theories and research address that form of maltreatment. The four most prominent theories of physical abuse will be presented, followed by a review of research on the topic.

Theories of Parental Maltreatment of Children

To date, four major theories of why parents commit physical abuse have been dominant. These theories are the psychiatric model, the sociological model, the social interaction model, and the ecological model.

The first theory of maltreatment was the *psychiatric model:* Maltreatment is inflicted by mentally ill or emotionally disturbed parents. According to this theory, abusive parents are substantially different from the rest of the parenting population in terms of their mental health. Some of the first studies in the area did confirm that psychopathology (e.g., psychosis, neurosis, schizophrenia, anxiety states, and depression) could be identified in abusive parents (Steele & Pollock, 1968). The implication of this theory was that maltreating parents shared a distinctive "child abuse personality."

In contrast to the psychiatric model, the *sociological model* takes the position that abusive parents are not abnormal but merely respond to the circumstances in which they live. Culture, social class, poverty, stress, isolation, and lack of social supports all conspire to predispose parents to abuse. In our society, individuals are constantly exposed to aggression and violence on television and at the movies. Moreover, most parents use physical punishment to discipline their children. Consequently, aggression and violence are commonplace and accepted in our society. It only takes a small step, according to the sociological model of abuse, to escalate from a disciplinary response to an abusive act.

A third theoretical approach to the causes of maltreatment is the *social interaction model,* which attempts to understand abuse by focusing on the quality of behavioral interactions (Reid, 1986). Because abuse occurs within social interactions, those events and the underlying processes must be the center of attention, according to this model. Efforts to reveal these processes have largely centered on careful observations of parent-child interactions and investigations into the beliefs of abusive parents.

The last major theoretical approach represents the most comprehensive model of abuse, because it was designed to encompass multiple explanations of abuse by integrating divergent etiological viewpoints. Based largely on Bronfenbrenner's (1979) theoretical approach, the *ecological model* provides a way of simultaneously considering (1) the characteristics of the parent (e.g., age, irritability); (2) the characteristics of the child (e.g., difficulty); (3) the ongoing interactions in the family (e.g., disciplinary practices, poor marital relations); (4) the neighborhood and community in which the family lives (e.g., sources of stress and support systems); and (5) the general culture and cultural beliefs that influence the other systems (e.g., attitudes toward violence and children's rights, society's acceptance of physical punishment as a legitimate form of discipline; Belsky, 1993). The model predicts that maltreatment is likely to occur when there is a mismatch, or conflict, between two or more of the components. The mismatch might be between the characteristics of the parent (e.g., stress level or personality) and the child (e.g., difficult temperament) or between aspects of the family (e.g., needing support) and the neighborhood or community (e.g., providing little support).

Empirical Evidence

How well are the four theories of the causes of maltreatment supported by the data? The theories will be evaluated by examining the results of investigations into the characteristics of parents, abused children, and families.

Parent Characteristics.   Four types of variables within the parent have received some systematic attention. These are the parents' psychological and emotional characteristics, biological predispositions, cognitive characteristics, and history of abuse. Much of the research concerning parents has followed the psychiatric model and investigated various mental health, psychological, and emotional characteristics of abusive parents. The early view that most abusive parents were mentally ill has not been substantiated by research. Although poor parental mental health has been associated with maltreatment, chronic mental illness in a parent is estimated to account for only about 10 percent of the cases (Starr, 1988). Schizophrenia is most commonly associated with the propensity to abuse, but the likelihood of abuse depends on the severity of the illness and its chronicity (Sameroff & Seifer, 1983).

More evidence has linked less severe psychological and emotional problems with physical abuse. In particular, feelings of anger, low self-esteem, rigidity, isolation, and stress, along with poor adjustment, impulsivity, and low frustration tolerance, have been linked to abuse (Bugental et al., 1989; Milner & Chilamkurti, 1991; Trickett & Kuczynski, 1986; Wolfe, 1987). Similarly, studies have found that abusive mothers are more depressed, anxious, unhappy, and apathetic than comparison mothers (Lahey, Conger, Atkinson, & Treiber, 1984; Milner & Robertson, 1990). However, not all investigations find significant differences on emotional variables; when such differences are found, it is not clear that the variables are causally related to the abuse.

Abusive parents have also been assessed on physiological indices to see whether they may have a biological predisposition for maltreatment. In particular, it is thought that some adults may be hyperreactive to their children's negative behavior and then lash out at them (Vasta, 1982). Some support for this hypothesis has been found in the physiological characteristics (e.g., skin conductance, respiration rates) of abusive parents and adults identified as at risk for abusive behavior (Bugental, Blue, & Cruzcosa, 1989; Frodi & Lamb, 1980; Pruitt & Erickson, 1985).

A number of investigators have adopted the parental beliefs approach in an effort to determine whether abusive parents perceive and think about their children differently from nonabusive parents. In particular, perceptions, attributions, knowledge, expectations, problem solving, beliefs, and attitudes have been studied. Early clinical reports suggested that this was a promising area of study: Abusive parents were found to hold negative views of their children and perceive them as intentionally disruptive and disobedient as well as to hold unrealistic and high expectations for their children (Helfer & Kempe, 1988).

Subsequent studies have found that physically abusive mothers are likely to attribute misbehavior to their children's personality and to view positive behaviors (e.g., successfully finishing a puzzle) as the consequence of external or situational factors (Larrance & Twentyman, 1983). Furthermore, abusive mothers in another sample were more likely than comparison mothers to perceive child misbehavior as designed intentionally to annoy them (Bauer & Twentyman, 1985). Similarly, abusing mothers rated videotaped scenes of child behavior as more negative than other mothers (Wood-Shuman & Cone, 1986). However, not all studies have found reliable differences between the attributions of abusive and normal mothers (Rosenberg & Reppucci, 1983).

Another area of social cognition that has received attention is child-rearing knowledge. Some studies have found that physically abusive mothers have less knowledge about child rearing than comparison mothers (Stainer & Thieman, 1991). That knowledge deficit may manifest itself in two other ways: inaccurate expectations and inability to effectively and efficiently solve child-rearing problems. Abusive mothers' expectations about their children have been repeatedly studied, with mixed results. Some studies have reported that abusive mothers do hold unrealistically high expectations for their children (Azar, Robinson, Hekimian, & Twentyman, 1984), yet other work has found that abusive mothers hold low expectations (Perry, Wells, & Doran, 1983). Other researchers have reported no differences or a mixture of expecting too little and too much of children given their ages (e.g., Kravitz & Driscoll, 1983). These conflicting results most likely reflect both methodological and conceptual problems with this area of inquiry.

Problem solving is yet another domain related to lack of knowledge about children and parenting. In one study, it was found that maltreating mothers were less adept at solving child-rearing problems than comparison mothers, in terms of being unable to generate as many solutions and types of solutions as nonabusing mothers (Azar et al., 1984). With regard to attitudes, abusive mothers have been found to hold harsher authoritarian attitudes and more positive attitudes toward the use of physical punishment than nonabusers (Simons, Whitbeck, Conger, & Chyi-In, 1991; Trickett & Susman, 1988). Abusive mothers also tend to perceive that they have less control over their children than other mothers (Bugental et al., 1989, 1990).

The final characteristic of abusive parents that has received some attention is the parents' history of abuse in their family of origin. It is commonly believed that a major cause of maltreatment is that the abusive parent was abused as a child. This history of childhood abuse, also called the *intergenerational transmission of abuse,* has frequently been mentioned in the literature. Empirical studies have reported rates of abuse by parents who were abused as children ranging from a low of 7 percent to a high of 100 percent (Gil, 1970; Steele & Pollock, 1968).

One of the reasons for such disparity is the poor quality of many of the studies (Widom, 1989). One estimate of the rate of intergenerational transmission is that approximately 30 ± 5 percent of abused children will grow up to abuse their offspring (Kaufman & Zigler, 1989). However, that estimate of 30 percent is based on only a few studies. Some investigators believe the rate is higher. Consider the results of a carefully conducted longitudinal study: It was found that 38 percent of abused mothers maltreated their children but that another 36 percent of the mothers provided only "borderline" care (Egeland et al., 1988). Evidently, being abused as a child puts one at risk for becoming an abusive parent, but as Joan Kaufman and Edward Zigler (1989) have argued, the path between these two points is not necessarily direct or inevitable.

It is easy to understand continuity in abuse across generations. Children who have been rejected, emotionally deprived, or physically or psychologically assaulted may not have been exposed to any adequate parenting models or developed secure attachments and the psychological resources needed to be giving, sensitive parents. But what about the majority of children raised in dysfunctional families who do not maltreat their own children? According to one study, mothers who break the cycle of abuse are more likely to be in intact, stable, and satisfying relationships; to have experienced a supportive relationship with an adult during childhood; and to have received long-term therapy that enables them to come to an understanding of their previous abuse (Egeland et al., 1988).

Several alternative mechanisms have been proposed to account for the intergenerational transmission of abuse. A behavioral genetics explanation might be that an "abuse gene" gets passed on; however, such an explanation cannot account for the observation that many times only one child in a family is singled out for abuse (Bugental et al., 1989). Better explanations for transmission come from social learning theory. Children learn about parenting from observing their own parents. If a parent uses excessive physical punishment or inappropriate sexual practices, the child may accept those behaviors as appropriate and normal. There is now evidence that attitudes toward the use of harsh parenting can be transferred directly from parents to children (Simons et al., 1991). Children may also learn from their parents inappropriate expectations of children and poor parent-child communication patterns.

Transmission of a high-stress lifestyle can also account for some of the abuse. The experience of growing up in a violent, abusive home could contribute to aggression in other ways. One longitudinal study determined that children who were physically abused as children developed biased and deficient forms of social information processing (Dodge, Bates, & Pettit, 1990). Those deficiencies then predicted the development of aggressive behavior and presumably will be linked to abusive parenting in the future.

The transactional theory helps to explain why not all children in a family are abused. Children with particular characteristics, such as those who are temperamentally difficult or at risk for some other reason (e.g., premature, disabled) are likely to be the victims. The transactional model suggests that parents who abuse such children do so only after a history of stressful and troublesome interactions that eventually escalate into abusive incidents.

Child Characteristics. Instead of looking for the cause of abuse in the parent, some researchers have argued that certain child characteristics are frequently associated with abuse (Friedrich & Einbender, 1983). Therefore, according to the child effects approach, it can be argued that children contribute to their own abuse by having characteristics that make them difficult to raise. The characteristics most commonly associated with physical abuse are the child's age, prematurity, difficult temperament, and mental or physical disabilities.

Younger children are more at risk for physical abuse owing to their impact on the stress level in the household, the sheer amount of time spent with parents or caregivers, and the fact that parents are more likely to become frustrated with a young child they cannot reason with. Young children also lack the physical strength or durability to withstand much physical punishment or force (Taylor & Maurer, 1985).

Another child characteristic associated with risk is difficult temperament. Abused children are sometimes observed to be difficult children in terms of being unresponsive, inappropriate, fussy, hyperactive, and resistant to control (Bugental et al., 1990; Trickett & Kuczynski, 1986). However, it is not known whether such children were born with difficult temperaments or the difficulty developed as a consequence of interacting with the abusive parent. One piece of evidence suggests the latter explanation. In the longitudinal study mentioned previously, no relation was found between children's early health problems or their mothers' perception of their temperament and the subsequent likelihood of physical abuse (Dodge et al., 1990).

Of the child characteristics associated with abuse, premature birth has received the most attention. Several reasons for the link between prematurity and abuse have been proposed. Parents initially are separated from the newborn, often for prolonged periods of time, resulting in difficulties in developing a close relationship and a secure attachment. Premature infants are also not as physically attractive as full-term infants and are more likely to have an especially aversive cry, which some researchers believe could precipitate an abusive incident (Frodi, 1983). Using a similar rationale, investigators have looked for abuse in children with other developmental handicaps, such as physical anomalies and mental or physical disabilities. A few studies have found links with abuse, but most studies are inconclusive, methodologically flawed, or have failed to find a consistent relation between handicap and abuse (Ammerman, 1991; Starr, 1988).

Family and Socioeconomic Characteristics.   Researchers following the social interaction theoretical approach have accumulated evidence concerning the distinct qualities of the parent-child interactions and relationships in physically abusive families. For instance, several studies have found that abusive families have less-satisfactory relationships and interactions than comparison families (Lahey, Conger, Atkinson, & Treiber, 1984). It directly follows from attachment theory that infants whose mothers are inaccessible, unresponsive, or inappropriately responsive to them should develop insecure attachments. Indeed, maltreated children are more likely to have insecure attachments with their mothers than comparison children. In a review of ten studies that used the Strange Situation procedure with maltreated children, it was found that 65 percent of physically abused children were insecurely attached to their abuser, in comparison to 39 percent of comparison children from nonabusive homes (Youngblade & Belsky, 1989).

When abusive mothers are observed interacting with their children, they exhibit significantly more negative physical behaviors (e.g., hitting, pushing) and aversive verbal behaviors (e.g., yelling and threatening) and emit fewer positive behaviors (e.g., hugs, approval; Crittenden, 1981;

Lahey et al., 1984; Mash, Johnston, & Kovitz, 1983; Reid, 1986). Besides having more negative and fewer positive interactions, physically abusive parents tend to be more controlling, exhibit less reasoning, and rely on physical punishment more than other parents (Trickett & Kuczynski, 1986).

Another characteristic of abusive families is the high level of stress or perceived stress that they experience (e.g., Rosenberg & Reppucci, 1983). A linear relation has been found between the amount of stress and amount of child abuse; as the number of stressors increase, so too does the likelihood of physical abuse (Gelles & Straus, 1988). Stressors in these families range from chronic, negative life events (unemployment, ill health, marital problems) to daily hassles and situational demands (Mash & Johnston, 1990). In conjunction with the heightened level of stress present in these families is an unavailability of social support to reduce the stress. Abusive parents are typically isolated and insulated from other people (Milner & Robertson, 1990).

The high level of stress is the main reason that maltreatment is far more prevalent in the lower than other SES groups. Although there is a reporting bias—lower SES abusive families are more likely to be detected and reported than middle SES abusive families—at the same time there is adequate evidence to indicate that abuse occurs more frequently in lower SES families. Low income or poverty usually means lower educational achievement, single-parent status, increased risk of psychopathology, and higher levels of stress.

Unemployment has also been linked to reports of child abuse. In southern California it was found that increasing unemployment rates preceded increased reports of child abuse (Steinberg, Catalano, & Dooley, 1981). Although low income is a risk factor, most low-income parents are not abusive. In a study that examined differences between low-income nonabusive and low-income abusive families, it was found that abusive families were more punitive, authoritarian, isolated, and conflict ridden than their nonabusive counterparts (Trickett, Aber, Carlson, & Cicchetti, 1991).

As this review of research has indicated, there is partial support for each of the theoretical models of abuse. Although severe psychopathology is rarely found in abusive parents, many abusive parents do have some emotional or psychological problems as suggested by the psychiatric model. Support has been found for the sociological model, which posits that maltreatment arises from economic and other sources of stress. However, there are several limitations to the sociological model of maltreatment: It fails to reveal the mechanisms through which societal variables lead to maltreatment; it does not account for why most financially disadvantaged parents do not maltreat their children; and it does not explain why abuse occurs at all socioeconomic levels. The social interaction model takes a more proximate view of abuse by examining parent and child characteristics as they interact together. As such, it has been successful in focusing attention on the poor quality of interaction in abusive families and some of the causes for those behaviors. Finally, the ecological theory attempts to integrate each of the theories by looking at the family as a system of interacting parts involving components of the individual, family, community, and culture. Support for this model has been found at a number of levels (Kaufman & Zigler, 1989); currently, the ecological theory provides the most comprehensive and inclusive model of the multiple causes of parental maltreatment.

Parents at Risk for Dysfunctional Child Rearing

It is now well recognized that certain characteristics of parents put them at risk for parenting problems or child maltreatment. Parents at greatest risk are adolescent mothers, single and poor parents, depressed mothers, and substance-abusing parents. It should be kept in mind that even though each of these characteristics represents a risk factor in itself, many families experience multiple problems that may interact or compound the severity of the dysfunction.

Adolescent Parents

Adolescent parents represent a heterogeneous category of individuals; a single 13-year-old teenager and a married 19-year-old woman can both be labeled "adolescent mother." But those primarily at risk are very young, single adolescent mothers. These mothers are at risk for inadequate parenting for three reasons. First, they face considerable stress, because they are typically poor, are often depressed, and have little social support. Second, they are faced with a "dual developmental crisis": having to rear a child when they are themselves just developing. It is believed that most young teenagers do not have the psychological resources, such as the patience and empathy, required for raising a young child. Third, it is thought that adolescent mothers do not have the child-rearing knowledge or skills to be effective parents.

Several studies have found a relation between teenage motherhood and child maltreatment, although the link has not been adequately studied. The younger the mother at her first birth, the more likely she is to abuse her child (Connelly & Straus, 1992). Presumably, adolescent fathers are also at risk for maltreatment for many of the same reasons, although to date there is little information about these parents.

Single Parents and Poor Parents

Both single parents and parents living in poverty are at risk for maltreating their children because of their heightened stress, as discussed previously. Some evidence supports this view: Single parents were almost twice as likely (9 versus 5 percent) as married parents to physically abuse their children (Sack, Mason, & Higgins, 1985). In a larger sample of 6,002 households, 13.6 percent of the single parents reported engaging in severe violence (defined by such behaviors as hitting, biting, kicking, beating up the child, burning, threatening the child with a gun or knife, or using a gun or knife) in contrast to 10.4 percent of the married parents (Gelles, 1989). The reason behind the relation between single parent status and abuse is presumably the high level of stress, attributable to low income and health problems (Angel & Angel, 1993). Approximately one-half of all single parents can be classified as poor (Gelles, 1989). Similarly, two-parent families living below the poverty line or with an unemployed father also have a greater likelihood of being physically abusive (Wolfner & Gelles, 1993).

Depressed Parents

Depression in mothers has been associated with a wide range of parenting deficiencies (Downey & Coyne, 1990). It is true that the effects of depression vary widely, depending in part on the diagnosis, effectiveness of medication, and phase of the depressive cycle the parent is in. However, on balance, depressed mothers' parenting mirrors the symptoms of their disorder. In general, depressed mothers feel ineffective as parents and often hostile toward their children. They rarely exhibit positive affect in their interactions. According to microanalytic studies of mother-child interactions, depressed mothers spend more time in negative than positive states, and their children do likewise (Field et al., 1990). Depressed mothers are also more critical toward their children and use more guilt-inducing methods of discipline (Webster-Stratton & Hammond, 1988). These mothers are more at risk for neglect or psychological maltreatment than for physical abuse.

Substance-Abusing Parents

To date, most attention to substance abuse has been devoted to alcoholism, the most prevalent mental health problem in the United States. A commonly cited estimate is that there are 10 million alcoholics (West & Prinz, 1987), and consequently about 7 million children, or about 10 percent of the population under the age of eighteen, live with an alcoholic parent (Roosa, Gensheimer, Ayers, & Short, 1990). A wide range of problems have been associated with being a child of an alcoholic parent. Several studies have found relations between alcoholism and child abuse (West & Prinz, 1987). For example, in a study of 409 adult children of alcoholic parents, 22.2 percent reported being physically abused, in contrast to 10.1 percent of a comparison group. According to reports of the children of alcoholics, more than 25 percent of the mothers and nearly 70 percent of the fathers were violent, in contrast to about 7 percent of the comparison parents (Black, Bucky, & Wilder-Padilla, 1986). Children of alcoholics are also more likely to experience a variety of problems, including externalizing problems, poor academic performance, lower self-esteem, anxiety, depression, and future alcohol abuse (Roosa et al., 1990; West & Prinz, 1987). There is also some evidence to indicate that alcoholic parents are more emotionally distant and provide less limit setting, less praise and encouragement, and less helpful advice than other parents (West & Prinz, 1987).

Several other variables have been associated with child abuse or dysfunctional parenting. The more children the parents have, the more likely they are to abuse one or more of them. Demographic studies have shown that parents with six children are twice as likely to physically abuse a child as parents with only one child (e.g., Connelly & Straus, 1992). There is some evidence indicating that fathers who batter their wives are also more likely to physically abuse their children (Gelles & Straus, 1988).

Why More Parents Do Not Maltreat Their Children

Despite the large number of parents at risk for maltreating their children, most parents do not. Fortunately, there are a number of compensatory factors that serve to reduce the likelihood of maltreatment. These mediators include parental, child, and environmental variables and can be seen to operate at each of the four levels of the ecological model (Bronfenbrenner, 1979). The major compensatory variables as summarized by Kaufman and Zigler (1989) are listed in Table 7.2.

Within individual parents, a high IQ, awareness of past abuse, beliefs and attitudes, and ways of coping with stress are examples of variables that can serve to reduce the likelihood that the parent might engage in child maltreatment. At the microsystem level, a supportive spouse or adequate finances can function as compensatory factors. At the next level up, a social support system, religious faith, or an intervention such as parenting classes can serve to mediate the likelihood of abuse. Finally, at the macrosystem level, economic prosperity and membership in a culture or subculture that opposes violence or values community responsibility for the care of children each can serve to lessen maltreatment in that society (Belsky, 1993; Gelles & Straus, 1988; Kaufman & Zigler, 1989).

Summary

Child maltreatment is a complex and heterogeneous problem. It is also pervasive in our society; although getting accurate counts is extremely difficult, it can be estimated that at least 20 percent of children in the United States endure some form of abuse or neglect. Maltreatment comes

TABLE 7.2   Compensatory Factors That Can Reduce the Likelihood of Maltreating at the Four Levels of the Ecological Model

Microsystem
   Healthy children
   Supportive spouse
   Economic security
   Received therapy
Mesosystem
   High IQ
   Awareness of past abuse
   Special talents
   Good interpersonal skills
Exosystem
   Good social support
   Few stressors
   Strong religious affiliation
   Positive school and peer relations as a child
Macrosystem
   Culture that opposes violence and promotes a sense of shared responsibility for
      children
   Economic prosperity

Source: J. Kaufman and E. Zigler, 1989, in D. Cicchetti and V. Carlson (Eds.), *Child Maltreatment* (pp. 129–152), New York: Cambridge University Press. Adapted with permission.

in various forms, with psychological maltreatment probably the most common manifestation and co-occurring with physical and sexual abuse as well as neglect. No one theory is capable of accounting for all of the causes of maltreatment. However, the single most common determinant of physical abuse appears to be vulnerability to environmental and child-induced stress in otherwise normal parents who are multistressed. Parents who are especially at risk for maltreatment or dysfunctional parenting include adolescent, single, poor, depressed, and substance-abusing parents. Fortunately, most parents at risk for abuse do not abuse, because there are several compensatory variables. Some of the ways in which our society can work to combat child maltreatment and other forms of dysfunctional parenting are addressed in Chapter 8.

8

Contemporary Family Problems and Social Policy

Most of the major contemporary social problems of our society are closely tied to how well families are functioning. Family violence, crime and juvenile delinquency, dropping out of school, poverty and unemployment, inadequate health care, teenage pregnancy and childbirth, substance abuse, and racism are problems that at some level are related to the family. This chapter takes a broader look at family problems through a sociological perspective. Recent changes in the structure of the American family will be examined and linked to various hazards in children's development. Some of the costs associated with those problems will be itemized, and social policy in the United States and other countries will be examined.

The Changing American Family

Dramatic sociological changes have occurred in the structure of the American family since the 1960s. The three most significant changes are increases in the rates of divorce, unwed motherhood, and maternal employment. The sharp escalation in the rate of divorce is the single most important change. The United States claims title to the highest divorce rate in the world with about half of all marriages ending in divorce; in about 60 percent of divorces, children are involved (Emery, 1988). This means that each year, about 1 million children witness the divorce of their parents. By the time they are sixteen years old, more than 40 percent of all children in the United States will have experienced their parents' divorce (Amato & Keith, 1991).

The second major change in American families is the increasing rate of births to unmarried women. Twenty-two percent of Caucasian women between the ages of fifteen and thirty-four have a first child before they are married. The comparable figure from 1960 was 9 percent. For African-American women, 70 percent have a child before their first marriage, a figure that is up from 42 percent in 1960 (U.S. Census Bureau, 1993). Most of these out-of-wedlock births are to adolescent women. In our society, adolescent childbirth results in problems not only for the offspring, as mentioned in Chapter 7, but also for the mothers. A single adolescent mother is often unable to complete her education, obtain an adequate-paying job, or develop a stable relationship with the child's father (Furstenberg et al., 1989). On the other hand, adolescent fathers all too often are absent and fail to take any parental responsibility or provide financial support.

The combination of divorces and out-of-wedlock births has resulted in a steep increase in the number of single parents since the 1960s, as is graphed in Figure 8.1. In 1992, about 26 percent of all children (about 16 million) were being reared by the 7 million single-parent families. The percentage of children being reared by single parents has almost tripled from 9 percent in 1959. Of the single parents, about 65 percent are divorced or separated, 25 percent have never been married, and the remaining 7 percent are widowed (U.S. Census Bureau, 1993).

The third family transformation is, in part, causally related to the first two changes. That social shift is the increasing rate of maternal employment. In 1970, less than one-third of mothers with children under the age of six worked outside the home. Twenty years later, that figure almost doubled to 58 percent (representing the mothers of 10.9 million children). Not only are more mothers working outside the home, but they are returning to the paid labor force sooner after childbirth than did women from previous generations. Figure 8.2 graphs the changes from 1950 to 1990 in the national trend of employment for mothers of children younger than six (Children's Defense Fund, 1992).

Not surprisingly, single working mothers are especially likely to be working outside the home. According to the U.S. Bureau of Labor Statistics, there were 2.1 million single working mothers in 1971, 4.4 million ten years later, and 5.8 million in 1991. Most of these mothers work to avoid receiving state aid. The children's fathers more often than not fail to provide child support: More than 70 percent of noncustodial parents do not make a monetary payment to the parent with custody (Children's Defense Fund, 1994). For example, of the 14 million mothers who were awarded child support in 1984, about 4 million received some payment and only 2.5 million received "full" payment (the average payment was only $2,341 annually). Getting these "deadbeat" fathers to help support their children has proved to be a difficult task, because many move out of state to avoid making payments.

One important consequence of maternal employment is the widespread need for alternative care. Affordable but high-quality day care is required in unprecedented rates. Parents pay an average of $3,000 per year for child care for one child; this cost represents about 10 percent of a middle-class family's budget (Stipek & McCroskey, 1989). However, for low-income single parents, day-care expenses can constitute one-third or more of their annual income. In addition to day-care needs for young children, some type of after-school care is necessary for older children in mother-headed families and families in which both parents are working.

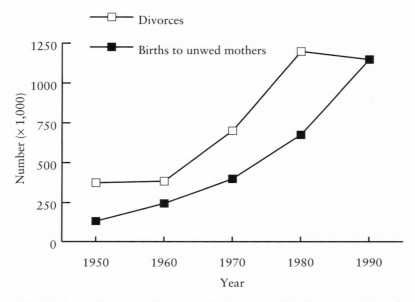

FIGURE 8.1 Changes in the Rates of Divorces and Births to Unwed Mothers in the United States. (From U.S. Bureau of the Census, 1993, *Statistical Abstract of the United States,* Washington, DC: Author.)

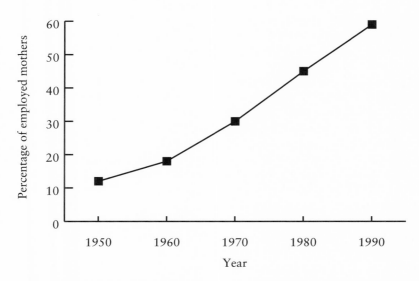

FIGURE 8.2 Changes in the Percentage of American Mothers With Children Under Age Six Working Outside the Home. (From Children's Defense Fund, 1994, *The State of America's Children: Yearbook 1994,* Washington, DC: Author.)

Parents who cannot afford before- or after-school care often let their children go unsupervised as "self-care" or "latchkey" children. Between 2 and 4 million children between the ages of six and thirteen years are left alone before or after school while their parents are at work. Typically, these children pass the time in unsupervised peer play or in front of the television. Consequently, these children are more likely to experience emotional problems, experiment with alcohol or drugs, or even set fire to their homes (Zigler & Finn-Stevenson, 1987).

Social Conditions That Pose Threats to Children's Development

Poverty

In addition to the three changes in the American family previously discussed, there are several other social trends that pose threats to children's development. The most pervasive problem for American families is chronic poverty. In 1993, 39.3 million Americans, or 15.1 percent of the population, lived in poverty (defined as living on less than $14,763 for a family of four). Children are especially likely to be from poor families; almost 22 percent of persons under 18 (or 14.3 million) were poor in 1992 (Children's Defense Fund, 1994). This statistic represents a considerable increase from 1970, when 15.1 percent of those under 18 were poor (Strawn, 1992). Phrased differently, 40 percent of those living in poverty are children. In contrast, the number of elderly living in poverty has decreased steadily over the past quarter century. Figure 8.3 is a graph of the changes from 1970 to 1993 in the percentage of children and the elderly (age 65 and older) living in poverty.

The increase in the number of children living in poverty is due to a combination of factors, including changes in family structure (i.e., increasing numbers of mother-only families), changes in the labor market and economy (e.g., the limited availability of adequate-paying, full-time jobs), and a decrease in governmental assistance to the poor (Duncan, 1991). The high rate of child poverty is especially evident where the poor are concentrated: in the inner city. In ten major U.S. cities (e.g., Detroit, New Orleans, Miami, Atlanta), 40 percent or more of the children are being raised in poverty. People in racial and ethnic minority groups are more likely than Caucasians to live in poverty: 32.7 percent of African-Americans, 28.7 percent of Hispanics, 13.8 percent of Asians, but only 10.7 percent of Caucasians are classified as poor. Among single female-headed families, 55 percent exist below the poverty line (Children's Defense Fund, 1992).

Poverty represents a constellation of risks for children's physical and mental health development. With regard to health, poverty often means a

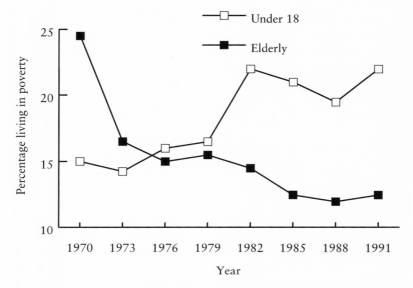

FIGURE 8.3   Changes in the Percentage of American Children Under Age Eighteen and the Elderly Living in Poverty. (U.S. Census Bureau, 1994, *Statistical Abstract of the United States,* Washington, DC: Author.)

lack of prenatal care, a relatively high rate of infant mortality, low-birthweight babies, and poor nutrition. Poor children usually do not have health insurance, and less than half of the people in poverty receive public health coverage, or Medicaid. Such children do not get periodic medical checkups or immunizations. As they grow, poor children experience a wide range of health problems, from infectious diseases to accidents. These health problems are likely to have long-term effects on the children's cognitive, social, and emotional development (Huston, 1991).

Children in poverty are raised in dangerous environments as well. They are often exposed to environmental hazards that include lead poisoning, drugs, gangs, and violence. It is no wonder that children from low-resource families are at risk for educational failure and feelings of helplessness and hopelessness. The 1991 National Commission on Children noted that "poor children face double jeopardy: they have the most health problems and least access to health care. They are growing up in families that experience the most stress, yet receive the least social support. They are at the highest risk for educational failure, and they often attend the worst schools. They are in the greatest danger of following paths that jeopardize their future, yet they enjoy the fewest legitimate job opportunities" (p. 36).

Another ramification of poverty or financial problems is the undermining of parental involvement and supportive parenting (McLoyd, 1990; Simons et al., 1992). Parents who have experienced job loss, severe income loss, or extended unemployment are less able to parent effectively, as described in Chapter 4. In turn, their children suffer. They are more likely to be depressed, withdrawn, or lonely, and they have more behavior problems and lower self-esteem than children of more financially stable parents (McLoyd & Wilson, 1990).

In cases of extreme poverty, homelessness occurs. It is estimated that on any given night, at least one hundred thousand children and their families are homeless (Masten, 1992). Homeless children face a wide range of problems, including hunger, high stress, developmental delays, and physical, mental health, behavioral, and academic problems (Rafferty & Shinn, 1991).

Substance Abuse and Violence

Besides the difficulties associated with poverty, substance abuse and violence represent two mental health problems endemic in our society that pose increasingly serious threats to families. Substance abuse impinges on children in two ways: when their parents use drugs and when the children themselves start using drugs as preadolescents and adolescents. Drugs ingested during pregnancy can have irreversible negative teratogenic effects on the developing fetus. The American Academy of Pediatrics estimates that 375,000 babies are born each year to mothers who have used drugs during the pregnancy (Zigler & Finn-Stevenson, 1987). Newborns of mothers who have used crack cocaine during pregnancy are faced with severe withdrawal symptoms and a variety of developmental problems.

More common than addiction to illegal drugs is the problem of alcoholism, the single most prevalent mental health problem in the United States. Children of alcoholic parents are at risk for a number of possible problems, including behavioral (aggression and delinquency), emotional (depression, anxiety, lower self-esteem), and academic problems. Children of alcoholics are also at increased risk for various forms of maltreatment, as mentioned in Chapter 7. Even when the children grow up, they continue to be at risk for experiencing various emotional and behavioral problems, including becoming alcohol-dependent, marrying an alcoholic, and entering into unstable relationships (Black et al., 1986; Roosa et al., 1990).

Yet another problem faced by an increasing number of children is violence, both in the home and in the community. Wife battering and child abuse are the two major manifestations of family violence. Twenty percent of all murders are committed by family members, and one-third of all female homicide victims are murdered by their husband or boyfriend (Emery, 1989). The National Research Council determined that among sixteen industrialized nations, the United States had the highest rates of marital assaults in 1988. One telephone survey that included a nationally representative sample of adults in the United States indicated that up to 16 percent of wives are at least occasionally beaten (Straus & Gelles, 1988). Community violence, especially for those living in inner cities, is becoming an increasingly serious mental and physical problem for children (Osofsky, 1995).

Children are also recipients of violence, as was made clear in Chapter 7. The fact that each year there are 1.8 million reports of child maltreatment in the United States is more than enough evidence to indicate that violence to children is a problem of epidemic proportions. The pervasive and multiple negative consequences of maltreatment attest to the severity of the problem.

Reduced Parental Involvement

In addition to poverty, substance abuse, and violence, the fourth threat to children's well-being is the reduction in parents' time and involvement with their children. A large part of this reduced involvement is a consequence of economics: single parents working, mothers working outside the home, and parents working two jobs or overtime to provide for their families. Furthermore, for people who work in a competitive job environment, many of the qualities needed for professional success (e.g., working long hours away from home, being mobile, focusing on oneself and job goals, performing at a high level) are antithetical to some of the central qualities of successful parents, including spending time together as a family, being empathic and child-centered, thinking about and dealing with child-rearing problems, and providing consistency for the child (Hewlett, 1991).

Many parents recognize the inadequacy of their involvement with their children. In a national survey of parents (National Commission on Children, 1991), 30 percent of parents said they need to spend "a lot more time" with their families, and another 29 percent said "a little more time." Thirty percent reported that they spend "about the right amount of time"; only 2 percent indicated they would like to spend "less time." Teachers have also recognized this reduced parental involvement. In a 1993 study called Survey of the American Teacher, conducted by Metropolitan Life, more than half of the one thousand teachers questioned reported that the biggest problem in American education today was the lack of parental involvement. Parents were not preparing their children for school entry, not supporting their children's education and teachers' efforts, and not adequately monitoring their children's school attendance (Chira, 1993).

The four threats to children's mental and physical health discussed previously do not represent all of the contemporary hazards to children's healthy development. Chronic and disabling physical conditions, such as birth defects, prematurity, or HIV infections, affect 10 to 15 percent of all children. Another 10 percent of children suffer from mental health disorders, ranging from autism to depression (National Commission on Children, 1991).

Among the many problems adolescents experience, school failure, delinquency, pregnancy, and substance abuse are four central risks to their development. For example, about 14 percent of students nationwide drop out of high school (Oakland, 1992). However, that rate varies considerably by ethnic or racial group and across states. Juvenile delinquency is becoming an increasingly prevalent problem, perpetrated mostly by male adolescents. The number of offenses committed by individuals under the age of eighteen has been rising steadily since 1979. In 1986, more than 1.4 million juveniles were arrested for "nonindex" crimes (e.g., vandalism, possession of drugs) and another 900,000 for "index" crimes (e.g., theft, robbery, rape; Patterson et al., 1989).

The Economic Costs of Family Problems

The problems encountered by children and parents result in a variety of costs to family members: physical and mental health problems, pain and trauma, and more abstractly, lost potential. Ultimately, many of those costs are passed on to society. Perhaps the most concrete way of demonstrating this is to show some of the economic costs resulting from family problems.

In the best of circumstances, child rearing is an expensive proposition. The U.S. Department of Agriculture figures that it costs approximately $4,330 (in 1990 dollars) to raise a child for his or her first year of life, the least expensive year. By the time a child celebrates a nineteenth birthday, middle-class parents have spent between $151,170 and $293,400 on that child (Hoffman, 1992). However, if things go wrong, those dollars represent only a fraction of the bill, a bill that the government often winds up paying. Four sources of excess costs will be discussed: premature births, children who contract a disease, child abuse victims, and juvenile delinquents.

Premature birth, a relatively common consequence of teenage pregnancy and inadequate prenatal care, represents a major economic burden to society. Women who do not receive adequate prenatal care (which costs about $1,400) are three times more likely to give birth to a premature infant (Hewlett, 1991). What would have been perhaps a $3,000 bill for a normal delivery at a hospital may explode to $150,000 or more, depending on the child's birthweight and the severity of medical problems. Each year the government spends $2.5 billion on medical care alone for premature and low-birthweight babies. The expenses do not stop there. Babies born to poor teenage mothers often require other social, health, and welfare services. In 1989, more than $21 billion was spent by the U.S. government for families begun by poor teenage mothers (Hooper, 1991).

Another cost that society bears is the medical expense incurred when children contract preventable diseases. Despite the efficacy and availability of preventive health care through childhood vaccinations, only about 50 to 60 percent of preschoolers are immunized against all eight major childhood diseases (e.g., polio, mumps, measles, rubella). This failure to immunize children has resulted in outbreaks of measles, rubella, and whooping cough (National Commission on Children, 1991). It is estimated that for every dollar spent immunizing children, ten dollars in later medical expenses are saved (Children's Defense Fund, 1992).

If medical expenses for sick infants and children are high, so too are the costs of not protecting children from child maltreatment. Investigations into reports of maltreatment require social workers, investigators, physicians, prosecutors, and foster parents. The cost to investigate, prosecute, and incarcerate one offender, as well as treat the victim, is estimated to be about $144,000 per child (Becker & Hunter, 1992). Further costs accrue from the long-term effects of abuse on untreated children. Maltreated children are more likely than other children to run away from home, become involved in prostitution, abuse drugs, or wind up in prison (Kendall-Tackett et al., 1993).

A fourth expense to taxpayers is juvenile delinquency. Some 1.75 million juveniles were arrested in 1990. If a youth is subsequently incarcerated, the expense averages over $40,000 per year. When the various costs are added up, it is estimated that the United States spends well over $1 billion each year on the juvenile justice system. In addition, up to a half billion dollars is spent annually on school vandalism alone (Patterson et al., 1989).

Society ultimately bears many of the financial expenses resulting from the problems of families. Money spent on dealing with the symptoms of the problem does not begin to address the source of the problem. Social policy and intervention as well as prevention programs are needed to avoid such expensive remedies as hospitalizations, foster care, and jail.

Social Policy Responses to Social Problems

Social policy refers to the principles that guide decisions or efforts to achieve desired goals (or avoid undesired ones). These most often are manifest as federal law, but they can also include business policies or community standards.

Early examples of laws and governmental policies designed to modify child-bearing and child-rearing practices occurred during the time of the Roman Empire. The first emperor of Rome (Augustus, ruling from 30 B.C. to A.D. 14) introduced laws to encourage family life and large families. For example, he established a law that limited parental rights to refuse consent to their children's marriage. In an effort to increase the population, he fined childless couples (Sommerville, 1982). Another legal milestone concerning child bearing occurred about three hundred years later when Constantine, the first Christian emperor of Rome, made it a crime to practice infanticide.

Since that time, social policy has been created around the globe to protect and benefit children. One of the most unusual laws designed to protect children prohibited parents from using a common disciplinary practice. In 1979, Sweden passed a law banning parents from spanking their children. Although many politicians did not think the law would accomplish its purpose, it has indeed been successful at changing Swedish parents' disciplinary attitudes and practices (Haeuser, 1990). The law has also served as a model; at least four countries have enacted similar laws.

Early Programs and Bills in the United States

Specifying social policy in the United States is difficult because there is no explicit national family policy. Instead, there exists a patchwork of bills, initiatives, and actions adopted at federal, state, and local levels that together form family policy (Silverstein, 1991).

Social policy toward children in the United States can be characterized as having two competing orientations. On the one hand, since colonial times there has been a doctrine of *parens patriae*: The state is the ultimate parent of every child (Hawes, 1991). This doctrine provided the foundation for child protection laws that were established as early as 1735. That was the year Massachusetts passed a law providing for removal of children from neglectful parents and placing them with caring foster families. During the 1800s, there were a number of private efforts made at establishing institutions for aiding and protecting children (e.g., the Children's Aid Society and the Society for the Prevention of Cruelty to Children), but it was not until the 1900s that the federal government got involved.

On the other hand, there has also been a strong tradition of noninterference with the rights of the family, such that government is leery to involve itself (Zigler, Kagan, & Krugman, 1983). Americans value individualism, self-sufficiency, and independence. Many citizens of the United States believe that any attempt by the government to tell them how to behave is an infringement on their constitutional rights. This belief creates problems in the attempt to legislate behavior, even behavior that is in the best interest of children.

Despite that conflicting orientation, Congress has passed many important bills designed to protect and enhance the lives of children. Five federal laws stand out as particularly significant. The first of many federal legislative efforts designed to protect children was the Keating-Owen bill of 1916, intended to regulate the type and amount of work a child could do.

The use of child labor was a particularly common practice in Southern cotton mills. One British reformer visited some of Alabama's mills during the winter of 1900 to 1901 and wrote the following: "I was prepared to find child labor, but one could hardly be prepared to find in America today white children six and seven years of age, working for twelve hours a day— aroused before daybreak and toiling, till long after sundown in winter, with only half an hour of rest and refreshment" (cited in Hawes, 1991). Although the Keating-Owen bill was declared unconstitutional two years after it became law, it set the stage for subsequent federal bills that, in conjunction with state compulsory school attendance laws (beginning with Massachusetts in 1852 and concluding with Mississippi in 1918), resulted in a rapid decline of child labor in the United States.

A second key bill was the Sheppard-Towner Maternal and Infancy Protection Act of 1922, designed to reduce infant mortality. The bill created community clinics for maternal and infant hygiene in an effort to establish preventive health care. This act marked the first use of federal grants to aid in development and maintenance of state and local social programs. Funds were also made available through this bill to provide prenatal care for pregnant women and hire public health nurses to teach women about prenatal and child health care.

During the 1930s, two congressional bills helped to establish children's rights. The Social Security Act of 1935 created the Aid to Dependent Children (ADC) program (now called Aid to Families with Dependent Children; AFDC). As part of the New Deal, it was intended to keep fatherless families together by providing payments to mothers to enable them to stay at home and raise their children. In addition, the act established various maternal and child health programs and other child welfare services.

A few years after that bill was passed, a new act concerning child labor was enacted. The Fair Labor Standards Act of 1938 prohibited employment of children under sixteen years in industries that engaged in interstate commerce. In addition, children under 18 were prohibited from working in dangerous occupations. These two acts established two precedents for children's rights: some degree of economic security and the freedom from the need to work in childhood.

A fifth important bill was the Child Abuse Prevention and Treatment Act passed in 1973. The act established the National Center on Child Abuse and Neglect (NCCAN) in an effort to provide federal leadership for the problem. Appropriations to the Center were intended to (1) develop reliable statistics about the incidence of abuse, (2) create a clearinghouse of information on abuse programs, and (3) sponsor research into the causes, identification, prevention, and treatment of child abuse. Unfortunately, the Act has consistently been underfunded; Zigler has described it as being like a Band-Aid on a cancer, and the small appropriation it receives virtually guarantees it will never be effective.

Many of these acts and other federal legislation were stimulated by a series of White House Conferences on Children. The first was held in 1909, designed to plan the government's role in protecting children. Since then, a new conference was held each decade to monitor and examine children's status in society. The last conference, convened in 1970, focused on child care as the single most serious problem for America's families. The fact that no White House Conference on Children has been convened since then reflects the lack of social policy devoted to children.

The White House Conferences resulted in various positive outcomes. The first conference led to the establishment of the Children's Bureau in 1912. The Children's Bureau was mandated to investigate and report on issues concerning the welfare of children, such as infant mortality, illegitimacy, child labor, and juvenile delinquency. Subsequently, the Bureau shifted its emphasis to public education, and it is best known for parent education publications. In 1913, *Prenatal Care* was printed; a year later, the popular manual *Infant Care* was published. The first two editions of *Infant Care* were based on Dr. Holt's popular treatise, although in subsequent editions (it went through twelve revisions), Holt's advice gave way to other, contemporary views. By 1921, 1.5 million copies of *Infant Care* had been distributed, most recently in 1980. The child rearing advice promoted in different editions of the pamphlet have changed over time, with a waning of Freudian influences and an increasing emphasis on the enjoyment of children (Wolfenstein, 1951).

The White House Conferences also provided the impetus for creation of a number of bills designed to help children and their families (Zigler & Muenchow, 1984). Besides establishing policy and legislation, the conferences served to reaffirm the right of children to parental love and respect. They also reiterated the shared goal of a society free of abject poverty and discrimination, in which there is equality of educational opportunities and the freedom to pursue different developmental paths based on choice or need (Beck, 1973).

Contemporary Family-Assistance Programs

Currently, a number of different government programs provide assistance to parents and their children; some are prophylactic, and others are intended to provide a "safety net" to combat the effects of poverty. Welfare programs provide food (food stamps, WIC), health care (Medicaid), work training (Family Support Act), supplemental income (AFDC), and early education for children (Head Start). Of these programs, two programs stand out as being particularly successful: The Special Supplemental Food Program for Women, Infants, and Children (WIC) and Head Start.

Developed in 1972, WIC was designed to combat the high incidence of inadequate nutritional care among poor pregnant women and malnutrition in young children. The prevention program provides vouchers for high-protein, iron-fortified foods and is available to low-income pregnant or breast-feeding women and mothers of children up to the age of five. Nutrition education and counseling are also included. Despite the program's laudable goals, support for the program has been at the mercy of politics rather than based on effectiveness (Rush, 1981).

Evaluation studies of the program have found it to be highly worthwhile. The United States General Accounting Office, in a 1992 study, determined that for each child in the program, $573 is saved by avoiding the prolonged hospitalization of low-birthweight babies and treatment of the sequelae to prematurity. Overall, it was estimated that the program results in a 25 percent reduction in the incidence of low-birthweight babies and a 44 percent reduction in the incidence of very low-birthweight babies. However, the program is underfunded; as many as 55 percent of women eligible to receive the benefits do not (Cummings, 1992).

The other widely acclaimed government prevention program is Project Head Start. Initially created in 1965, it began as a summer program for four- and five-year-old children. Within a few years it had expanded into a year-round program, and today it serves more than 621,000 children at two thousand sites. Besides providing the children with a preschool education, Head Start provides meals and medical services to children and involves parents in the process. This program and many others were designed on the premise of a cycle involving early childhood and adult outcomes as illustrated in Figure 8.4 (Laosa, 1984). By providing a remedial educational experience to counteract deficient home environments, Head Start was intended to make children more likely to succeed at school and thus break the cycle of poverty.

Evaluation studies of Head Start and other preschool intervention programs have found that the intervention is successful according to many criteria. Although Head Start has not been found to be effective at keeping IQ scores elevated, their graduates are more likely to be ready for school, perform better in school, and exhibit higher cognitive competence and are less likely to be put in remedial classes than comparison children who did not attend Head Start (Lazar & Darlington, 1982; Zigler et al., 1992). In addition, it is likely that there are other positive, long-term consequences for Head Start graduates, such as increased likelihood of graduating from high school, becoming and staying employed, and avoiding juvenile delinquency (Woodhead, 1988).

Head Start appears to set a child on a positive developmental course that yields feelings of efficacy and generates success in school and other social contexts. Graduates of Head Start are thought to be more likely to form

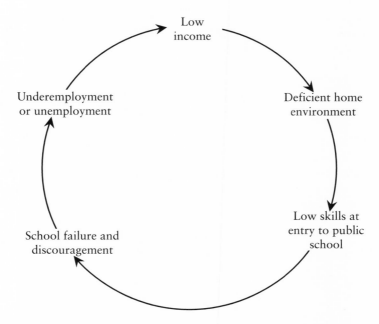

FIGURE 8.4   The Assumed Cycle of Poverty. (Reprinted, with permission, from L. M. Laosa, 1984, in H. W. Stevenson and A. E. Siegel [Eds.], *Child Development Research and Social Policy* [Vol. 1, pp. 1–109], Chicago: University of Chicago Press.)

positive relationships with teachers and to adopt teachers' conventional value system. The major limitation of Head Start is that, like the WIC program, it is underfunded. For every child in the program, there are more than three other children eligible.

All fifty states have participated in another successful social policy experiment: reducing childhood injuries and fatalities through the adoption of mandatory car seat restraints for children. About 43 percent of the sixteen thousand fatalities and forty thousand injuries to infants and children each year are due to automobile accidents. By the end of the 1980s, each state had passed laws requiring infants and children to ride in child safety seats. It is estimated that 90 percent of all traffic-related deaths to children are preventable and that 70 percent of injuries to children would be avoided if the children were restrained. However, owing to noncompliance or improper use of the child seats, the reduction in the rate of injury or death has been significantly less than it could be (Treiber, 1986).

One program that has not been so successful is the massive AFDC program, commonly called "welfare" but actually only one of a number of welfare programs. In 1988, the AFDC program provided 11 million people with food, shelter, and clothing at a cost of about $18 billion. Of those people, 7.3 million were children (Levine & Levine, 1992). One of the problems with the program is that only about 50 percent of children living in poverty received AFDC, because twenty-five states do not offer AFDC to two-parent families. A second problem is that the entitlements are not generous. Many states have not increased benefits to match inflation, and it is not uncommon for a recipient to receive an average of 49 cents per meal (Stipek & McCroskey, 1989). Monthly payments for a family of three range from a high of $950 in Alaska to a low of $120 in Mississippi; in Texas, a welfare mother must support her child on less than $2 a day (Ward, 1994). A third problem is that owing to the cost of day care, many mothers are financially better off to stay home and collect the AFDC payments than to try to get a job. These and other limitations have been well recognized by politicians and social scientists; efforts are currently under way to revamp the program.

Innovative Programs to Help Families

Across the nation, individuals and communities have created numerous programs to assist parents and children in need. For example, there are now many family support programs operating in the United States. Such programs serve important needs, but their significance for nationwide family social change is limited by their scope. In contrast, there are several innovative programs that hold considerable promise for improving the quality of life for parents and their children. These programs concern changing the nature of the public school system and modifying the way Americans work.

Changing the Public Schools. Periodically there are calls to reform the education system in an effort to make it more effective in producing literate and competent adults. Since the late 1960s, there have been at least two well-publicized efforts at modifying schools. The first effort was directed by James Comer in a poorly functioning, inner-city school in New Haven, Connecticut. Comer developed a new approach to organization and functioning of the school to improve its effectiveness and raise the level of student and teacher involvement, performance, and enthusiasm. Over a period of years, he was able to show considerable improvement in the school, through increasing involvement and control of faculty, students, and parents (Comer, 1980).

A more comprehensive effort at reconceptualizing the role of schools has been developed by developmental psychologist Edward Zigler. He has redesigned public schools with his concept of the "School of the 21st Century." He believes that public schools are outdated; they need to be revamped by being open longer hours and serving younger children. The School of the 21st Century model provides all-day care for children aged three to five years and before- and after-school as well as vacation care for children from kindergarten through sixth grade. In addition to those childcare components, the model for the new school includes (1) family support through home visitation for parents with children from birth to three years of age, (2) information about infant day-care facilities and other family services in the community, (3) parent education, and (4) support for family day care in the neighborhood.

The School of the 21st Century is already operating in about two hundred schools, including programs across the state of Missouri and in seven other states. Full implementation of the concept is expensive; Zigler has estimated that, nationwide, it would cost $75 to $100 billion dollars. However, as he has pointed out, the cost of doing nothing will be much higher.

Changing How Parents Work.   Innovative programs for families have also cropped up in the business sector. Corporations are slowly coming to the realization that providing assistance to employees who are parents is good business because it results in improved employee performance and morale. Businesses can become more "family friendly" in a variety of ways. Innovations for working families include flexible hours, flexible leave, job sharing, work at home, providing child-care information and referral, financial aid for child care, and on-site child care. Currently, the percentage of businesses that offer these forms of assistance ranges from a high of 45 percent for flexible hours provided in small businesses to a low of 1.5 percent for on-site day care (U.S. Bureau of Labor Statistics, 1988).

Changes in business practices can result in tangible improvements in parents' lives. Parents in more flexible job situations report greater job satisfaction and experience less conflict between work and family roles (Marshall and Barnett, 1993). Added job flexibility enables parents to fulfill their parenting responsibilities (such as attending to sick children or meeting with teachers) without sacrificing job performance.

Social Policy in Other Countries

The United States has been slow and reluctant to provide assistance to families. In Europe, as early as 1870 Otto Bismarck instituted Germany's first social insurance program for those who become disabled or unable to work, such as pregnant women. Since then, Western European countries have continued to be world leaders in supporting the family. Currently, European countries provide guaranteed parental leave after the birth of a child, family allowances based on number of children in the family, national health insurance, subsidized housing for most families, and academic and vocational education for all children (Kamerman & Kahn, 1989).

Benefits in France, where children are considered a part of public responsibility, are particularly generous. Mothers are given four months of paid maternity leave and are guaranteed health care; each month, parents with two children receive $123 to help offset the cost of child rearing. The drawback of the program is its expense: Forty-four percent of French workers' paychecks goes toward family benefits (including social security), in contrast with 29 percent in the United States (Smolowe, 1992).

The United States compares poorly to a number of other countries in terms of the amount of resources it devotes to children and parents. The United States invests a smaller percentage of its gross national product in child health needs than do eighteen other industrialized nations (Children's Defense Fund, 1994). Even more surprising is that the United States is not among the seventy countries that provide medical care and financial assistance to pregnant women. It is likely that the relatively high rate of infant mortality in the United States is directly attributable to that lack of prenatal care. In 1990, the United States was tied for twentieth among countries in the rate of infant mortality, with 10 per 1,000 live births. Japan had the lowest rate, with 5 deaths per 1,000 live births, followed by Finland, Sweden, Canada, Germany, and Hong Kong (UNICEF, cited in Children's Defense Fund, 1992).

The United States also measures up poorly to other industrialized countries with regard to maternity leave and child-care subsidies. Of one hundred countries surveyed, the United States is the only one that does not have paid, job-protected maternity leave as a national policy (Scarr et al., 1989). Although the Family and Medical Leave Act of 1993 requires employers to provide up to twelve weeks of leave for employees to care for a newborn (or a newly adopted child, a child in foster care, or a sick relative), employees are not paid during their leave. Working mothers in many other countries also receive subsidized child care. For example, France, Italy, Spain, and all of the Eastern European countries provide subsidized child care for more than half of their infants, toddlers, and preschoolers. There are no comparable figures for the United States, in part because other than Head Start, there are no federal programs (Scarr et al., 1989).

Many countries have enacted policies to curb violence against children; once again, the United States lags behind. Corporal punishment in schools was banned by Poland in 1783. Today, more than thirty other countries (e.g., England, Germany, China, Turkey) also have outlawed the practice. In contrast, as of 1993, less than half of the states in the United States had banned corporal punishment in their public schools. Furthermore, as mentioned earlier in this chapter, Sweden, Denmark, and several other countries have undertaken the additional bold step of banning parents from using physical punishment on their children. Inspired in part by those Scandinavian laws, a worldwide organization called End Physical Punishment of Children (EPOCH) has been created with the mission of ending physical punishment of children in school and at home through educational initiatives and legal reforms.

Child and Parent Advocacy

An advocate is someone who identifies a problem and then informs others about it. Child advocates are persons who recognize children as individuals with rights, distinct from their parents, and then provide the catalyst for social policy initiatives. In the United States, the child advocacy movement has a long history. The Society for the Prevention of Cruelty to Children was founded in 1874. Fifteen years later, the family and child advocate Jane Addams opened Hull House in Chicago, the first settlement house for families. In 1897, the first National Congress of Mothers, an advocacy group, met and eventually grew into the Parent-Teacher Associations.

A more recent example of an advocacy group was Action for Children's Television, formed in the 1960s to improve scheduling, reduce the amount of violence, and limit the amount of advertising on children's TV. One of the newest family advocacy groups is Parent Action, begun in 1989 to identify and articulate the needs of parents, to lobby politicians, to gather and disseminate information about the needs of families, and to promote actions to help parents effectively raise their children.

Perhaps the single most important advocacy group of recent times has been the bipartisan, thirty-four-member National Commission on Children that spent two and a half years investigating and deliberating a new agenda for U.S. families in the 1990s. Their final report, published in 1991, had eight broad recommendations about how to improve the lives of U.S. children. These were (1) ensuring economic security for families; (2) improving health and health insurance coverage; (3) increasing educational achievement of youth (expanding Head Start, reducing the high school dropout rate); (4) supporting the transition to adulthood (preventing high-risk behavior such as drug use, linking school with work opportunities); (5) strengthening and supporting families (e.g., parent education, high-quality day care, support groups); (6) protecting vulnerable children and their families (providing access and referrals to a broad range of preventive and intervention services); (7) making existing policies and programs work better; and (8) creating a better moral climate for children to develop in (by encouraging parents, TV producers, and communities to promote values).

The commission recognized that both parents and society must be made more responsible for the healthy development of children. But the cost to society is high, with a midrange estimate of $54 billion for the first year of new programs. However, failure to act "only defers to the next generation the rising social, moral, and financial costs of our neglect" (National Commission on Children, 1991, p. 390). A shift in resources from other programs to programs for children is needed. In 1990, less than 7 percent of the federal budget was devoted to programs to help children. Although many needy children did not receive any aid, on average, children under eighteen years received $1,020 worth of benefits. In comparison, the elderly are much more likely to receive benefits; programs for senior citizens consumed 28 percent of the federal budget, and on average, each senior citizen received $11,350 in benefits (Strawn, 1992). Largely for this reason, the number of elderly living in poverty has decreased dramatically over the past twenty years, as was illustrated earlier in this chapter in Figure 8.2.

Summary

Much can and needs to be done in the United States to support families and aid parents in their profound responsibility of rearing their young. But this will happen only with the recognition that the foundation for a healthy and stable society begins at home. Recent societal shifts have resulted in changes in parents and the experience of child rearing. These modifications necessitate action and new social policy initiatives.

If the United States is to have a strong future, our society in general, and parents in particular, must devote more resources to nurturing children from the prenatal period through adolescence and even through parenthood. A commitment to the well-being of children means that both children and parents must become a central priority. As the attachment theorist John Bowlby (1951) recognized a long time ago, "if a community values its children it must cherish their parents" (p. 54).

9

Summary and Implications
of a Dynamic View of Parents

As this book has documented, a considerable body of research concerning parents and child rearing has accumulated over the past fifty years. That work has served to move our understanding from idiosyncratic, mere beliefs to empirically supported facts. Although these facts are constructions of scientists (Scarr, 1985), current conceptualizations about parents and the nature of child rearing are now derived from a rich empirical base.

Many of the themes of recent parenting research reflect an increasing appreciation for different forms of variation and change associated with child rearing. Besides change in views about children and child rearing, researchers are increasingly recognizing different forms of behavioral variation that are intrinsic to parenting. Change is also apparent in parent-child relationships as a consequence of exposure to certain contextual or environmental influences; child rearing is not immune from external forces. Another theme involving change concerns the expanding view of the characteristics that are considered important for effective parenting.

The sources of and potential for change in the parent-child relationship provide an underlying organizational framework for the book. The first chapter gave examples of how our views and understanding of parents have changed dramatically over time. The chapter addressed how views about child rearing have shifted from impressions derived from unsubstantiated beliefs to conceptualizations informed by the results of scientific investigation.

Over the past half century, research into parenting has been guided by five major theoretical orientations. Ethology, attachment, social learning, ecological systems, and behavioral genetics theories have directed attention to different aspects of the parent-child relationship and led to different questions and types of investigations. However, these theories have only partially recognized and accounted for the dynamics of child rearing. In contrast, narrower theories involving child rearing, such as Vygotsky's concept of the zone of proximal development, the control system model, and attribution theory, explicitly focus on the ongoing change and variation within interactions.

Empirical investigations into parent-child relationships have been guided by the six competing conceptualizations of the nature of parents that were described in Chapter 3. The trait, social address, learning, microanalytic, child effects, and parental beliefs approaches each developed their own focus on particular aspects of the parent-child relationship. Of those, it was the three newest approaches (microanalytic, child effects, and parental beliefs) that emphasized the variations that are fundamental to the task of parenting.

Results of research based on the six approaches have revealed a wealth of different determinants of parenting. Those multiple influences on child rearing were organized around the ecological systems model in Chapter 4. The multiplicity of influences attests to the many potential sources of change of parental behavior, ranging from cultural prescriptions or admonitions to subtle behavioral and cognitive variations induced by parental mood changes.

The single most important question of the book, concerning the likely effects of child-rearing practices, was addressed in Chapter 5. A variety of parental characteristics and behaviors were linked with positive and negative outcomes in children. However, the evidence indicates that the associations are not inevitable. Rather, there are parent, child, and family characteristics that may moderate the associations. Thus, a focus on the dynamic processes through which child-rearing influences may occur is advocated.

Chapter 6 summarized what is known about the attributes of effective parents in five arenas of influence: attachment, social learning, social interactions, teaching, and structuring of the environment. A dialectic model of effective parenting that incorporates the constant adjustments that are required in child rearing was presented. Such a dynamic model best reflects the common process that effective parents must frequently use when interacting with their children. The chapter concluded with an overview of parent education and a description of contemporary efforts to help individuals become better parents.

In contrast to the focus on effective parents, the focus of Chapter 7 was on individuals who mistreat their children. The underlying question was what contributes to transforming these individuals into abusive parents. Although there are competing views, investigations into the topic have isolated a set of contributing factors within the parent, the child, and the environment that contribute to the development of dysfunctional parenting.

Chapter 8 concerned how changes in society have affected parenting and families. Relatively recent social shifts in U.S. families (i.e., increasing rates of single-parent families and maternal employment) and social changes such as poverty and violence have had negative impacts on contemporary families. Examples of social policies intended to address the changing needs of families were discussed.

The Need for a Dynamic Perspective on Parents

The preceding eight chapters reviewed the scientific evidence with an orientation toward the changing nature of parent-child relationships. Such a dynamic orientation to parents is not new; one of the first calls for such a view consisted of the need to recognize the bidirectionality in parent-child relations (Sears, 1951). But a full acceptance of the dynamic perspective has been slow in coming.

Researchers of parenting are only beginning to recognize the extent of the variation inherent in parenting and to develop adequately complex models of parent-child relationships. Although there are some exceptions (e.g., Bugental et al., 1990; Grusec & Goodnow, 1994), much of the work over the past half-century has reflected a static model of parenting. The implicit assumption still held by many researchers is that parents do not change, or if they do modify their behavior, that it is not in a meaningful way. This book has marshaled evidence supporting the view that variation and change are fundamental attributes of parents and child rearing.

Regarding virtually every topic discussed in this book, there has been a growing awareness of the complexity and inherent variability in parent-child relationships. An orientation that fails to recognize the mutable nature of parental behavior can never adequately describe or account for parenting. Similarly, recognition of moderating and mediating characteristics of children and parents necessitates a more sophisticated underlying conceptualization of the nature of child rearing and its effects. Perhaps the dynamic perspective is best suited to reveal the characteristics of effective parents. An effective parent cannot act the same way across situations, to different children, or across time and still be effective. Rather, parenting changes from moment to moment. Effective parents take into account the competing ideas, concerns, or needs of the moment. Using a dialectic model is a way of recognizing the change that parents routinely exhibit and the flexibility that effective parenting requires.

The need for a dynamic, process-oriented view of child rearing may be most evident in the research into the stability and change of parenting. If one assumes the traditional, static view of parenting, child-rearing beliefs and practices should be characterized by a relatively high degree of stability. To be sure, there is some evidence to support such a view. A longitudinal study of child-rearing attitudes found reliable correlations over time, leading the authors to conclude that "parents have fundamental, pervasive, and enduring child-rearing orientations" (Roberts, Block, & Block, 1984). However, the balance of evidence does not support such a view.

Information about parental stability and change can be obtained from three types of studies: (1) child rearing across time, (2) child rearing across different situations, and (3) child rearing across different children. In a meta-analytic review (Holden & O'Dell, 1995), examination of correlation coefficients and difference scores revealed that there is almost as much evidence for change as there is for stability.

Change is particularly evident in studies assessing parenting across different situations (e.g., the home and the laboratory) or different tasks (playing versus teaching), suggesting that parents are sensitive to changes in the environment. In contrast, the strongest evidence for stability comes from studies across time, but that finding is qualified by the type of variable assessed. Parents show most across-time stability for such variables as control or negative affect. But child-rearing practices were observed to change markedly over time for such variables as caregiving or stimulation, variables that are highly dependent on the child's developmental level.

Evidently, a strict view of either stability or change is not supported by the evidence. How does one reconcile the evidence of both stability and change? One solution is to focus on the processes that contribute to stability or change in the individual parent. The best theoretical model to account for this is a theory about personality that has recently been proposed by Walter Mischel and Yuichi Shoda (1995). They have argued that it is futile to search for invariants of behavior over time or situations. Instead, behavior is the result of a system of mediating processes involving cognitions and affects that are related in a way that is psychologically meaningful to the individual. According to this view, parenting is the dynamic interplay of the individuals' tendencies, developed over time, with the specific cognitive-affective processes activated at a particular moment and context.

Such a view can help to explain the potential dynamics in parenting. Consider the question of whether the use of corporal punishment is stable over time in a parent. Stability over years could occur only if the parent continued to believe that spanking is a useful solution, maintained the conviction that it is an appropriate disciplinary practice to use with older children, and remained committed to disciplining the child; all the while, the child must continue to engage in behaviors that elicit a spanking.

On the other hand, change in the use of corporal punishment can be induced by a variety of factors such as admonitions of a spouse, bidirectional effects from a child's reactions to being spanked, change in level of stress, attendance in a parent education program, or behavioral change in the child. Only a view informed by a dynamic orientation that appreciates the multiple and potentially changing influences on behavior can provide a full answer concerning the stability of the behavior.

This example is intended to illustrate the point that to understand parenting, a focus on the mechanisms is needed. Process models, such as the ones described in earlier chapters, provide the best avenue for appreciating the active nature of parenting: the models by Belsky (1984) for understanding determinants of parenting, by McLoyd (1989) for revealing the effects of economic stress on parenting, and by Dix (1991) for showing how parents' affect and beliefs are three prime examples.

Implications of a Dynamic Perspective

A dynamic view of child rearing has several implications. Besides reflecting the phenomenon more accurately, it is likely to result in new discoveries. A focus on the processes through which child-rearing influences occur and qualities of the dynamic interchanges such as power sharing and reciprocity may result in new understandings about how child rearing is associated with outcomes in children. It is also likely that new attributes of parents or the parent-child relationship will be discovered from such a perspective.

Although it is necessary, such an approach is conceptually and methodologically more difficult to investigate. Currently, much of our knowledge about parents is at the level of main effects. We know working-class parents value obedience more than parents who are professionals (Kohn, 1979; Luster et al., 1989). But such social address approaches provide little information about the variation within the social class or the parenting variables that likely interact with social class. Similarly, it is well documented that authoritative parenting is associated with competent children. However, little is known about how particular child characteristics may interact with or modify the association. Holding a dynamic view that focuses on processes is the best way to move beyond main effects and reveal the workings of interactions.

Another implication of a dynamic perspective on parenting is an optimistic one: It assumes that parents can and do change. Such an orientation is amenable for discovering how best to change an individual's child rearing. An appreciation of the dynamics inherent in child rearing will give new life to the study of parent education.

In conclusion, viewing parents from a dynamic perspective is beginning to provide a new framework with which to understand child rearing. Such a perspective may prove to be useful in integrating different approaches and theories. Ultimately, it should result in a more complete answer to the enduring and fundamental question of what role parents play in their children's development.

References

Aboud, F. (1988). *Children and prejudice.* New York: Basil Blackwell.

Acock, A. C., & Bengtson, V. L. (1980). On the relative influence of mothers and fathers: A covariance analysis of political and religious socialization. *Journal of Marriage and the Family, 42,* 519–530.

Ainsworth, M. D. S. (1989). Attachments beyond infancy. *American Psychologist, 44,* 709–716.

Ainsworth, M. D. S., & Bell, S. M. (1977). Infant crying and maternal responsiveness: A rejoinder to Gewirtz and Boyd. *Child Development, 48,* 1208–1216.

Ainsworth, M. D. S., Blehar, M. C., Waters, E., & Wall, S. (1978). *Patterns of attachment.* Hillsdale, NJ: Erlbaum.

Ainsworth, M. D. S., & Bowlby, J. (1991). An ethological approach to personality development. *American Psychologist, 46,* 333–341.

Alwin, D. F. (1986). Religion and parental child-rearing orientations: Evidence of a Catholic-Protestant convergence. *American Journal of Sociology, 92,* 412–440.

Amato, P. R. (1989). Family processes and the competence of adolescents and primary school children. *Journal of Youth and Adolescence, 18,* 39–53.

Amato, P. R., & Keith, B. (1991). Parental divorce and the well being of children: A meta-analysis. *Psychological Bulletin, 110,* 26–46.

Ammerman, R. T. (1991). The role of the child in physical abuse: A reappraisal. *Violence and Victims, 6,* 87–101.

Anderson, K. E., Lytton, H., & Romney, D. M. (1986). Mothers' interactions with normal and conduct-disordered boys: Who affects whom? *Developmental Psychology, 22,* 604–609.

Angel, R. J., & Angel, J. L. (1993). *Painful inheritance: Health and the new generation of fatherless families.* Madison: University of Wisconsin Press.

Arend, R. A., Gove, F. L., & Sroufe, L. A. (1979). Continuity of early adaptation: From attachment in infancy to ego-resiliency and curiosity at age 5. *Child Development, 50,* 950–959.

Ariès, P. (1962). *Centuries of childhood: A social history of family life* (Robert Baldick, Trans.). New York: Vintage Books.

Azar, S. T., Robinson, D. R., Hekimian, E., & Twentyman, C. T. (1984). Unrealistic expectations and problem-solving ability in maltreating and comparison mothers. *Journal of Consulting and Clinical Psychology, 52,* 687–691.

Azuma, H. (1986). Why study child development in Japan? In H. Stevenson, H. Azuma, & K. Hakuta (Eds.), *Child development and education in Japan* (pp. 3–12). New York: Freeman.

Bacon, M. K., & Ashmore, R. D. (1986). A consideration of the cognitive activities of parents and their role in the socialization process. In R. D. Ashmore & D. M.

Brodzinsky (Eds.), *Thinking about the family: Views of parents and children* (pp. 3–33). Hillsdale, NJ: Erlbaum.

Baker, H. S., & Baker, M. N. (1987). Heinz Kohut's self psychology: An overview. *American Journal of Psychiatry, 144,* 1–9.

Baldwin, A. L. (1948). Socialization and the parent-child relationship. *Child Development, 19,* 127–136.

Baldwin, A. L., Cole, R. E., & Baldwin, C. P. (1982). Parental pathology, family interaction, and the competence of the child in school. *Monographs of the Society for Research in Child Development, 47*(5, Serial No. 197).

Baldwin, A. L., Kalhorn, J., & Breese, F. (1945). Patterns of parent behavior. *Psychological Monographs, 58*(3, Whole No. 268).

Bandura, A. (1965). Vicarious processes: A case of no-trial learning. In L. Berkowitz (Ed.), *Advances in experimental social psychology* (Vol. 2, pp. 1–55). San Diego: Academic Press.

Bandura, A. (1989). Social cognitive theory. In R. Vasta (Ed.), *Annals of child development* (Vol. 6, pp. 1–60). Greenwich, CT: Jai Press.

Bandura, A., Ross, D., & Ross, S. A. (1963). Imitation of film-mediated aggressive models. *Journal of Abnormal and Social Development, 66,* 3–11.

Bandura, A., & Walters, R. H. (1959). *Adolescent aggression.* New York: Ronald Press.

Barkley, R. A., & Cunningham, C. E. (1979). Stimulant drugs and activity level in hyperactive children. *American Journal of Orthopsychiatry, 49,* 491–499.

Barnard, K. E., Bee, H. L., & Hammond, M. A. (1984). Developmental changes in maternal interactions with term and preterm infants. *Infant Behavior and Development, 7,* 101–113.

Barnes, G. M., Farrell, M. P., & Cairns, A. (1986). Parental socialization factors and adolescent drinking behaviors. *Journal of Marriage and the Family, 48,* 27–36.

Barnett, M. A. (1986). Empathy and related responses in children. In N. Eisenberg & J. Strayer (Eds.), *Empathy and its development* (pp. 146–162). New York: Cambridge University Press.

Bates, J. E. (1989). Concepts and measures of temperament. In G. A. Kohnstamm, J. E. Bates, & M. K. Rothbart (Eds.), *Temperament in childhood* (pp. 3–26). New York: Wiley.

Bates, J. E., & Bayles, K. (1984). Objective and subjective components in mothers' perceptions of their children from age 6 months to 3 years. *Merrill-Palmer Quarterly, 30,* 111–130.

Bauer, W. D., & Twentyman, C. T. (1985). Abusing, neglectful, and comparison mothers' responses to child-related and non-child-related stressors. *Journal of Consulting and Clinical Psychology, 53,* 335–343.

Baumrind, D. (1971). Current patterns of parental authority. *Developmental Psychology Monographs, 4* (No. 1, Pt. 2).

Baumrind, D. (1973). The development of instrumental competence through socialization. *Minnesota symposia on child psychology* (Vol. 7, pp. 3–46). Minneapolis: University of Minnesota Press.

Baumrind, D. (1982). Are androgynous individuals more effective persons and parents? *Child Development, 53,* 44–75.

Baumrind, D. (1983). Rejoinder to Lewis' reinterpretation of parental firm control effects: Are authoritative families really harmonious? *Psychological Bulletin, 94,* 132–142.

Baumrind, D. (1991). The influence of parenting style on adolescent competence and substance use. *Journal of Early Adolescence, 11,* 56–95.

Beck, R. (1973). The White House Conferences on Children: An historical perspective. *Harvard Educational Review, 43,* 653–668.

Becker, J. V., & Hunter, J. A. (1992). Evaluation of treatment outcome for adult perpetrators of child sexual abuse. *Criminal Justice and Behavior, 19,* 74–92.

Beckwith, L., Rodning, C., & Cohen, S. (1992). Preterm children at early adolescence and continuity and discontinuity in maternal responsiveness from infancy. *Child Development, 63,* 1198–1208.

Beekman, D. (1977). *The mechanical baby: A popular history of the theory and practice of child raising.* Westport, CT: Lawrence Hill.

Bell, R. Q. (1968). A reinterpretation of the direction of effects in studies of socialization. *Psychological Review, 75,* 81–95.

Bell, R. Q. (1971). Stimulus control of parent or caretaker behavior by offspring. *Developmental Psychology, 4,* 63–72.

Bell, R. Q. (1979). Parent, child, and reciprocal influences. *American Psychologist, 34,* 821–826.

Bell, R. Q., & Chapman, M. (1986). Child effects in studies using experimental or brief longitudinal approaches to socialization. *Developmental Psychology, 22,* 595–603.

Bell, R. Q., & Harper, L. (1977). *Child effects on adults.* Hillsdale, NJ: Erlbaum.

Belsky, J. (1980). Child maltreatment: An ecological integration. *American Psychologist, 35,* 320–335.

Belsky, J. (1984). The determinants of parenting: A process model. *Child Development, 55,* 83–96.

Belsky, J. (1993). Etiology of child maltreatment: A developmental-ecological analysis. *Psychological Bulletin, 114,* 413–434.

Belsky, J., Steinberg, L., & Draper, P. (1991). Childhood experience, interpersonal development, and reproductive strategy: An evolutionary theory of socialization. *Child Development, 62,* 647–670.

Belsky, J., & Vondra, J. (1985). Characteristics, consequences, and determinants of parenting. In L. L'Abate (Ed.), *The handbook of family psychology and therapy* (Vol. 1, pp. 523–556). Homewood, IL: Dorsey.

Berkowitz, B. P., & Graziano, A. M. (1972). Training parents as behavior therapists: A review. *Behavioral Research & Therapy, 10,* 297–317.

Bettelheim, B. (1987). *A good enough parent.* New York: Knopf.

Bijou, S. W. (1989). Behavior analysis. In R. Vasta (Ed.), *Annals of child development* (Vol. 6, pp. 61–83). Greenwich, CT: Jai Press.

Bijou, S. W., & Baer, D. M. (1961). *Child development: A systematic and empirical theory* (Vol. 1). New York: Appleton-Century-Crofts.

Biringen, Z. (1990). Direct observation of maternal sensitivity and dyadic interactions in the home: Relations to maternal thinking. *Developmental Psychology, 26,* 278–284.

Biringen, Z. & Robinson, J. (1991). Emotional availability in mother-child interactions: A reconceptualization for research. *American Journal of Orthopsychiatry, 61,* 258–271.

Bishop, B. M. (1951). Mother-child interaction and the social behavior of children. *Psychological Monographs, 65,* 1–34.

Black, C., Bucky, S. F., & Wilder-Padilla, S. (1986). The interpersonal and emotional consequences of being an adult child of an alcoholic. *The International Journal of the Addictions, 21,* 213–231.

Bleckman, E. A., & McEnroe, M. J. (1985). Effective family problem solving. *Child Development, 56,* 429–437.

Block, J., Block, J. H., & Keyes, S. (1988). Longitudinally foretelling drug usage in adolescence: Early childhood personality and environmental precursors. *Child Development, 59,* 336–355.

Bloom, B. S. (Ed.). (1985). *Developing talent in young people.* New York: Ballantine Books.

Bloom, L. Z. (1972). *Doctor Spock: Biography of a conservative radical.* New York: Bobbs-Merrill.

Bornstein, M. H. (1985). How infant and mother jointly contribute to developing cognitive competence in the child. *Proceedings of the National Academy of Sciences, 82,* 7470–7473.

Bornstein, M. H. (Ed.). (1991). *Cultural approaches to parenting.* Hillsdale, NJ: Erlbaum.

Bornstein, M. H. (Ed.). (1995). *Handbook of parenting.* Mahwah, NJ: Erlbaum.

Bornstein, M. H., & Tamis-LeMonda, C. S. (1989). Maternal responsiveness and cognitive development in children. In M. H. Bornstein (Ed.), *Maternal responsiveness: Characteristics and consequences* (pp. 49–61). San Francisco: Jossey-Bass.

Bornstein, M. H., Tamis-LeMonda, C. S., Tal, J., Lundeman, P., Toda, S., Rahn, C. W., Pecheux, M.-G., Azuma, H., & Vardi, D. (1992). Maternal responsiveness to infants in three societies: The United States, France, and Japan. *Child Development, 63,* 808–821.

Borstelmann, L. J. (1983). Children before psychology: Ideas about children from antiquity to the late 1800s. In P. H. Mussen (Ed.), *History, theory, and methods* (Vol. 1, pp. 1–40). New York: Wiley.

Bowlby, J. (1951). *Maternal care and mental health.* Geneva: World Health Organization.

Bowlby, J. (1969). *Attachment and loss: Vol. 1. Attachment.* New York: Basic Books.

Bowlby, J. (1988). *A secure base: Parent-child attachment and healthy human development.* New York: Basic Books.

Boyce, W. T., Jensen, E. W., James, S. A., & Peacock, J. L. (1983). The family routines inventory: Theoretical origins. *Social Science Medicine, 17,* 193–200.

Bradley, R. H., & Caldwell, B. M. (1984). The relation of infants' home environments to achievement test performance in the first grade: A follow-up study. *Child Development, 55,* 803–809.

Bradley, R. H., Caldwell, B. M., & Rock, S. L. (1988). Home environment and school performance: A ten-year follow-up and examination of three models of environmental action. *Child Development, 59,* 852–867.

Brassard, M. R., Germain, R., & Hart, S. N. (1987). *Psychological maltreatment of children and youth*. New York: Pergamon Press.

Brazelton, T. B., Koslowski, B., & Main, M. (1974). The origin of reciprocity: The early mother-infant interaction. In M. Lewis & L. Rosenblum (Eds.), *The effect of the infant on its caregiver* (pp. 49–76). New York: Wiley.

Bristol, M. M., Gallagher, J. J., & Schopler, E. (1988). Mothers and fathers of young developmentally disabled and nondisabled boys: Adaptation and spousal support. *Developmental Psychology, 24,* 441–451.

Brody, G. H., & Shaffer, D. R. (1982). Contributions of parents and peers to children's moral socialization. *Developmental Review, 2,* 31–75.

Bronfenbrenner, U. (1979). *The ecology of human development: Experiments by nature and design*. Cambridge, MA: Harvard University Press.

Bronfenbrenner, U. (1986). Ecology of the family as a context for human development: Research perspectives. *Developmental Psychology, 22,* 723–742.

Bronfenbrenner, U. (1989). Ecological systems theory. In R. Vasta (Ed.), *Annals of child development* (Vol. 6, pp. 187–249). Greenwich, CT: Jai Press.

Bronfenbrenner, U., & Crouter, A. C. (1983). The evolution of environmental models in developmental research. In W. Kessen (Ed.), *Handbook of child psychology: Vol. 1. History, theory, and methods* (4th ed., pp. 357–414). New York: Wiley.

Broussard, W. R., & Hartner, M. S. S. (1971). Further considerations regarding maternal perception of the first born. In J. Hellmuth (Ed.), *Exceptional infant* (Vol. 2). New York: Brunner/Mazel.

Brown, B. B., Mounts, N., Lamborn, S. D., & Steinberg, L. (1993). Parenting practices and peer group affiliation in adolescence. *Child Development, 64,* 467–482.

Brunnquell, D., Crichton, L., & Egeland, B. (1981). Maternal personality and attitude in disturbances of child rearing. *American Journal of Orthopsychiatry, 51,* 680–691.

Bugental, D. B., Blue, J., & Cruzcosa, M. (1989). Perceived control over caregiving outcomes: Implications for child abuse. *Developmental Psychology, 25,* 532–539.

Bugental, D. B., Blue, J., & Lewis, J. (1990). Caregiver beliefs and dysphoric affect directed to difficult children. *Developmental Psychology, 26,* 631–638.

Bugental, D. B., Caporael, L., & Shennum, W. A. (1980). Experimentally produced child uncontrollability: Effects on the potency of adult communication patterns. *Child Development, 52,* 520–528.

Bugental, D. B., & Cortez, V. L. (1988). Physiological reactivity to responsive and unresponsive children as moderated by perceived control. *Child Development, 59,* 686–693.

Bugental, D. B., & Shennum, W. A. (1984). "Difficult" children as elicitors and targets of adult communication patterns: An attributional-behavioral transactional analysis. *Monographs of the Society for Research in Child Development, 4* (1, Serial No. 205).

Buhrmester, D., Camparo, L., Christensen, A., Gonzalez, L. S., & Hinshaw, S. P. (1992). Mothers and fathers interacting in dyads and triads with normal and hyperactive sons. *Developmental Psychology, 28,* 500–509.

Cairns, R. B. (1979). *Social Development: The origins and plasticity of interchanges*. San Francisco: Freeman.

Cairns, R. B. (1983). The emergence of developmental psychology. In P. Mussen (Ed.), *Handbook of child psychology: Vol. 1. History and methods* (pp. 41–102). New York: Wiley.

Cairns, R. B. (1991). Multiple metaphors for a singular idea. *Developmental Psychology, 27,* 23–26.

Calvin, J. (1965). *Calvin's commentary on Ephesians* (T. H. L. Parker, Trans.). Grand Rapids, MI: William B. Eerdmanf. (Original work published 1556.)

Campagna, D. S., & Poffenberger, D. L. (1988). *The sexual trafficking in children: An investigation of the child sex trade.* Dover, MA: Auburn House.

Campos, R., Raffaelli, M., Ude, W., Greco, M., Ruff, A., Rolf, J., Antunes, C. M., Halsey N., Greco, D., & Street Youth Study Group (1994). Social networks and daily activities of street youth in Belo Horizonte, Brazil. *Child Development, 65,* 319–330.

Caplan, P. J., & Hall-McCorquodale, I. (1985). Mother-blaming in major clinical journals. *American Journal of Orthopsychiatry, 55,* 345–353.

Ceci, S. J., & Bruck, M. (1993). Child witnesses: Translating research into policy. *Social Policy Report* (Society for Research in Child Development), 7, 1–30.

Children's Defense Fund. (1992). *The health of America's children: Maternal and child health data book.* Washington, DC: Author.

Children's Defense Fund (1994). *The state of America's children: Yearbook 1994.* Washington, DC: Author.

Chira, S. (1993, June 23). What do teachers want most? Help from parents. *The New York Times,* p. B6.

Chiu, L. H. (1987). Child-rearing attitudes of Chinese, Chinese-American, and Anglo-American mothers. *International Journal of Psychology, 22,* 409–419.

Clarke, A. M., & Clarke, A. D. B. (1976). *Early experience: Myth and evidence.* New York: Free Press.

Clarke-Stewart, K. A. (1978a). Evaluating parental effects on child development. In L. S. Shulman (Ed.), *Review of research in education* (Vol. 6, pp. 47–119). Itasca, IL: Peacock.

Clarke-Stewart, K. A. (1978b). Popular primers for parents. *American Psychologist, 33,* 359–369.

Clarke-Stewart, K. A. (1988). Parents' effects on children's development: A decade of progress? *Journal of Applied Developmental Psychology, 9,* 41–84.

Clausen, A. H., & Crittenden, P. M. (1991). Physical and psychological maltreatment: Relations among types of maltreatment. *Child Abuse & Neglect, 15,* 5–18.

Clifford, E. (1959). Discipline in the home: A controlled observational study of parental practices. *Journal of Genetic Psychology, 95,* 45–82.

Cohn, D. A. (1990). Child-mother attachment of six-year-olds and social competence at school. *Child Development, 61,* 152–162.

Cohn, J. F., & Tronick, E. Z. (1983). Three-month-old infants' reaction to simulated maternal depression. *Child Development, 54,* 185–193.

Collins, N. L., & Read, S. J. (1990). Adult attachment, working models, and relationship quality in dating couples. *Journal of Personality and Social Psychology, 58,* 644–663.

Comer, J. P. (1980). *School power.* New York: Free Press.

Conger, R. D., McCarty, J. A., Yang, R. K., Lahey, B. B., & Burgess, R. L. (1984). Mother's age as a predictor of observed maternal behavior in three independent samples of families. *Journal of Marriage and the Family, 46,* 411–424.

Connelly, C. D., & Straus, M. A. (1992). Mother's age and risk for physical abuse. *Child Abuse & Neglect, 16,* 709–718.

Coombs, R. H., & Landsverk, J. (1988). Parenting styles and substance use during childhood and adolescence. *Journal of Marriage and the Family, 50,* 473–482.

Cooper, C. R., Grotevant, H. D., & Condon, S. M. (1983). Individuality and connectedness in the family as a context for adolescent identity formation and role-taking skill. *New Directions for Child Development, 22,* 43–59.

Coverman, S., & Sheley, J. F. (1986). Change in men's housework and child-care time, 1965–1975. *Journal of Marriage and the Family, 48,* 413–422.

Cowan, C. P., & Cowan, P. A. (1988). Who does what when partners become parents: Implications for men, women, and marriage. In R. Palkovitz & M. B. Sussman (Eds.), *Transitions to parenthood* (pp. 105–131). New York: Haworth Press.

Cowan, C. P., & Cowan, P. A. (1992). *When partners become parents: The big life change for couples.* New York: Basic Books.

Cox, M. J., Owen, M. T., Lewis, J. M., & Henderson, V. K. (1989). Marriage, adult adjustment, and early parenting. *Child Development, 60,* 1015–1024.

Crittenden, P. M. (1981). Abusing, neglecting, problematic, and adequate dyads: Differentiating by patterns of interaction. *Merrill-Palmer Quarterly, 27,* 201–218.

Crnic, K. A., Greenberg, M. T., Ragozin, A., Robinson, N., & Basham, R. (1983). Effects of stress and social support on mothers and premature and full-term infants. *Child Development, 54,* 209–217.

Crockenberg, S. B. (1981). Infant irritability, mother responsiveness, and social support influences on the security of infant-mother attachment. *Child Development, 52,* 857–865.

Crockenberg, S., & Litman, C. (1991). Effects of maternal employment on maternal and two-year-old child behavior. *Child Development, 62,* 930–953.

Crockenberg, S. B., & McCluskey, K. (1986). Change in maternal behavior during the baby's first year of life. *Child Development, 57,* 746–753.

Crouter, A. C., MacDermid, S. M., McHale, S. M., Perry-Jenkins, M. (1990). Parental monitoring and perceptions of children's school performance and conduct in dual- and single-earner families. *Child Development, 26,* 649–657.

Crouter, A. C., & McHale, S. M. (1993). Temporal rhythms in family life: Seasonal variation in the relation between parental work and family processes. *Developmental Psychology, 29,* 198–205.

Crouter, A. C., Perry-Jenkins, M., Huston, T., & McHale, S. M. (1987). Processes underlying father involvement in dual-earner and single-earner families. *Developmental Psychology, 23,* 431–440.

Cummings, E. M., & Davies, P. (1994). *Children and marital conflict: The impact of family dispute and resolution.* New York: Guilford Press.

Cummings, J. (1992, May 6). Prenatal program is cost-saver in long run, GAO report says. *Austin American-Statesman,* p. A20.

Curtis, S. (1977). *Genie: A psycholinguistic study of a modern day wild child.* New York: Academic Press.

Cutrona, C. E., & Troutman, B. R. (1986). Social support, infant temperament, and parenting self-efficacy: A mediational model of postpartum depression. *Child Development, 57,* 1507–1518.

Darling, N., & Steinberg, L. (1993). Parenting style as context: An integrative model. *Psychological Bulletin, 113,* 487–496.

Daro, D. (1992). *World perspectives on child abuse: An international resource book.* Chicago: National Center on Child Abuse Prevention Research.

Darwin, C. (1877). A biographical sketch of an infant. *Mind, 2,* 285–294.

Davies, P. T., & Cummings, E. M. (1994). Marital conflict and child adjustment: An emotional security hypothesis. *Psychological Bulletin, 116,* 387–411.

Davis, A., & Havighurst, R. J. (1946). Social class and color differences in child-rearing. *American Sociological Review, 11,* 698–710.

Dekovic, M., & Janssens, M. M. A. M. (1992). Parents' child-rearing style and child's sociometric status. *Child Development, 28,* 925–932.

deMause, L. (Ed.). (1974). *The history of childhood.* New York: Harper & Row.

DeMeis, D. K., Hock, E., & McBride, S. L. (1986). The balance of employment and motherhood: Longitudinal study of mothers' feelings about separation from their first-born infants. *Developmental Psychology, 22,* 627–632.

Dinkmeyer, D., & McKay, G. (1976). *Systematic training for effective parenting.* Circle Pines, MN: American Guidance Service.

Dix, T. (1991). The affective organization of parenting: Adaptive and maladaptive processes. *Psychological Bulletin, 110,* 3–25.

Dix, T. (1992). Parenting on behalf of the child: Empathic goals in the regulation of responsive parenting. In I. E. Sigel, A. V. McGillicuddy-DeLisi, & J. J. Goodnow (Eds.), *Parental belief systems: The psychological consequences for children* (2nd ed., pp. 319–346). Hillsdale, NJ: Erlbaum.

Dix, T., & Grusec, J. E. (1985). Parent attribution processes in the socialization of children. In I. E. Sigel (Ed.), *Parental Belief Systems: The psychological consequences for children* (pp. 201–234). Hillsdale, NJ: Erlbaum.

Dix, T., & Reinhold, D. P. (1991). Chronic and temporary influences on mothers' attributions for children's disobedience. *Merrill-Palmer Quarterly, 37,* 251–271.

Dix, T., Reinhold, D. P., & Zambarano, R. (1990). Mothers' judgement in moments of anger. *Merrill-Palmer Quarterly, 36,* 465–486.

Dix, T., Ruble, D. N., Grusec, J., & Nixon, J. (1986). Social cognition in parents: Inferential and affective reactions to children of three age levels. *Child Development, 57,* 879–894.

Dix, T., Ruble, D. N., & Zambarano, R. J. (1989). Mothers' implicit theories of discipline: Child effects, parent effects, and the attribution process. *Child Development, 60,* 1373–1391.

Dobson, J. (1970). *Dare to discipline.* New York: Bantam Books.

Dodge, K. A. (1990). Nature versus nurture in childhood conduct disorder: It is time to ask a different question. *Developmental Psychology, 26,* 698–701.

Dodge, K. A., Bates, J. E., & Pettit, G. S. (1990). Mechanisms in the cycle of violence. *Science, 250,* 1678–1683.

Dollard, J., Doob, L. W., Miller, N. E., Mowrer, O. H., & Sears, R. R. (1939). *Frustration and aggression.* New Haven: Yale University Press.

Donovan, W. L., & Leavitt, L. A. (1989). Maternal self efficacy and infant attachment: Integrating physiology, perceptions, and behavior. *Child Development, 60,* 460–472.

Downey, G., & Coyne, J. C. (1990). Children of depressed parents: An integrative review. *Psychological Bulletin, 108,* 50–76.

Duncan, G. J. (1991). The economic environment of childhood. In A. C. Huston (Ed.), *Children in poverty* (pp. 23–50). New York: Cambridge University Press.

Dunn, J., & Plomin, R. (1990). *Separate lives: Why siblings are so different.* New York: Basic Books.

Easterbrooks, M. A., & Emde, R. N. (1988). Marital and parent-child relationships: The role of affect in the family system. In R. A. Hinde & J. Stevenson-Hinde (Eds.), *Relationships within families: Mutual influences* (pp. 83–103). New York: Oxford University Press.

Eckenrode, J., Laird, M., & Doris, J. (1993). School performance and disciplinary problems among abused and neglected children. *Developmental Psychology, 29,* 53–62.

Egeland, B., Jacobvitz, D., & Sroufe, L. A. (1988). Breaking the cycle of abuse. *Child Development, 59,* 1080–1088.

Egeland, B., Sroufe, L. A., & Erickson, M. F. (1983). The developmental consequence of different patterns of maltreatment. *Child Abuse and Neglect, 7,* 459–469.

Eibl-Eibesfeldt, I. (1970). *Ethology: The biology of behavior.* New York: Holt, Rinehart & Winston.

Eiden, R. D., Teti, D. M., & Corns, K. M. (1995). Maternal working models of attachment, marital adjustment, and the parent-child relationship. *Child Development, 66,* 1504–1518.

Eisenberg, N., Fabes, R. A., Carlo, G., Troyer, D., Speer, A. L., Karbon, M., & Switzer, G. (1992). The relations of maternal practices and characteristics to children's vicarious emotional responsiveness. *Child Development, 63,* 583–602.

Elder, G. H., Jr., Caspi, A., & Downey, G. (1986). Problem behavior and family relationships: Life course and intergenerational themes. In A. B. Sorensen, F. E. Weinert, & L. R. Sherrod (Eds.), *Human development and the life course: Multidisciplinary perspectives* (pp. 293–340). Hillsdale, NJ: Erlbaum.

Elder, G. H., Jr., Nguyen, T. V., & Caspi, A. (1985). Linking family hardship to children's lives. *Child Development, 56,* 361–375.

Emde, R. N. (1992). Individual meaning and increasing complexity: Contributions of Sigmund Freud and Rene Spitz to Developmental Psychology. *Developmental Psychology, 28,* 347–359.

Emery, R. E. (1982). Interparental conflict and the children of discord and divorce. *Psychological Bulletin, 92,* 310–330.

Emery, R. E. (1988). *Marriage, divorce, and children's adjustment.* Newbury Park, CA: Sage.

Emery, R. E. (1989). Family violence. *American Psychologist, 44,* 321–328.

Emery, R. E., Fincham, F., & Cummings, E. M. (1992). Parenting in context: Systemic thinking about parental conflict and its influence on children. *Journal of Consulting and Clinical Psychology, 60,* 909–912.

Emmerich, W. (1969). The parental role: A functional cognitive approach. *Monographs of the Society for Research in Child Development, 34*(8, Serial No. 132).

Endsley, R. C., Hutcherson, M. A., Garner, A. P., & Martin, M. J. (1979). Interrelationships among selected maternal behaviors, authoritarianism, and preschool children's verbal and nonverbal curiosity. *Child Development, 50,* 331–339.

Erickson, M. F., Egeland, B., & Pianta, R. (1989). The effects of maltreatment on the development of young children. In D. Cicchetti & V. Carlson (Eds.), *Child maltreatment* (pp. 647–684). New York: Cambridge University Press.

Erlanger, H. S. (1974). Social class and corporal punishment in childrearing: A reassessment. *American Sociological Review, 39,* 68–85.

Eron, L. D., Huesman, L. R., & Zelli, A. (1991). The role of parental variables in the learning of aggression. In D. Pepler & K. Rubin (Eds.), *The development and treatment of child aggression* (pp. 169–188). Hillsdale, NJ: Erlbaum.

Eron, L. D., Walder, L. O., & Lefkowitz, M. M. (1971). *The learning of aggression in children.* Boston: Little, Brown.

Eyer, D. E. (1992). *Mother-infant bonding: A scientific fiction.* New Haven, CT: Yale University Press.

Fagot, B. I. (1978). The influence of sex on parental reactions to toddler children. *Child Development, 49,* 30–36.

Fagot, B. I., & Kavanagh, K. (1990). The prediction of antisocial behavior from avoidant attachment classifications. *Child Development, 61,* 864–873.

Fagot, B. I., & Kavanagh, K. (1993). Parenting during the second year: Effects of children's age, sex, and attachment classification. *Child Development, 64,* 258–271.

Fagot, B. I., Leinbach, M. D., & O'Boyle, C. (1992). Gender labeling, gender stereotyping, and parenting behaviors. *Developmental Psychology, 28,* 225–230.

Feldman, D. H., & Goldsmith, L. T. (1986). Transgenerational influences on the development of early prodigious behavior: A case study approach. In W. Fowler (Ed.), *Early experience and the development of competence* (pp. 67–85). *New directions for child development, No. 32.* San Francisco: Jossey-Bass.

Feldman, S. S., & Brown, N. L. (1993). Family influences on adolescent male sexuality: The mediational role of self-restraint. *Social Development, 2,* 15–35.

Ferber, R. (1985). *Solving your child's sleep problems.* New York: Simon & Schuster.

Feshbach, N. D. (1987). Parental empathy and children's adjustment/maladjustment. In N. Eisenberg & J. Strayer (Eds.), *Empathy and its development* (pp. 271–291). Cambridge: Cambridge University Press.

Field, M. (1940). Maternal attitudes found in twenty-five cases of children with behavior primary disorders. *American Journal of Orthopsychiatry, 10,* 293–311.

Field, T. M., Healy, B., Goldstein, S., & Guthertz, M. (1990). Behavior-state matching and synchrony in mother-infant interactions of non-depressed versus depressed dyads. *Developmental Psychology, 26,* 7–14.

Fine, M. J., & Henry, S. A. (1989). Professional issues in parent education. In M. J. Fine (Ed.), *The second handbook on parent education* (pp. 3–20). New York: Academic Press.

Finkelhor, D. (1987). The sexual abuse of children: Current research reviewed. *Psychiatric Annals, 17*, 233–241.

Finkelstein, N. W., & Ramey, C. T. (1977). Learning to control the environment in infancy. *Child Development, 48*, 806–819.

Fishbein, H. D. (1976). *Evolution, development, and children's learning.* Pacific Palisades, CA: Goodyear.

Fitzgerald, H. E., Sullivan, L. A., Ham, H. P., Zucker, R. A., Bruckel, S., Schneider, A. M., & Noll, R. B. (1993). Predictors of behavior problems in three-year-old sons of alcoholics: Early evidence for the onset of risk. *Child Development, 64*, 110–123.

Flax, D. K., Ficher, I., Masterpasqua, F., & Joseph, G. (1995). Lesbians choosing motherhood: A comparative study of lesbian and heterosexual parents and their children. *Developmental Psychology, 31*, 105–114.

Fletcher, A. C., Darling, N. E., Dornbusch, S. M., & Steinberg, L. (1995). The company that they keep: Relation of adolescents' adjustment and behavior to their friends' perception of authoritative parenting in the social network. *Developmental Psychology, 31*, 300–310.

Fogel, A., & Melson, G. F. (Eds.). (1986). *Origins of nurturance: Developmental, biological, and cultural perspectives on caregiving.* Hillsdale, NJ: Erlbaum.

Fonagy, P., Steele, H., & Steele, M. (1991). Maternal representations of attachment during pregnancy predict the organization of infant-mother attachment at one year of age. *Child Development, 62*, 891–905.

Fraiberg, S. (1987). Ghosts in the nursery: A psychoanalytic approach to the problems of impaired infant-mother relationships. In L. Fraiberg (Ed.), *Selected writings of Selma Fraiberg.* Columbus: Ohio State University Press.

Frankel, D. G., & Roer-Bornstein, D. (1982). Traditional and modern contributions to changing infant-rearing ideologies of two ethnic communities. *Monographs of the Society for Research in Child Development, 47*(4, Serial No. 196).

Frankel, K. A., & Bates, J. E. (1990). Mother-toddler problem solving: Antecedents in attachment, home behavior, and temperament. *Child Development, 61*, 810–819.

Freeman, D. (1983). *Margaret Mead and Samoa: The making and unmaking of an anthropological myth.* Cambridge, MA: Harvard University Press.

French, V. (1977). History of the child's influence: Ancient Mediterranean civilizations. In R. Q. Bell & L. V. Harper (Eds.), *Child effects on adults* (pp. 3–29). New York: Erlbaum.

Freud, S. (1936). *The problem of anxiety* (H. A. Bunker, Trans.). New York: Norton.

Friedrich, W. N., & Einbender, A. J. (1983). The abused child: A psychological review. *Journal of Clinical Child Psychology, 12*, 244–256.

Frodi, A. (1983). When empathy fails: Aversive infant crying and child abuse. In B. Lester & Z. Boukydis (Eds.), *Infant crying: Theoretical and research perspectives* (pp. 263–277). New York: Plenum Press.

Frodi, A. M., & Lamb, M. E. (1980). Child abusers' responses to infant smiles and cries. *Child Development, 51*, 238–241.

Frodi, A. M., Lamb, M. E., Leavitt, L. A., & Donovan, W. L. (1978). Fathers' and mothers' responses to infant smiles and cries. *Infant Behavior and Development, 1*, 187–198.

Fuligni, A. J., & Eccles, J. S. (1993). Perceived parent-child relationships and early adolescents' orientation toward peers. *Developmental Psychology, 29,* 622–632.

Furstenberg, F. F., Brooks-Gunn, J., & Chase-Lansdale, L. (1989). Teenaged pregnancy and childbearing. *American Psychologist, 44,* 313–320.

Garbarino, J., Kosstelny, K., & Dubrow, N. (1991). *No place to be a child: Growing up in a war zone.* Lexington, MA: Heath.

Gardner, F. E. M. (1989). Inconsistent parenting: Is there evidence for a link with children's conduct problems? *Journal of Abnormal Child Psychology, 17,* 223–233.

Gardner, F. E. M. (1992). Parent-child interaction and conduct disorder. *Educational Psychology Review, 4,* 135–163.

Gecas, V. (1979). The influence of social class on socialization. In W. R. Burr, R. Hill, F. I. Nye, & I. L. Reiss (Eds.), *Contemporary theories about the family: Research based theories* (pp. 365–404). New York: Free Press.

Gecas, V., & Nye, F. I. (1974). Sex and class differences in parent-child interaction: A test of Kohn's hypothesis. *Journal of Marriage and the Family, 36,* 742–749.

Gelfand, D. M., & Teti, D. M. (1990). The effects of maternal depression on children. *Clinical Psychology Review, 10,* 329–353.

Gelles, R. J. (1989). Child abuse and violence in single-parent families: Parental absence and economic deprivation. *American Journal of Orthopsychiatry, 59,* 492–501.

Gelles, R. J., & Straus, M. A. (1988). *Intimate violence.* New York: Simon & Schuster.

George, C., & Main, M. (1979). Social interactions of young abused children. *Child Development, 50,* 306–318.

Gewirtz, J. L., & Boyd, E. F. (1977). Infant crying? A critique of the 1972 Bell and Ainsworth report. *Child Development, 18,* 1200–1207.

Gewirtz, J. L., & Pelaez-Nogueras, M. (1992). B. F. Skinner's legacy to human infant behavior and development. *American Psychologist, 47,* 1411–1422.

Gil, D. G. (1970). *Violence against children.* Cambridge, MA: Harvard University Press.

Glenn, N. D. (1987). The marriages and divorces of the children of divorce. *Journal of Marriage and the Family, 49,* 811–825.

Goldberg, W. A. (1990). Marital quality, parental personality, and spousal agreement about perceptions and expectations for children. *Merrill-Palmer Quarterly, 36,* 531–556.

Goldsmith, H. H. (1994, Winter). The behavior-genetic approach to development and experience: Contexts and constraints. *SRCD Newsletter,* pp. 1–11.

Goldsmith, H. H., Buss, A. H., Plomin, R., Rothbart, M. K., Thomas, A., Chess, S., Hinde, R. A., & McCall, R. B. (1987). Roundtable: What is temperament? Four approaches. *Child Development, 58,* 505–529.

Goldstein, M. J. (1988). The family and psychopathology. *Annual Review of Psychology, 39,* 283–299.

Goodman, S. H., Brogan, D., Lynch, M. E., & Fielding, B. (1993). Social and emotional competence in children of depressed mothers. *Child Development, 64,* 516–531.

Goodman, S. H., & Brumley, H. E. (1990). Schizophrenic and depressed mothers: Relational deficits in parenting. *Developmental Psychology, 26,* 31–39.

Goodnow, J. J. (1984). Parents' ideas about parenting and development: A review of issues and recent work. In M. Lamb, A. Brown, & B. Rogoff (Eds.), *Advances in developmental psychology* (pp. 193–242). Hillsdale, NJ: Erlbaum.

Goodnow, J. J. (1988a). Children's household work: Its nature and functions. *Psychological Bulletin, 103,* 5–26.

Goodnow, J. J. (1988b). Parents' ideas, actions, and feelings: Models and methods from developmental and social psychology. *Child Development, 59,* 286–320.

Goodnow, J. J., & Collins, W. A. (1990). *Development according to parents: The nature, sources, and consequences of parents' ideas.* Hillsdale, NJ: Erlbaum.

Gordon, T. (1976). *P.E.T. in action.* New York: Wyden Books.

Gottesman, I. I., & Shields, J. (1982). *Schizophrenia: The epigenetic puzzle.* Cambridge: Cambridge University Press.

Graziano, W. (1994). The development of Agreeableness as a dimension of personality. In C. F. Halverson, Jr., G. A. Kohnstamm, & R. P. Martin (Eds.), *The developing structure of temperament and personality from infancy to adulthood* (pp. 339–354). Hillsdale, NJ: Erlbaum.

Greenberger, E., & Goldberg, W. A. (1989). Work, parenting, and the socialization of children. *Developmental Psychology, 25,* 22–35.

Greenberger, E., Goldberg, W. A., Hamill, S., O'Neil, R., & Payne, C. K. (1989). Contributions of a supportive work environment to parents' well-being and orientation to work. *American Journal of Community Psychology, 17,* 755–783.

Greven, P. (1973). *Child-rearing concepts, 1628–1861.* Itasca, IL: Peacock.

Greven, P. (1977). *The Protestant temperament: Patterns of child-rearing, religious experience, and the self in early America.* New York: Knopf.

Grolnick, W. S., & Ryan, R. M. (1989). Parent styles associated with children's self-regulation and competence in school. *Journal of Educational Psychology, 81,* 143–154.

Grusec, J. E., & Kuczynski, L. (1980). Direction of effect in socialization: A comparison of the parent's vs. the child's behavior as determinants of disciplinary techniques. *Developmental Psychology, 6,* 1–9.

Grusec, J. E. (1991). Socializing concern for others in the home. *Developmental Psychology, 27,* 338–342.

Grusec, J. E. (1992). Social learning theory and developmental psychology: The legacies of Robert Sears and Albert Bandura. *Developmental Psychology, 28,* 776–786.

Grusec, J. E., & Goodnow, J. J. (1994). Impact of parental discipline methods on the child's internalization of values: A reconceptualization of current points of view. *Developmental Psychology, 30,* 4–19.

Grusec, J. E., & Lytton, H. (1988). *Social development: History, theory, and research.* New York: Springer-Verlag.

Grych, J. H., & Fincham, F. D. (1990). Marital conflict and children's adjustment: A cognitive-contextual framework. *Psychological Bulletin, 108,* 267–290.

Haeuser, A. A. (1990). *Banning parental use of physical punishment: Success in Sweden.* Paper presented at the Eighth International Congress on Child Abuse and Neglect, Hamburg, Germany.

Halpern, R. (1990). Poverty and early childhood parenting: Toward a framework for intervention. *American Journal of Orthopsychiatry, 60,* 6–18.

Hannan, K., & Luster, T. (1991). Influence of parent, child and contextual factors on the home environment. *Infant Mental Health Journal, 12,* 17–30.

Harkness, S., & Super, C. (1995). Culture and parenting. In M. H. Bornstein (Ed.), *Handbook of parenting: Vol. 2. Biology and ecology of parenting* (pp. 211–234). Mahwah, NJ: Erlbaum.

Harlow, H., Dodsworth, R. O., & Harlow, M. K. (1965). Total social isolation in monkeys. *Proceedings of the National Academy of Sciences, 54,* 90–96.

Harmon, D., & Brim, O. G. J. (1980). *Learning to be parents: Principles, programs, and methods.* Beverly Hills, CA: Sage.

Hart, C. H., Ladd, G. W., & Burleson, B. R. (1990). Children's expectations of the outcomes of social strategies: Relations with sociometric status and maternal disciplinary styles. *Child Development, 61,* 127–137.

Hart, S. N., & Brassard, M. R. (1987). A major threat to children's mental health: Psychological maltreatment. *American Psychologist, 42,* 160–165.

Hart, S. N., & Brassard, M. R. (1994). *Draft guidelines for psychosocial evaluation of suspected psychological maltreatment in children and adolescents.* American Professional Society on the Abuse of Children, Chicago, IL.

Hartup, W. W. (1989). Social relationships and their developmental significance. *American Psychologist, 44,* 120–126.

Hausfater, G., & Hrdy, S. B. (Eds.). (1984). *Infanticide: Comparative and evolutionary perspectives.* New York: Aldine.

Hawes, J. M. (1991). *The children's rights movement: A history of advocacy and protection.* Boston: Twayne.

Helfer, R. E., & Kempe, C. (1988). *The battered child* (4th ed.). Chicago: University of Chicago Press.

Hess, R. D., & Holloway, S. D. (1984). Family and school as educational institutions. In R. D. Parke (Ed.), *Review of child development research: Vol. V. The family* (pp. 179–222). Chicago: University of Chicago Press.

Hetherington, E. M., & Clingempeel, W. G. (1992). Coping with marital transitions: A family systems perspective. *Monographs of the Society for Research in Child Development, 57* (2–3, Serial No. 227).

Hewlett, S. A. (1991). *When the bough breaks: The cost of neglecting our children.* New York: Basic Books.

Himelstein, S., Graham, S., & Weiner, B. (1991). An attributional analysis of maternal beliefs about the importance of child-rearing practices. *Child Development, 62,* 301–310.

Hinde, R. A. (1976). On describing relationships. *Journal of Child Clinical Psychology and Psychiatry, 17,* 1–19.

Hinde, R. A. (1989). Ethological relationships and approaches. In R. Vasta (Ed.), *Annals of child development* (Vol. 6, pp. 251–285). Greenwich, CT: Jai Press.

Hodapp, R. M., Goldfield, E. C., & Boyatzis, C. J. (1984). The use and effectiveness of maternal scaffolding in mother-infant games. *Child Development, 55,* 772–781.

Hoffman, L. W. (1989). Effects of maternal employment in the two-parent family. *American Psychologist, 44,* 283–292.

Hoffman, L. W. (1991). The influence of the family environment on personality: Accounting for sibling differences. *Psychological Bulletin, 110,* 187–203.

Hoffman, M. L. (1975). Moral internalization, parental power and the nature of parent-child interaction. *Developmental Psychology, 11,* 228–239.

Hoffman, M. L., & Saltzstein, H. D. (1967). Parent discipline and the child's moral development. *Journal of Personality and Social Psychology, 5,* 45–57.

Hoffman, M. S. (Ed.). (1992). *The world almanac and book of facts: 1992.* New York: Pharos Books.

Holden, G. W. (1983). Avoiding conflict: Mothers as tacticians in the supermarket. *Child Development, 54,* 233–240.

Holden, G. W. (1985). How parents create a social environment via proactive behavior. In T. Gärling & J. Valsiner (Eds.), *Children within environments: Towards a psychology of accident prevention* (pp. 193–215). New York: Plenum Press.

Holden, G. W. (1988). Adults' thinking about a child-rearing problem: Effects of experience, parental status, and gender. *Child Development, 59,* 1623–1632.

Holden, G. W. (1995). Parent attitudes toward child rearing. In M. H. Bornstein (Ed.), *Handbook of parenting* (Vol. 3, pp. 359–392). Hillsdale, NJ: Erlbaum.

Holden, G. W., Coleman, S., & Schmidt, K. L. (1995). Why 3-year-old children get spanked: Parent and child determinants in a sample of college-educated mothers. *Merrill-Palmer Quarterly, 41,* 431–452.

Holden, G. W., & Edwards, J. (1989). Parental attitudes toward child rearing: Instruments, issues, and implications. *Psychological Bulletin, 106,* 29–58.

Holden, G. W., Lavigne, V. V., & Cameron, A. M. (1990). Probing the continuum of effectiveness in parent training: Characteristics of parents and preschoolers. *Journal of Clinical Child Psychology, 19,* 2–8.

Holden, G. W., Nelson, P. B., Velasquez, J., & Ritchie, K. L. (1993). Cognitive, psychosocial, and reported sexual behavior differences between pregnant and nonpregnant adolescents. *Adolescence, 28,* 557–572.

Holden, G. W., & O'Dell, P. (1995). *The stability of parental behavior: A meta-analysis and reformulation.* Manuscript under review, University of Texas at Austin.

Holden, G. W., & Ritchie, K. L. (1988). Child rearing and the dialectics of parental intelligence. In J. Valsiner (Ed.), *Children's development within socio-culturally structured environments* (pp. 30–59). Norwood, NJ: Ablex.

Holden, G. W., & Ritchie, K. L. (1991). Linking extreme marital discord, child rearing, and child behavior problems: Evidence from battered women. *Child Development, 62,* 311–327.

Holden, G. W., Ritchie, K. L., & Coleman, S. D. (1992). The accuracy of maternal self-reports: Agreement between reports on a computer simulation compared with observed behaviour in the supermarket. *Early Development and Parenting, 1,* 109–119.

Holden, G. W., & West, M. J. (1989). Proximate regulation by mothers: A demonstration of how differing styles affect young children's behavior. *Child Development, 60,* 64–69.

Holden, G. W., & Zambarano, R. J. (1992). Passing the rod: Similarities between parents and their young children in orientations toward physical punishment. In I. E. Sigel, A. V. McGillicuddy-Delisi, & J. J. Goodnow (Eds.), *Parental belief sys-*

tems: The psychological consequences for children (2nd ed., pp. 143–172). Hillsdale, NJ: Erlbaum.

Holt, L. (1914). *The Care and feeding of children*. New York: Appleton.

Hooper, C. (1991). The birds, the bees, and human sexual strategies. *Journal of NIH Research, 3,* 54–60.

Horn, J., Loehlin, J., & Willerman, L. (1979). Intellectual resemblance among adoptive and biological relatives: The Texas Adoption project. *Behavior Genetics, 9,* 177–207.

Horney, K. (1933). Maternal conflicts. *American Journal of Orthopsychiatry, 3,* 455–463.

Horowitz, F. D. (1992). John B. Watson's legacy: Learning and environment. *Developmental Psychology, 28,* 360–367.

Hosken, F. P. (1978). Female circumcision in Africa. *Victimology, 2,* 487–498.

Huston, A. C. (Ed.). (1991). *Children in poverty: Child development and public policy*. New York: Cambridge University Press.

Huttenlocher, J., Haight, W., Bryk, A., Seltzer, M., & Lyons, T. (1991). Early vocabulary growth: Relation to language input and gender. *Developmental Psychology, 27,* 236–248.

Isabella, R. (1993). Origins of attachment: Maternal interactive behavior across the first year. *Child Development, 64,* 605–621.

Itard, J. M. G. (1962). *The wild boy of Aveyron* (G. Humphrey & M. Humphrey, Trans.). New York: Appleton-Century-Crofts.

Izard, C. E., Haynes, O. M., Chisholm, G., & Baak, K. (1991). Emotional determinants of infant-mother attachment. *Child Development, 62,* 906–917.

Jaffe, P. G., Wolfe, D. A., & Wilson, S. K. (1990). *Children of battered women*. Newbury Park, CA: Sage.

Jennings, K. D., Stagg, V., & Connors, R. E. (1991). Social networks and mothers' interactions with their preschool children. *Child Development, 62,* 966–978.

Johnson, C. F., & Showers, J. (1985). Injury variables in child abuse. *Journal of Child Abuse & Neglect, 9,* 207–215.

Johnston, C., & Mash, E. (1989). A measure of parenting satisfaction and efficacy. *Journal of Clinical Child Psychology, 18,* 167–175.

Jones, E. (1923). The phantasy of the reversal of generations. *Papers on psychoanalysis* (pp. 674–679). New York: Wood.

Jouriles, E. N., Murphy, C. M., & O'Leary, K. D. (1989a). Effects of maternal mood on mother-son interaction patterns. *Journal of Abnormal Child Psychology, 17,* 513–525.

Jouriles, E. N., Murphy, C. M., & O'Leary, K. D. (1989b). Interspousal aggression, marital discord, and child problems. *Journal of Consulting and Clinical Psychology, 57,* 453–455.

Kamerman, S., & Kahn, A. (1989). Family policy: Has the United States learned from Europe? *Policy Studies Review, 8,* 581–598.

Kaufman, J., & Zigler, E. (1989). The intergenerational transmission of child abuse. In D. Cicchetti & V. Carlson (Eds.), *Child maltreatment* (pp. 129–152). New York: Cambridge University Press.

Kaye, K. (1982). *The mental and social life of babies: How parents create persons.* Chicago: University of Chicago Press.

Kaye, K., & Fogel, A. (1980). The temporal structure of face-to-face communication between mothers and infants. *Developmental Psychology, 16,* 454–464.

Kazdin, A. E. (1987). Treatment of antisocial behavior in children: Current status and future directions. *Psychological Bulletin, 102,* 187–203.

Kelley, M. L., Power, T. G., & Wimbush, D. D. (1992). Determinants of disciplinary practices in low-income Black mothers. *Child Development, 63,* 573–582.

Kempe, C. H., Silverman, F. N., Steele, B. B., Droegemueller, W., & Silver, H. K. (1962). The battered child syndrome. *Journal of the American Medical Association, 181,* 17–24.

Kendall-Tackett, K. A., Williams, L. M., & Finkelhor, D. (1993). Impact of sexual abuse on children: A review and synthesis of recent empirical studies. *Psychological Bulletin, 113,* 164–180.

Kenny, D. A. (1990). The analysis of data from two-person relationships. In S. Duck (Ed.), *Handbook of interpersonal relations* (pp. 57–77). London: Wiley.

Kessen, W. (1965). *The child.* New York: Wiley.

Kessen, W. (1979). The American child and other cultural inventions. *American Psychologist, 34,* 815–820.

Klaus, M. H., Jerauld, R., Kreger, N. C., McAlpine, W., Steffa, M., & Kennell, J. H. (1972). Maternal attachment: Importance of the first post-partum days. *The New England Journal of Medicine, 286,* 460–463.

Klaus, M. H., & Kennell, J. H. (1976). *Maternal-infant bonding.* St. Louis: Mosby.

Kobak, R. R., & Sceery, A. (1988). Attachment in late adolescence: Working models, affect regulation, and representations of self and others. *Child Development, 59,* 135–146.

Kochanska, G. (1991). Socialization and temperament in the development of conscience. *Child Development, 62,* 1379–1392.

Kochanska, G. (1992). Children's interpersonal influence with mothers and peers. *Developmental Psychology, 28,* 491–499.

Kochanska, G. (1993). Toward a synthesis of parental socialization and child temperament in early development of conscience. *Child Development, 64,* 325–347.

Kochanska, G. (1995). Children's temperament, mothers' discipline, and security of attachment: Multiple pathways to emerging internalization. *Child Development, 66,* 597–615.

Kochanska, G., DeVet, K., Goldman, M., Murray, K., & Putnam, S. P. (1994). Maternal reports of conscience development and temperament in young children. *Child Development, 65,* 852–868.

Kohn, M. L. (1979). The effects of social class on parental values and practices. In D. Reiss & H. Hoffman (Eds.), *The American family: Dying or developing* (pp. 45–68). New York: Plenum Press.

Kohn, M. L., Naoi, A., Shoenbach, C., Schooler, C., & Slomczynski, K. M. (1990). Position in the class structure and psychological functioning: A comparative analysis of the United States, Japan, and Poland. *American Journal of Sociology, 90,* 964–1008.

Kopp, C. (1982). The antecedents of self-regulation: A developmental perspective. *Developmental Psychology, 18,* 199–214.

Kravitz, R. I., & Driscoll, J. M. (1983). Expectations for childhood development among child-abusing and nonabusing parents. *American Journal of Orthopsychiatry, 53,* 336–343.

Kristof, N. D. (1993, July 21). Ultrasound gives China way to weed out girls. *Austin American Statesman,* p. A17.

Kuczynski, L. (1984). Socialization goals and mother-child interaction: Strategies for long-term and short-term compliance. *Developmental Psychology, 20,* 1061–1073.

Kuo, Z.-Y. (1967). *The dynamics of behavioral development: An epigenetic view.* New York: Plenum Press.

Ladd, G. W., & Golter, B. S. (1988). Parents' management of preschooler's peer relations: Is it related to children's social competence? *Developmental Psychology, 24,* 109–117.

Ladd, G. W., Profilet, S. M., & Hart, C. H. (1992). Parents' management of children's peer relations: Facilitating and supervising children's activities in the peer culture. In R. D. Parke & G. W. Ladd (Eds.), *Family-peer relationships* (pp. 215–253). Hillsdale, NJ: Erlbaum.

LaFreniere, P. J., & Sroufe, L. A. (1985). Profiles of peer competence in the preschool: Interrelations between measures, influence of social ecology, and relation to attachment history. *Developmental Psychology, 21,* 56–69.

Lahey, B. B., Conger, R. D., Atkinson, B. M., & Treiber, F. A. (1984). Parenting behavior and emotional status of physically abusive mothers. *Journal of Consulting and Clinical Psychology, 52,* 1062–1071.

Lamb, M. E. (1977). Father-infant and mother-infant interaction in the first year of life. *Child Development, 48,* 167–181.

Lamb, M. E., & Easterbrooks, M. A. (1981). Individual differences in parental sensitivity: Origins, components, and consequences. In M. E. Lamb & L. R. Sherrod (Eds.), *Infant social cognition: Empirical and theoretical considerations* (pp. 127–154). Hillsdale, NJ: Erlbaum.

Lamb, M. E., Hwang, C.-P., & Broberg, A. (1989). Associations between parental agreement regarding child-rearing and the characteristics of families and children in Sweden. *International Journal of Behavioral Development, 12,* 115–129.

Lamb, M. E., & Nash, A. (1989). Infant-mother attachment, sociability, and peer competence. In T. J. Berndt & G. W. Ladd (Eds.), *Peer relationships in child development* (pp. 219–246). Hillsdale, NJ: Erlbaum.

Lamb, M. E., Thompson, R. A., Gardner, W., & Charnov, E. L. (1985). *Infant-mother attachment: The origins and developmental significance of individual differences in Strange Situation behavior.* Hillsdale, NJ: Erlbaum.

Lamborn, S., Mounts, N., Steinberg, L., & Dornbusch, S. (1991). Patterns of competence and adjustment among adolescents from authoritative, authoritarian, indulgent, and neglectful homes. *Child Development, 62,* 1049–1065.

Lang, A. R., Pelham, W. E., Johnston, C., & Gelernter, S. (1989). Levels of alcohol consumption induced by interactions with child confederates exhibiting normal versus externalizing behaviors. *Journal of Abnormal Psychology, 98,* 294–299.

Langlois, J. H., & Downs, A. C. (1980). Mothers, fathers, and peers as socialization agents of sex-typed play behaviors in young children. *Child Development, 51,* 1217–1247.

Laosa, L. M. (1978). Maternal teaching strategies in Chicano families of varied educational and socioeconomic levels. *Child Development, 49,* 1129–1135.

Laosa, L. M. (1984). Social policies toward children of diverse ethnic, racial, and language groups in the United States. In H. W. Stevenson & A. E. Siegel (Eds.), *Child development research and social policy* (Vol. 1, pp. 1–109). Chicago: University of Chicago Press.

Larrance, D. T., & Twentyman, C. T. (1983). Maternal attributions and child abuse. *Journal of Abnormal Psychology, 92,* 449–457.

Lasko, J. K. (1954). Parent behavior toward first and second children. *Genetic Psychology Monographs, 49,* 97–137.

Lawrence, J. A., & Valsiner, J. (1993). Conceptual roots of internalization: From transmission to transformation. *Human Development, 36,* 150–167.

Laws, G. (1927). *Parent-child relationships.* New York: Columbia University Press.

Lazar, I. & Darlington, R. (1982). Lasting effects of early education: A report from the consortium for longitudinal studies. *Monographs of the Society for Research in Child Development, 47* (2–3, Serial No. 195).

Lee, C. L., & Bates, J. E. (1985). Mother-child interaction at age two years and perceived difficult temperament. *Child Development, 56,* 1314–1325.

Lepper, M. R. (1983). Social-control processes and the internalization of social values: An attributional perspective. In E. T. Higgins, D. N. Ruble, & W. W. Hartup (Eds.), *Social cognition and social development* (pp. 294–330). New York: Cambridge University Press.

Levine, M., & Levine, A. (1992). *Helping children: A social history.* New York: Oxford University Press.

LeVine, R. A., Miller, P. M., & West, M. M. (Eds.). (1988). *Parental behavior in diverse societies* (Vol. 40). San Francisco: Jossey-Bass.

Levy, D. (1943). *Maternal overprotection.* New York: Columbia University Press.

Lewin, K. (1935). *A dynamic theory of personality.* New York: McGraw-Hill.

Lewis, C. C. (1981). The effects of parental firm control: A reinterpretation of the findings. *Psychological Bulletin, 90,* 547–563.

Lewis, M., & Kreitzberg, V. S. (1979). Effects of birth order and spacing on mother-infant interactions. *Developmental Psychology, 15,* 617–625.

Lin, C.-Y. C., & Fu, V. R. (1990). A comparison of child-rearing practices among Chinese, immigrant Chinese, and Caucasian-American parents. *Child Development, 61,* 429–433.

Locke, J. (1978). *Some thoughts concerning education.* New York: Oxford University Press. (Original work published 1693.)

Loeber, R., & Dishion, T. (1983). Early predictors of male delinquency: A review. *Psychological Bulletin, 94,* 68–99.

Loehlin, J. C. (1992). *Genes and environment in personality development.* Newbury Park, CA: Sage.

Lollis, S. P., Ross, H. S., & Tate, E. (1992). Parents' regulation of children's peer interactions: Direct influences. In R. D. Parke & G. W. Ladd (Eds.), *Family-peer relationships* (pp. 255–281). Hillsdale, NJ: Erlbaum.

Lomax, E. M. R., Kagan, J., & Rosenkrantz, B. G. (1978). *Science and patterns of child care.* San Francisco: Freeman.

Lounsbury, M. L., & Bates, J. E. (1982). The cries of infants of differing levels of perceived temperamental difficultness: Acoustic properties and effects on listeners. *Child Development, 53,* 677–686.

Luster, R., & Okagaki, L. (Eds.). (1993). *Parenting: An ecological perspective.* Hillsdale, NJ: Erlbaum.

Luster, T., Rhoades, K., & Haas, B. (1989). The relation between parental values and parenting behavior: A test of the Kohn hypothesis. *Journal of Marriage and the Family, 51,* 139–147.

Lynd, R. S., & Lynd, H. M. (1929). *Middletown: A study in contemporary American culture.* New York: Harcourt, Brace.

Lyons-Ruth, K., Alpern, L., & Repacholi, B. (1993). Disorganized infant attachment classification and maternal psychosocial problems as predictors of hostile-aggressive behavior in the preschool classroom. *Child Development, 64,* 572–585.

Lytton, H. (1979). Disciplinary encounters between young boys and their mothers and fathers: Is there a contingency system? *Developmental Psychology, 15,* 256–268.

Lytton, H. (1980). *Parent-child interaction: The socialization process observed in twin and singleton families.* New York: Plenum Press.

Lytton, H., & Romney, D. M. (1991). Parents' differential socialization of boys and girls: A meta-analysis. *Psychological Bulletin, 109,* 267–296.

Maccoby, E. E. (1984). Socialization and developmental change. *Child Development, 55,* 317–328.

Maccoby, E. E. (1992). The role of parents in the socialization of children: An historical overview. *Developmental Psychology, 28,* 1006–1017.

Maccoby, E. E., & Gibbs, P. K. (1954). Methods of child-rearing in two social classes. In W. E. Martin & C. B. Stendler (Eds.), *Readings in child development* (pp. 380–396). New York: Harcourt, Brace & World.

Maccoby, E. E., & Jacklin, C. N. (1974). *The psychology of sex differences.* Stanford: Stanford University Press.

Maccoby, E. E., & Martin, J. A. (1983). Socialization in the context of the family: Parent-child interaction. In E. M. Hetherington (Ed.), *Handbook of child psychology: Vol. 4. Socialization, personality, and social development* (4th ed., pp. 1–102). New York: Wiley.

MacDonald, K. (1987). Parent-child physical play with rejected, neglected, and popular boys. *Developmental Psychology, 23,* 705–711.

MacDonald, K. (1992). Warmth as a developmental construct: An evolutionary analysis. *Child Development, 63,* 753–773.

MacDonald, K., & Parke, R. D. (1984). Bridging the gap: Parent-child play interaction and peer interactive competence. *Child Development, 55,* 1265–1277.

MacPhee, D., Ramey, C. T., & Yeates, K. O. (1984). Home environment and early cognitive development: Implications for intervention. In A. W. Gottfried (Ed.), *Home environment and early cognitive development* (pp. 343–369). New York: Academic Press.

Main, M., & Goldwyn, R. (1984). Predicting rejection of her infant from mother's representation of her own experience: Implications for the abused-abusing intergenerational cycle. *Child Abuse & Neglect, 8,* 203–217.

Main, M., Kaplan, N., & Cassidy, J. (1985). Security in infancy, childhood, and adulthood: A move to the level of representation. In I. Bretherton & E. Waters (Eds.), *Growing points of attachment theory and research. Monographs of the Society for Research in Child Development, 50* (1–2, Serial No. 209, pp. 66–104).

Margolin, G., & Patterson, G. R. (1975). Differential consequences provided by mothers and fathers of their sons and daughters. *Developmental Psychology, 11,* 537–538.

Marshall, N. L., & Barnett, R. C. (1993). Work-family strain and gains among two-earner couples. *Journal of Community Psychology, 21,* 64–78.

Martin, B. (1975). Parent-child relations. In F. D. Horowitz (Ed.), *Review of child development research* (Vol. 4, pp. 463–540). Chicago: University of Chicago Press.

Martin, J. A. (1989). Personal and interpersonal components of responsiveness. In M. H. Bornstein (Ed.), *Maternal responsiveness: Characteristics and consequences* (pp. 5–14). San Francisco: Jossey-Bass.

Mash, E. J., & Johnston, C. (1990). Determinants of parenting stress: Illustrations from families of hyperactive children and families of physically abused children. *Journal of Clinical Child Psychology, 19,* 313–328.

Mash, E. J., Johnston, C., & Kovitz, K. (1983). A comparison of the mother-child interactions of physically abused and non-abused children during play and task situations. *Journal of Clinical Child Psychology, 12,* 337–346.

Masten, A. S. (1992). Homeless children in the United States: Mark of a nation at risk. *Current Directions in Psychological Science, 1,* 41–44.

Matas, L., Arend, R. A., & Sroufe, L. A. (1978). Continuity of adaptation in the second year: The relationship between quality of attachment and later competence. *Child Development, 49,* 547–556.

McBride, S., & Belsky, J. (1988). Characteristics, determinants, and consequences of maternal separation anxiety. *Developmental Psychology, 24,* 407–414.

McCord, J. (1988). Parental aggressiveness and physical punishment in long-term perspective. In G. T. Hotaling, D. Finkelhor, J. T. Kirpatrick, & M. A. Straus (Eds.), *Family abuse and its consequences: New directions in research* (pp. 93–98). Beverly Hills, CA: Sage.

McHale, J. P. (1995). Coparenting and triadic interactions during infancy: The roles of marital distress and child gender. *Developmental Psychology, 31,* 985–996.

McHale, S. M., Bartko, W. T., Crouter, A. C., & Perry-Jenkins, M. (1990). Children's housework and psychosocial functioning: The mediating effects of parents' sex role behaviors and attitudes. *Child Development, 61,* 1413–1426.

McLanahan, S. S. (1989). Mother-only families: Problems, prospects, and politics. *Journal of Marriage and the Family, 51,* 557–580.

McLoyd, V. C. (1989). Socialization and development in a changing economy: The effects of paternal job and income loss on children. *American Psychologist, 44,* 293–302.

McLoyd, V. C. (1990). The impact of economic hardship on Black families and children: Psychological distress, parenting, and socioemotional development. *Child Development, 61,* 311–346.

McLoyd, V. C., & Wilson, L. (1990). Maternal behavior, social support, and economic conditions as predictors of distress in children. *New Directions for Child Development, 46,* 49–69.

Mead, M. (1928). *Coming of age in Samoa*. New York: Morrow.

Medway, F. J. (1989). Measuring the effectiveness of parent education. In M. J. Fine (Ed.), *The second handbook on parent education: Contemporary perspectives* (pp. 237–255). New York: Academic Press.

Miller, G. E., & Prinz, R. J. (1990). Enhancement of social learning family interventions for childhood conduct disorder. *Psychological Bulletin, 108,* 291–307.

Miller, N. B., Cowan, P. A., Cowan, C. P., Hetherington, E. M., & Clingempeel, W. G. (1993). Externalizing in preschoolers and early adolescents: A cross-study replication of a family model. *Developmental Psychology, 29,* 3–18.

Miller, N. E., & Dollard, J. (1941). *Social learning and imitation*. New Haven: Yale University Press.

Miller, P. H. (1989). *Theories of developmental psychology* (2nd ed.). New York: Freeman.

Miller, S., & Scarr, S. (1989). Diagnosis of behavior problems in two-year-olds. *Journal of Clinical Child Psychology, 18,* 290–298.

Miller, S. A. (1988). Parents' beliefs about children's cognitive development. *Child Development, 63,* 259–285.

Miller, S. A. (1995). Parents' attributions for their children's behavior. *Child Development, 66,* 1557–1584.

Milner, J. S., & Chilamkurti, C. (1991). Physical child abuse perpetrator characteristics: A review of the literature. *Journal of Interpersonal Violence, 6,* 345–366.

Milner, J. S., & Robertson, K. R. (1990). Comparison of physical child abusers, intrafamilial sexual child abusers, and child neglecters. *Journal of Interpersonal Violence, 5,* 15–34.

Minturn, L., & Lambert, W. W. (1964). *Mothers of six cultures: Antecedents of child rearing*. New York: Wiley.

Mintz, S., & Kellogg, S. (1988). *Domestic revolutions: A social history of American family life*. New York: Free Press.

Minuchin, P. (1985). Families and individual development: Provocations from the field of family therapy. *Child Development, 56,* 289–302.

Mischel, W. & Shoda, Y. (1995). A cognitive-affective system theory of personality: Reconceptualizing situations, dispositions, dynamics, and invariance in personality structure, *Psychological Review, 102,* 246–268.

Mulhern, R. K. J., & Passman, R. H. (1981). Parental discipline as affected by the sex of the parent, the sex of the child, and the child's apparent responsiveness to discipline. *Developmental Psychology, 17,* 604–613.

National Center for the Prevention of Child Abuse. (1991). *Current trends in child abuse reporting and fatalities: Results of the 1990 annual fifty state survey*. Washington, DC: National Center on Child Abuse Prevention Research.

National Center on Child Abuse and Neglect. (1993). *Summary data component*: Working Paper 2, 1991. U.S. Department of Health and Human Services. Washington, DC.

National Commission on Children. (1991). *Beyond rhetoric: A new American agenda for children and families*. Washington, DC: Author.

National Committee for Prevention of Child Abuse. (1993, May). *Current trends in child abuse reporting and fatalities: The results of the 1992 annual fifty state survey*. *Working paper #808.* Chicago: Author.

National Research Council. (1993). *Losing generations: Adolescents in high-risk settings*. Washington, DC: National Academy Press.

Newcomb, M. D., & Bentler, P. M. (1989). Substance use and abuse among children and teenagers. *American Psychologist, 44*, 242–248.

Ninio, A. (1979). The naive theory of the infant and other maternal attitudes in two subgroups in Israel. *Child Development, 50*, 976–980.

Ninio, A., & Rinott, N. (1988). Fathers' involvement in the care of their infants and their attributions of cognitive competence to infants. *Child Development, 59*, 652–663.

Noll, R. B., Zucker, R. A., & Greenberg, G. S. (1990). Identification of alcohol by smell among preschoolers: Evidence for early socialization about drugs occurring in the home. *Child Development, 61*, 1520–1527.

Oakland, T. (1992). School drop-outs: Characteristics and prevention. *Applied and Preventive Psychology, 1*, 201–208.

Ogbu, J. U. (1981). Origins of human competence: A cultural-ecological perspective. *Child Development, 55*, 1913–1925.

Ogbu, J. U. (1988). Cultural diversity and human development. In D. T. Slaughter (Ed.), *Black children and poverty: A developmental perspective* (Series Vol. No. 42, pp. 11–28). San Francisco: Jossey-Bass.

Okagaki, L., & Sternberg, R. J. (1991). Cultural and parental influences on cognitive development. In L. Okagaki & R. J. Sternberg (Eds.), *Directors of development: Influences on the development of children's thinking* (pp. 101–120). Hillsdale, NJ: Erlbaum.

Okagaki, L., & Sternberg, R. J. (1993). Parental beliefs and children's school performance. *Child Development, 64*, 36–56.

Olvera-Ezzell, N., Power, T. G., & Cousins, J. H. (1990). Maternal socialization of children's eating habits: Strategies used by obese Mexican-American mothers. *Child Development, 61*, 395–400.

Osofsky, J. (1995). The effects of exposure to violence on young children. *American Psychologist, 50*, 782–788.

Paikoff, R. L., & Brooks-Gunn, J. (1991). Do parent-child relationships change during puberty? *Psychological Bulletin, 110*, 47–66.

Palisin, H. (1980). The Neonatal Perception Inventory: Failure to replicate. *Child Development, 51*, 737–742.

Papoušek, H., & Papoušek, M. (1987). Intuitive parenting: A dialectic counterpart to the infant's integrative competence. In J. D. Osofsky (Ed.), *Handbook of infant development* (2nd ed., pp. 669–720). New York: Wiley.

Papoušek, H., & Papoušek, M. (1995). Intuitive parenting. In M. H. Bornstein (Ed.), *Handbook of parenting: Vol. 2. Biology and ecology of parenting* (pp. 117–136). Mahwah, NJ: Erlbaum.

Parke, R. D. (1974). Rules, roles, and resistance to deviation: Recent advances in punishment, discipline, and self-control. In A. D. Pick (Ed.), *Minnesota symposia on child psychology* (Vol. 8, pp. 111–143). Minneapolis: University of Minnesota.

Parke, R. D. (1978). Parent-infant interaction: Progress, paradigms, and problems. In G. P. Sackett (Ed.), *Observing behavior* (Vol. 1, pp. 69–94). Baltimore: University Park Press.

Parke, R. D., & Ladd, G. W. (Eds.). (1992). *Family-peer relationships: Modes of linkage.* Hillsdale, NJ: Erlbaum.

Parke, R. D., & Slaby, R. G. (1983). The development of aggression. In P. H. Mussen & E. M. Hetherington (Eds.), *Handbook of child psychology: Vol. 4. Socialization, personality, and social development* (pp. 547–642). New York: Wiley.

Parpal, M., & Maccoby, E. E. (1985). Maternal responsiveness and subsequent child compliance. *Child Development, 56,* 1326–1334.

Parsons, J. E., Adler, T. F., & Kaczala, C. M. (1982). Socialization of achievement attitudes and beliefs: Parental influences. *Child Development, 53,* 310–321.

Patterson, C. J. (1995). Lesbian and gay parenthood. In M. H. Bornstein (Ed.), *Handbook of parenting: Vol. 3. Status and social conditions of parenting* (pp. 255–274). Mahwah, NJ: Erlbaum.

Patterson, C. J., Cohn, D. A., & Kao, B. T. (1989). Maternal warmth as a protective factor against risks associated with peer rejection among children. *Development and Psychopathology, 1,* 21–38.

Patterson, G. R. (1980). Mothers: The unacknowledged victims. *Monographs of the Society for Research in Child Development, 45* (5, Serial No. 186).

Patterson, G. R. (1982). *Coercive family process.* Eugene, OR: Castalia.

Patterson, G. R. (1986). Performance models for antisocial boys. *American Psychologist, 41,* 432–444.

Patterson, G. R., DeBaryshe, B. D., & Ramsey, E. (1989). A developmental perspective on antisocial behavior. *American Psychologist, 44,* 329–335.

Patterson, G. R., & Stouthamer-Loeber, M. (1984). The correlation of family management practices and delinquency. *Child Development, 55,* 1299–1307.

Perry, M. A., Wells, E. A., & Doran, L. D. (1983). Parent characteristics in abusing and nonabusing families. *Journal of Clinical Child Psychology, 12,* 329–336.

Peschel, E. R., & Peschel, R. E. (1987). Medical insights into the castrati in opera. *American Scientist, 75,* 578–583.

Pettit, G. S., & Bates, J. E. (1989). Family interaction patterns and children's behavior problems from infancy to 4 years. *Developmental Psychology, 25,* 413–420.

Pettit, G. S., Dodge, K. A., & Brown, M. M. (1988). Early family experience, social problem solving patterns, and children's social competence. *Child Development, 59,* 107–120.

Phares, V., & Compas, B. E. (1992). The role of fathers in child and adolescent psychopathology: Make room for daddy. *Psychological Bulletin, 111,* 387–412.

Pianta, R. C., Sroufe, L. A., & Egeland, B. (1989). Continuity and discontinuity in maternal sensitivity at 6, 24, and 42 months in a high-risk sample. *Child Development, 60,* 481–487.

Pinneau, S. R. (1955). The infantile disorders of hospitalism and anaclitic depression. *Psychological Bulletin, 52,* 429–452.

Plato. (1970). *The laws* (T. J. Saunders, Trans.). Harmonsworth, England: Penguin Books. (Original work published circa 360 B.C.)

Plomin, R. (1990). *Nature and nurture: An introduction to human behavioral genetics.* Pacific Grove, CA: Brooks/Cole.

Plomin, R. (1994). Nature, nurture, and social development. *Social Development, 3,* 37–52.

Pollock, L. A. (1983). *Forgotten children: Parent-child relations from 1500 to 1900*. New York: Cambridge University Press.

Power, T. G. (1985). Mother- and father-infant play: A developmental analysis. *Child Development, 56,* 1514–1524.

Power, T. G., & Chapieski, M. L. (1986). Childrearing and impulse control in toddlers: A naturalistic investigation. *Developmental Psychology, 22,* 271–275.

Power, T. G., & Shanks, J. A. (1989). Parents as socializers: Maternal and paternal views. *Journal of Youth and Adolescence, 18,* 203–220.

Pratt, M. W., Kerig, P., Cowan, P. A., & Cowan, C. P. (1988). Mothers and fathers teaching 3-year-olds: Authoritative parenting and adult scaffolding of young children's learning. *Developmental Psychology, 24,* 832–839.

Preyer, W. (1893). *The mind of the child*. New York: Appleton.

Pruitt, D. L., & Erickson, M. T. (1985). The Child Abuse Potential Inventory: A study of concurrent validity. *Journal of Clinical Psychology, 41,* 104–111.

Pulkkinen, L. (1982). Self control and continuity from childhood to adolescence. In P. B. Baltes & O. B. Brim (Ed.), *Life span development and behavior* (Vol. 4, pp. 63–105). New York: Academic Press.

Pumroy, D. K., & Pumroy, S. S. (1978). *Modern childrearing: A behavioral approach*. Chicago: Nelson-Hall.

Putallaz, M. (1987). Maternal behavior and children's sociometric status. *Child Development, 58,* 324–340.

Putallaz, M., & Heflin, A. H. (1990). Parent-child interaction. In S. R. Asher & J. D. Coie (Eds.), *Peer rejection in childhood* (pp. 189–216). New York: Cambridge University Press.

Radford, J. (1990). *Child prodigies and exceptional early achievers*. New York: Free Press.

Radke-Yarrow, M., & Zahn-Waxler, C. (1986). The role of familial factors in the development of prosocial behavior: Research findings and questions. In D. Olweus, J. Block, & M. Radke-Yarrow (Eds.), *Development of antisocial and prosocial behavior* (pp. 207–233). New York: Academic Press.

Radke-Yarrow, M., Zahn-Waxler, C. Z., & Chapman, M. (1983). Children's prosocial dispositions and behavior. In E. M. Hetherington (Ed.), *Handbook of child psychology: Vol. 4. Socialization, personality, and social development* (4th ed., pp. 469–545). New York: Wiley.

Rafferty, Y., & Shinn, M. (1991). The impact of homelessness on children. *American Psychologist, 46,* 1170–1179.

Ragozin, A. S., Basham, R. B., Crnic, K. A., Greenberg, M. T., & Robinson, N. M. (1982). Effects of maternal age on parenting role. *Developmental Psychology, 18,* 627–634.

Reid, J. B. (1986). Social-interactional patterns in families of abused and nonabused children. In C. Zahn-Waxler, E. M. Cummings, & R. Iannotti (Eds.), *Altruism and aggression: Biological and social origins* (pp. 238–255). New York: Cambridge University Press.

Reis, J., Barbera-Stein, L., & Bennett, S. (1986). Ecological determinants of parenting. *Family Relations, 35,* 547–554.

Rheingold, H. L. (1969). The social and socializing infant. In D. A. Goslin (Ed.), *Handbook of socialization theory and research* (pp. 779–790). Chicago: Rand McNally.

Rheingold, H. L. (1982). Little children's participation in the work of adults: A nascent prosocial behavior. *Child Development, 53,* 114–125.

Rhodes, R. (1990). *A hole in the world: An American boyhood.* New York: Simon & Schuster.

Richman, A. L., Miller, P. M., & LeVine, R. A. (1992). Cultural and educational variations in maternal responsiveness. *Developmental Psychology, 28,* 614–621.

Riegel, K. F. (1976). The dialectics of human development. *American Psychologist, 10,* 689–700.

Roberts, G. C., Block, J. H., & Block, J. (1984). Continuity and change in parents' child-rearing practices. *Child Development, 55,* 586–597.

Roberts, W. L. (1986). Nonlinear models of development: An example from the socialization of competence. *Child Development, 57,* 1166–1178.

Roberts, W. L., & Strayer, J. (1987). Parents' responses to the emotional distress of their children: Relations with children's competence. *Developmental Psychology, 23,* 415–422.

Rogoff, B., Ellis, S., & Gardner, W. (1984). Adjustment of adult-child instruction according to child's age and task. *Developmental Psychology, 20,* 193–199.

Rohner, R. P. (1986). *The warmth dimension: Foundations of parental acceptance-rejection theory.* Beverly Hills, CA: Sage.

Rollins, B. C., & Thomas, D. L. (1979). Parental support, power, and control techniques in the socialization of children. In W. R. Burr, R. Hill, F. I. Nye, & I. L. Reiss (Eds.), *Contemporary theories about the family: Vol. 1. Research-based theories* (pp. 317–364). New York: Free Press.

Roopnarine, J. L., & Carter, D. B. (Eds.). (1992). *Parent-child socialization in diverse cultures.* Hillsdale, NJ: Erlbaum.

Roopnarine, J. L., Talukder, E., Jain, D., Josi, P., & Srivastav, P. (1990). Characteristics of holding, patterns of play, and social behaviors between parents and infants in New Delhi, India. *Developmental Psychology, 26,* 667–673.

Roosa, M. W., Gensheimer, L. K., Ayers, T. S., & Short, J. L. (1990). Development of a school-based prevention program for children in alcoholic families. *Journal of Primary Prevention, 11,* 119–141.

Rosenberg, M. S., & Reppucci, N. D. (1983). Abusive mothers: Perceptions of their own and their children's behavior. *Journal of Consulting and Clinical Psychology, 51,* 674–682.

Rosenthal, R. (1991). *Meta-analytic procedures for social science research* (Rev. ed.). Newbury Park, CA: Sage.

Rost, K., & Gielen, A. (1986). Car safety seat legislation: Enforcement and increased restraint use. *Journal of Police Science and Administration, 14,* 62–66.

Rothbart, M. K. (1971). Birth order and mother-child interaction in an achievement situation. *Journal of Personality and Social Psychology, 17,* 113–120.

Rothbart, M. K., & Goldsmith, H. H. (1985). Three approaches to the study of infant temperament. *Developmental Review, 5,* 237–260.

Rothbart, M. K., & Maccoby, E. E. (1966). Parents' differential reaction to sons and daughters. *Journal of Personality and Social Psychology, 4,* 237–243.

Rothbaum, F., & Weisz, J. R. (1994). Parental caregiving and child externalizing behavior in nonclinical samples: A meta-analysis. *Psychological Bulletin, 116,* 55–74.

Rousseau, J. J. (1956). *Emile* (W. Boyd, Trans.). New York: Columbia University Press. (Original work published 1762.)

Rowe, D. C. (1994). *The limits of family influence: Genes, experience, and behavior.* New York: Guilford Press.

Rubin, J., Provenzano, R., & Luria, Z. (1974). The eye of the beholder: Parents' views on sex of newborns. *American Journal of Orthopsychiatry, 44,* 512–519.

Ruhrah, J. (1925). *Pediatrics of the past.* New York: Hoeber.

Rush, D. (1981). Is WIC worthwhile? *American Journal of Public Health, 72,* 1101–1103.

Russell, A., & Russell, G. (1982). Mother, father, and child beliefs about child development. *Journal of Psychology, 110,* 297–306.

Russell, A., & Russell, G. (1989). Warmth in the mother-child and father-child relationships in middle childhood. *British Journal of Developmental Psychology, 7,* 219–235.

Russell, A., & Russell, G. (1992). Child effects in socialization research: Some conceptual and data analysis issues. *Social Development, 1,* 163–184.

Russell, D. E. H. (1984). The prevalence and seriousness of incestuous abuse: Stepfathers vs. biological fathers. *Child Abuse & Neglect, 8,* 15–22.

Russell, G. (1986). Primary caretaking and role-sharing fathers. In M. E. Lamb (Ed.), *The father's role: Applied perspectives* (pp. 29–57). New York: Wiley.

Rutter, M. (1979). Maternal deprivation, 1972–1978: New findings, new concepts, new approaches. *Child Development, 50,* 283–305.

Rutter, M. (1985). Family and school influences on behavioural development. *Journal of Child Psychology and Psychiatry, 26,* 349–368.

Rutter, M. (1987). Psychosocial resilience and protective mechanisms. *American Journal of Orthopsychiatry, 57,* 316–331.

Rymer, R. (1993). *Genie: An abused child's flight from silence.* New York: Harper-Collins.

Saarni, C. (1985). Indirect processes in affect socialization. In M. Lewis & C. Saarni (Eds.), *The socialization of emotions* (pp. 187–209). New York: Plenum Press.

Sack, W. H., Mason, R., & Higgins, J. E. (1985). The single-parent family and abusive child punishment. *American Journal of Orthopsychiatry, 55,* 252–259.

Salzinger, S., Feldman, R. S., Hammer, M., & Rosario, M. (1993). The effects of physical abuse on children's social relationships. *Child Development, 64,* 169–187.

Sameroff, A. J., & Chandler, M. J. (1975). Reproductive risk and the continuum of caretaking casualty. In F. Horowitz (Ed.), *Review of child development research* (Vol. 4, pp. 187–244). Chicago: University of Chicago Press.

Sameroff, A. J., & Seifer, R. (1983). Familial risk and child competence. *Child Development, 54,* 1254–1268.

Scarr, S. (1985). Constructing psychology: Making facts and fables for our times. *American Psychologist, 40,* 499–512.

Scarr, S. (1992). Developmental theories for the 1990s: Development and individual differences. *Child Development, 63,* 1–19.

Scarr, S., & McCartney, K. (1983). How people make their own environments: A theory of genotype environment effects. *Child Development, 54,* 424–435.

Scarr, S., Phillips, D., & McCartney, K. (1989). Working mothers and their families. *American Psychologist, 44,* 1402–1409.

Schaefer, C. E., & Briesmeister, J. M. (1989). *Handbook of parent training: Parents as co-therapists for children's behavior problems.* New York: Wiley.

Schaefer, E. S. (1959). A circumplex model for maternal behavior. *Journal of Abnormal and Social Psychology, 59,* 226–235.

Schaffer, H. R., & Crook, C. K. (1979). Maternal control techniques in a directed play situation. *Child Development, 50,* 989–996.

Schultz, S. J. (1984). *Family systems theory.* New York: Aronson.

Sears, C. H. (1899). Home and school punishments. *Pedagogic Seminary, 6,* 159–187.

Sears, R. R. (1951). A theoretical framework for personality and social behavior. *American Psychologist, 6,* 476–483.

Sears, R. R. (1975). Your ancients revisited: A history of child development. In E. M. Hetherington (Ed.), *Review of child development research* (Vol. 5, pp. 1–73). Chicago: University of Chicago Press.

Sears, R. R., Maccoby, E. E., & Levin, H. (1957). *Patterns of child rearing.* Evanston, IL: Row, Peterson.

Sears, R. R., Rau, L., & Alpert, R. (1965). *Identification and child rearing.* Stanford: Stanford University Press.

Seginer, R. (1983). Parents' educational expectations and children's academic achievement: A literature review. *Merrill-Palmer Quarterly, 29,* 1–23.

Seiner, S. H., & Gelfand, D. M. (1995). Effects of mothers' simulated withdrawal and depressed affect on mother-toddler interactions. *Child Development, 66,* 1519–1528.

Seligman, M. E. P. (1991). *Learned optimism.* New York: Knopf.

Sewell, W. H., & Mussen, P. H. (1952). The effects of feeding, weaning, and scheduling procedures on childhood adjustment and the formation of oral symptoms. *Child Development, 23,* 185–191.

Shahar, S. (1990). *Childhood in the middle ages.* New York: Routledge.

Sigel, I. E. (1985). *Parental belief systems: The psychological consequences for children.* Hillsdale, NJ: Erlbaum.

Sigel, I. E. (1986). Reflections on the belief-behavior connection: Lessons learned from a research program on parental belief systems and teaching strategies. In R. D. Ashmore & D. M. Brodzinsky (Eds.), *Thinking about the family: Views of parents and children* (pp. 35–65). Hillsdale, NJ: Erlbaum.

Sigel, I. E., McGillicuddy-DeLisi, A. V., & Goodnow, J. J. (Eds.). (1992). *Parental belief systems: The psychological consequences for children* (2nd ed.). Hillsdale, NJ: Erlbaum.

Sigel, I. E., Stinson, E. T., & Flaugher, J. (1991). Socialization of representational competence in the family: The distancing paradigm. In L. Okagaki & R. J. Sternberg (Eds.), *Directors of development: Influences on the development of children's thinking* (pp. 121–144). Hillsdale, NJ: Erlbaum.

Silverstein, L. B. (1991). Transforming the debate about child care and maternal employment. *American Psychologist, 46,* 1025–1032.

Simons, R. L., Lorenz, F. O., Conger, R. D., & Wu, C.-I. (1992). Support from spouse as mediator and moderator of the disruptive influence of economic strain on parenting. *Child Development, 63,* 1282–1301.

Simons, R. L., Whitbeck, L. B., Conger, R. D., & Chyi-In, W. (1991). Intergenerational transmission of harsh parenting. *Developmental Psychology, 27,* 159–171.

Simons, R. L., Whitbeck, L. B., Conger, R. D., & Melby, J. N. (1990). Husband and wife differences in determinants of parenting: A social learning and exchange model of parental behavior. *Journal of Marriage and the Family, 52,* 375–392.

Simpson, J. A., Rholes, W. S., & Nelligan, J. S. (1992). Support seeking and support giving within couples in an anxiety-provoking situation: The role of attachment styles. *Journal of Personality and Social Psychology, 62,* 434–446.

Skinner, B. F. (1963). Operant behavior. *American Psychologist, 18,* 503–515.

Smetana, J. G. (1989). Toddlers' social interactions in the context of moral and conventional transgressions in the home. *Developmental Psychology, 25,* 499–508.

Smith, T. E. (1982). The case of parental transmission of educational goals: The importance of accurate offspring perceptions. *Journal of Marriage and the Family, 44,* 661–674.

Smolowe, J. (1992, Nov. 9). Where children come first. *Time,* pp. 58–59.

Snyder, J. J. (1977). Reinforcement analysis of interaction in problem and nonproblem families. *Journal of Abnormal Psychology, 86,* 528–535.

Sommerville, C. J. (1982). *The rise and fall of childhood.* Beverly Hills, CA: Sage.

Spence, J. T., & Helmreich, R. L. (1978). *Masculinity & femininity: Their psychological dimensions, correlates, and antecedents.* Austin: University of Texas Press.

Spitz, R. A. (1945). Hospitalism: An inquiry into the genesis of psychiatric conditions in early childhood. *Psychoanalytic Study of the Child, 1,* 53–74.

Spock, B., & Morgan, M. (1989). *Spock on Spock: A memoir of growing up with the century.* New York: Pantheon Books.

Spock, B., & Rothenberg, M. B. (1992). *Dr. Spock's baby and child care* (6th ed.). New York: Pocket Books.

Sprunger, L. W., Boyce, W. T., & Gaines, J. A. (1985). Family-infant congruence: Routines and rhythmicity in family adaptations to a young infant. *Child Development, 56,* 564–572.

Sroufe, L. A. (1979). The coherence of individual development: Early care, attachment, and subsequent developmental issues. *American Psychologist, 34,* 834–841.

Sroufe, L. A., & Fleeson, J. (1986). Attachment and the construction of relationships. In W. W. Hartup & Z. Rubin (Eds.), *Relationships and development* (pp. 51–71). Hillsdale, NJ: Erlbaum.

St. Peters, M., Fitch, M., Huston, A. C., Wright, J. C., & Eakins, D. J. (1991). Television and families: What do young children watch with their parents? *Child Development, 62,* 1409–1423.

Stainer, K. E., & Thieman, A. (1991, March). *The relation of child, parent, and family characteristics to the severity of child maltreatment.* Paper presented at the Society for Research in Child Development, Seattle, WA.

Starr, R. H. J. (1988). Physical abuse of children. In V. B. V. Hasselt, R. L. Morrison, A. S. Bellack, & M. Hersen (Eds.), *Handbook of family violence* (pp. 119–155). New York: Plenum Press.

Stattin, H., & Klackenberg-Larsson, I. (1991). The short and long-term implications for parent-child relations of parents' prenatal preferences for their child's gender. *Developmental Psychology, 27,* 141–147.

Steele, B. F. (1970). Parental abuse of infants and small children. In E. J. Anthony & T. Benedek (Eds.), *Parenthood: Its psychology and psychopathology* (pp. 449–477). Boston: Little, Brown.

Steele, B. F., & Pollock, C. B. (1968). A psychiatric study of parents who abuse infants and small children. In R. E. Helfer & C. H. Kempe (Eds.), *The battered child* (pp. 103–147). Chicago: University of Chicago Press.

Stein, J. A., Newcomb, M. D., & Bentler, P. M. (1993). Differential effects of parent and grandparent drug use on behavior problems of male and female children. *Developmental Psychology, 29,* 31–43.

Steinberg, L., Catalano, R., & Dooley, D. (1981). Economic antecedents of child abuse and neglect. *Child Development, 52,* 975–985.

Steinberg, L., Elmer, J. D., & Mounts, N. S. (1989). Authoritative parenting, psychosocial maturity, and academic success among adolescents. *Child Development, 60,* 1424–1436.

Steinberg, L., Lamborn, S. D., Darling, N., Mounts, N. S., & Dornbusch, S. M. (1994). Over-time changes in adjustment and competence among adolescents from authoritative, authoritarian, indulgent, and neglectful families. *Child Development, 65,* 754–770.

Steinberg, L., Lamborn, S. D., Dornbusch, S. M., & Darling, N. (1992). Impact of parenting practices on adolescent achievement: Authoritative parenting, school involvement, and encouragement to succeed. *Child Development, 63,* 1266–1281.

Steinberg, L., & Silverberg, S. B. (1986). The vicissitudes of autonomy in early adolescence. *Child Development, 57,* 841–851.

Stern, D. (1971). A micro-analysis of mother-infant interaction: Behavior regulating contact between a mother and her $3\frac{1}{2}$ month-old twins. *American Academy of Child Psychiatry, 10,* 501–517.

Stern, D. (1977). *The first relationship: Infant and mother.* Cambridge, MA: Harvard University Press.

Stern, M., & Hildebrandt, K. A. (1984). Prematurity stereotype: Effects of labeling on adults' perceptions of infants. *Developmental Psychology, 20,* 360–362.

Stern, M., & Karraker, K. H. (1989). Sex stereotyping of infants: A review of gender labeling studies. *Sex Roles, 20,* 501–522.

Stevenson, D. L., & Baker, D. P. (1987) The family-school relation and the child's school performance. *Child Development, 58,* 1348–1357.

Stevenson, M. R., & Black, K. N. (1988). Paternal absence and sex-role development: A meta-analysis. *Child Development, 59,* 793–814.

Stevenson, R. D. (1992). Failure to thrive. In D. E. Greydanus & M. L. Wolraich (Eds.), *Behavioral pediatrics* (pp. 298–313). New York: Springer-Verlag.

Stipek, D., & McCroskey, J. (1989). Investing in children: Government and workplace policies for parents. *American Psychologist, 44,* 416–423.

Stocker, C., Dunn, J., & Plomin, R. (1989). Sibling relationships: Links with child temperament, maternal behavior, and family structure. *Child Development, 60,* 715–727.

Stolz, L. M. (1967). *Influences on parental behavior.* Stanford: Stanford University Press.

Stott, L. H. (1940). Parental attitudes of farm, town, and city parents in relation to certain personality adjustments in their children. *Journal of Social Psychology, 11,* 325–339.

Straus, M. A., & Gelles, R. J. (1988). How violent are American families? In G. T. Hotaling, D. Finkelhor, J. T. Kirkpatrick, & M. A. Straus (Eds.), *Family abuse and its consequences: New directions in research* (pp. 14–36). Beverly Hills, CA: Sage.

Strawn, J. (1992). The states and the poor: Child poverty rises as the safety net shrinks. *Social Policy Report, Society for Research in Child Development, 6,* 1–19.

Sturm, L., & Drotar, D. (1989). Predictions for weight for height following intervention in three-year-old children with early histories of nonorganic failure to thrive. *Child Abuse and Neglect, 13,* 19–28.

Symonds, P. (1938). A study of parental acceptance and rejection. *American Journal of Orthopsychiatry, 8,* 679–688.

Symonds, P. (1949). *The dynamics of parent-child relationships.* New York: Columbia University.

Taylor, L., & Maurer, A. (1985). *Think twice: The medical effects of physical punishment.* Berkeley, CA: Generation Books.

Teti, D. M., & Gelfand, D. M. (1991). Behavioral competence among mothers of infants in the first year: The mediational role of maternal self-efficacy. *Child Development, 62,* 918–929.

Thelen, E., & Adolph, K. E. (1992). Arnold L. Gesell: The paradox of nature and nurture. *Developmental Psychology, 28,* 368–380.

Thomas, A., & Chess, S. (1977). *Temperament and development.* New York: Brunner/Mazel.

Thomas, R. M. (1992). *Comparing theories of child development.* Belmont, CA: Wadsworth.

Tinsley, B. J. (1992). Multiple influences on the acquisition and socialization of children's health attitudes and behavior: An integrative review. *Child Development, 63,* 1043–1069.

Treiber, F. A. (1986). A comparison of the positive and negative consequences approaches upon car restraint usage. *Journal of Pediatric Psychology, 11,* 15–24.

Trevarthen, C. (1977). Descriptive analyses of infant communicative behavior. In H. R. Schaffer (Ed.), *Studies in mother-infant interaction* (pp. 227–270). New York: Academic Press.

Trickett, P. K., Aber, J. L., Carlson, V., & Cicchetti, D. (1991). Relationship of socioeconomic status to the etiology and developmental sequelae of physical child abuse. *Developmental Psychology, 27,* 148–158.

Trickett, P. K., & Kuczynski, L. (1986). Children's misbehaviors and parental discipline strategies in abusive and nonabusive families. *Developmental Psychology, 22,* 115–123.

Trickett, P. K., & Susman, E. J. (1988). Parental perceptions of child-rearing practices in physically abusive and nonabusive families. *Developmental Psychology, 24,* 270–276.

Trivers, R. L. (1974). Parent-offspring conflict. *American Zoologist, 14,* 249–264.

U.S. Bureau of the Census. (1993). *Statistical abstract of the United States.* Washington, DC: Author.

U.S. Bureau of the Census. (1994). *Poverty in the U.S., 1993.* Washington, DC: U.S. Department of Commerce.

U.S. Bureau of Labor Statistics. (1988). *Statistical abstract of the United States* (108th ed.). Washington, DC: U.S. Department of Commerce.

Valsiner, J. (1985). Parental organization of children's cognitive development within home environment. *Psychologia, 28,* 131–143.

Valsiner, J. (1989). *Human development and culture: The social nature of personality and its study.* Lexington, MA: Heath.

Valsiner, J., & Lightfoot, C. (1987). Process structure of parent-child-environment relations and the prevention of children's injuries. *Journal of Social Issues, 43,* 61–72.

Vandell, D. L., & Wilson, K. S. (1987). Infants' interactions with mother, sibling, and peer: Contrasts and relations between interaction systems. *Child Development, 58,* 176–186.

Van der Veer, R., & Valsiner, J. (1988). Lev Vygotsky and Pierre Janet: On the origin of the concept of sociogenesis. *Developmental Review, 8,* 52–65.

Van IJzendoorn, M. H. (1992). Intergenerational transmission of parenting: A review of studies in nonclinical populations. *Developmental Review, 12,* 76–99.

Vasta, R. (1982). Physical child abuse: A dual-component analysis. *Developmental Review, 2,* 125–149.

Vuchinich, S., Bank, L., & Patterson, G. R. (1992). Parenting, peers, and the stability of antisocial behavior in preadolescent boys. *Developmental Psychology, 28,* 510–521.

Wachs, T. D. (1992). *The nature of nurture.* Newbury Park, CA: Sage.

Wachs, T. D., Bishry, Z., Sobhy, A., McCabe, B., Galal, O., & Shaheen, F. (1993). Relation of rearing environment to adaptive behavior of Egyptian toddlers. *Child Development, 64,* 586–604.

Wachs, T. D., & Gruen, G. E. (1982). *Early experience and human development.* New York: Plenum Press.

Wagner, M. E., Schubert, H. J. P., & Schubert, D. S. P. (1985). Family size effects: A review. *Journal of Genetic Psychology, 146,* 65–78.

Wahler, R. G., & Dumas, J. E. (1989). Attentional problems in dysfunctional mother-child interactions: An interbehavioral model. *Psychological Bulletin, 105,* 116–130.

Walker, E., Downey, G., & Bergman, A. (1989). The effects of parental psychopathology and maltreatment on child behavior: A test of the diathesis-stress model. *Child Development, 60,* 15–24.

Ward, P. (1994, February 21). "Welfare moms" at vortex of reform-minded storm. *Austin American Statesman,* p. A8.

Waters, E., & Sroufe, L. A. (1983). Social competence as a developmental construct. *Developmental Review, 3,* 79–97.

Watson, J. B. (1924). *Behaviorism.* New York: Norton.

Watson, J. B. (1926). What the nursery has to say about instincts. In C. Murchison (Ed.), *Psychologies of 1925* (pp. 1–35). Worcester, MA: Clark University Press.

Watson, J. B. (1928). *Psychological care of infant and child.* New York: Norton.

Watson, J. B. (1930). *Behaviorism* (Rev. ed.). New York: Norton.

Wauchope, B., & Straus, M. A. (1990). Age, gender, and occupational class in physical punishment and physical abuse of American children. In M. A. Straus & R. J. Gelles (Eds.), *Physical violence in American families: Risk factors and adaptations in 8,145 families* (pp. 133–148). New Brunswick, NJ: Transaction.

Webster-Stratton, C., & Hammond, M. (1988). Maternal depression and its relationship to life stress, perceptions of child behavior problems, parenting behaviors, and child conduct problems. *Journal of Abnormal Child Psychology, 16,* 299–315.

Weiss, B., Dodge, K. A., Bates, J. E., & Pettit, G. S. (1992). Some consequences of early harsh discipline: Child aggression and a maladaptive social information processing style. *Child Development, 63,* 1321–1335.

Weisz, J. R., Rothbaum, F. M., & Blackburn, T. C. (1984). Standing out and standing in: The psychology of control in America and Japan. *American Psychologist, 39,* 955–969.

Werner, E. E., & Smith, R. S. (1989). *Vulnerable but invincible: A longitudinal study of resilient children and youth.* New York: Adams, Bannister, Cox.

Wertsch, J. V. (1985). *Vygotsky and the social formation of the mind.* Cambridge, MA: Harvard University Press.

West, M. O., & Prinz, R. J. (1987). Parental alcoholism and childhood psychopathology. *Psychological Bulletin, 102,* 204–218.

Westerman, M. A. (1990). Coordination of maternal directives with preschoolers' behavior in compliance-problem and healthy dyads. *Developmental Psychology, 26,* 621–630.

Whitehurst, G. J., Falco, F. L., Lonigan, C. J., Fischel, J. E., DeBaryshe, B. D., Valdez-Menchaca, M. C., & Caulfield, M. (1988). Accelerating language development though picture book reading. *Developmental Psychology, 24,* 552–559.

Whiting, B. (Ed.). (1963). *Six cultures: Studies of child rearing.* New York: Wiley.

Whiting, B., & Edwards, C. P. (1988). *Children of different worlds: The formation of social behavior.* Cambridge, MA: Harvard University Press.

Whiting, J. W. M., & Child, I. L. (1953). *Child training and personality: A cross-cultural study.* New Haven: Yale University Press.

Wickes, I. G. (1953). A history of infant feeding. *Archives of Diseases in Childhood, 28,* 151–158.

Widom, C. S. (1989). Does violence beget violence? A critical examination of the literature. *Psychological Bulletin, 106,* 3–28.

Wierson, M., & Forehand, R. (1994). Parent behavioral training for child noncompliance: Rationale, concepts, and effectiveness. *Current Directions in Psychological Science, 3,* 146–150.

Winnicott, D. W. (1967). Mirror-role of mother and family in child development. In P. Lomas (Ed.), *The predicament of the family: A psycho-analytical symposium* (pp. 111–119). London: Hogarth Press.

Wolfe, D. A. (1987). *Child abuse: Implications for child development and psychopathology.* Beverly Hills, CA: Sage.

Wolfenstein, M. (1951). Fun morality: An analysis of recent American child-training literature. *Journal of Social Issues, 7,* 15–25.

Wolfner, G. D., & Gelles, R. J. (1993). A profile of violence toward children: A national study. *Child Abuse and Neglect, 17,* 197–212.

Woodhead, M. (1988). When psychology informs public policy: The case of early childhood intervention. *American Psychologist, 43,* 443–454.

Wood-Shuman, S., & Cone, J. D. (1986). Differences in abusive, at-risk for abuse, and control mothers' descriptions of normal child behavior. *Child Abuse and Neglect, 10,* 397–405.

Yarrow, A. L. (1991). *Latecomers: Children of parents over 35.* New York: Free Press.

Yeates, K. O., MacPhee, D., Campbell, F. A., & Ramey, C. T. (1983). Maternal IQ and home environment as determinants of early childhood intellectual competence: A developmental analysis. *Developmental Psychology, 19,* 731–739.

Young, K. T. (1990). American conceptions of infant development from 1955 to 1984: What the experts are telling parents. *Child Development, 61,* 17–28.

Youngblade, L. M., & Belsky, J. (1989). Child maltreatment, infant-parent attachment security, and dysfunctional peer relationships in toddlerhood. *Topics in Early Childhood Special Education, 9,* 1–15.

Youngblade, L. M., & Belsky, J. (1992). Parent-child antecedents of 5-year-olds' close friendships: A longitudinal analysis. *Developmental Psychology, 28,* 700–713.

Zahn-Waxler, C., McKnew, D. H., Cummings, E. M., Davenport, Y. B., & Radke-Yarrow, M. (1984). Problem behaviors and peer interactions of young children with a manic-depressive parent. *American Journal of Psychiatry, 2,* 236–240.

Zahn-Waxler, C., Radke-Yarrow, M., & King, R. A. (1979). Child rearing and children's prosocial initiations toward victims of distress. *Child Development, 50,* 319–330.

Zahn-Waxler, C., Radke-Yarrow, M., Wagner, E., & Chapman, M. (1992). Development of concern for others. *Developmental Psychology, 28,* 126–136.

Zigler, E., & Finn-Stevenson, M. (1987). *Children: Development and social issues.* Lexington, MA: Heath.

Zigler, E., & Hall, N. W. (1989). Physical child abuse in America: Past, present, and future. In D. Cicchetti & V. Carlson (Eds.), *Child maltreatment* (pp. 38–75). New York: Cambridge University Press.

Zigler, E., Kagan, S. L., & Krugman, E. (Eds.). (1983). *Children, families, and government: Perspectives on American social policy.* Cambridge: Cambridge University Press.

Zigler, E., & Muenchow, S. (1984). How to influence social policy affecting children and families. *American Psychologist, 39,* 415–420.

Zuravin, S. J. (1988). Child maltreatment and teenage first births: A relationship mediated by chronic sociodemographic stress? *American Journal of Orthopsychiatry, 58,* 91–103.

Zuravin, S. J., & DiBlasio (1992). Child-neglecting adolescent mothers: How do they differ from their nonmaltreating counterparts? *Journal of Interpersonal Violence, 7,* 471–489.

Zussman, J. U. (1978). Relationship of demographic factors to parental discipline techniques. *Developmental Psychology, 14,* 685–686.

Zussman, J. U. (1980). Situational determinants of parental behavior: Effects of competing cognitive activity. *Child Development, 51,* 792–800.

About the Book and Author

Research into parent-child relationships is a diverse field of inquiry, attracting investigators from a variety of disciplines and subdisciplines. This book integrates and synthesizes the literature by focusing on issues concerning the parent. The text is organized around four key questions: What determines parental behavior? What are the effects of parenting on children? What makes some parents more effective than others? Why do some parents maltreat their children?

George Holden adopts a dynamic rather than a static perspective on parenting. This dynamic approach reflects parents' capacity to modify their behavior as they respond to changes in their children and in their own lives. Throughout the text, historical antecedents as well as methodological and theoretical issues are highlighted. Although the book is designed for advanced courses focusing on the parent-child relationship, it also provides a good overview for those interested in current research concerning parenting.

George W. Holden is associate professor of psychology at the University of Texas at Austin and is director of the Institute of Human Development and Family Studies.

Index